Quick Reference
for Band Directors

Ronald E. Kearns

Published in partnership with
MENC: The National Association for Music Education

ROWMAN & LITTLEFIELD EDUCATION
A division of

ROWMAN & LITTLEFIELD PUBLISHERS, INC.
Lanham • New York • Toronto • Plymouth, UK

Published in partnership with MENC: The National Association for Music Education

Published by Rowman & Littlefield Education
A division of Rowman & Littlefield Publishers, Inc.
A wholly owned subsidary of The Rowman & Littlefield Publishing Group, Inc.
4501 Forbes Boulevard, Suite 200, Lanham, Maryland 20706
http://www.rowmaneducation.com

Estover Road, Plymouth PL6 7PY, United Kingdom

British Library Cataloguing in Publication Information Available

Library of Congress Cataloging-in-Publication Data

Kearns, Ronald E., 1952-
 Quick reference for band directors / Ronald E. Kearns.
 p. cm.
 Includes bibliographical references.
 ISBN 978-1-61048-345-2 (cloth : alk. paper) — ISBN 978-1-61048-346-9 (pbk. : alk. paper) — ISBN 978-1-61048-347-6 (electronic)
 1. Bands (Music)—Instruction and study. 2. School music—Instruction and study. I. Title.
 MT733.K43 2011
 784.071—dc23   2011019966

♾™ The paper used in this publication meets the minimum requirements of American National Standard for Information Sciences—Permanence of Paper for Printed Library Materials, ANSI/NISO Z39.48-1992. Printed in the United States of America

Contents

PART ONE

Contents   v

PART TWO

Acknowledgments

If you ever see a "turtle on a fence" you know he didn't get there by himself. The same is true of me and this book. I'd like to thank my wife Lillie for her assistance proofing and listening to me bounce off ideas for chapters. I'd like to thank my daughter Tiffany for her inspiration as a music student. Being a father of a band student helped me to realize how important being a band director is.

I'd also like to thank my students for allowing me to share my passion for music with them and for giving me so many fond memories to draw from for this book. The support I have received from family and colleagues helped me to survive thirty years of teaching music in public schools. Thanks to Mr. Z. E. Holmes, Mr. James McGinnis, and the music faculty of Knoxville College for Laying the foundation for a successful career in music education.

I sincerely appreciate MENC for giving me an opportunity to share my experiences with other teachers who may need that extra boost to bring music to life for their students. I am also grateful to my co-publisher with MENC, Rowman & Littlefield Education, for making this book a reality.

Purpose

The purpose of this book is to give band directors a quick reference for building and maintaining a band program. It is written for the high school band program but since a lot of high school band directors have to teach elementary and middle school bands, information has been included to help those directors. The idea is to provide the band director with a virtual mentor or advisor. The information found within this book has been gathered from over thirty years of teaching experience, discussions with young directors, reflections of former colleagues and friends, and responding to queries I received while serving as a mentor for online forums of MENC: The National Association for Music Education.

There will invariably be questions not answered here or issues not addressed that some readers wish to have addressed but it is my hope that I will provide direction for where to go or what to do to get answers. I reference throughout this book how important MENC is to music teachers in the United States and around the world, not because this is an MENC publication but because over my years of teacher training and teaching, MENC and its affiliates have been of immense help for me.

Attending music conferences and in-service activities over the years gave me an opportunity to interact one on one with some of the greatest minds in music education. Drs. Charles Gary and Charles Benner were two of my mentors and helped me to understand how MENC and its members helped shape the American band movement. Their work with the Yale Seminar and other activities to bring professional musicians and music educators together with other educators and intellectuals helped to standardize music education with the realization that all music students will not be professional musicians, but that music will be an important part of every American's life.

Keeping this in mind, we as band directors have to realize the significance of what we do with our students and how it will impact their lives. It can be a bit overwhelming when you step into a school and you are the music authority for that school. Balancing educational value and recreational aspects of band participation is something every band director faces, but when you are alone in front of your class it is easy to believe that you are the only one facing this challenge.

That is where this book comes in. I want you to be aware that you are not alone and that issues facing you are not new or unique. Someone else has confronted some variation of every problem you will face and so there are answers out there that you can find if you know where to look. Fortunately, Internet search engines have made finding some answers as simple as typing in the problem. Once you search for the problem it is up to you to sift through the resources and determine which resource will help you.

I have chosen to write this book in such a way that it doesn't have a sterile, academic approach to problems but reads as though I'm addressing you and your problems. Be assured that issues and problems addressed in the subsequent pages have been researched or have resulted from personal experiences by me or other band directors. Through the use of e-mails, search engines, attendance at conferences, and in-service meetings, your ability to receive assistance is limitless.

You are not alone in your quest to provide your students and school community with the best band program possible, and reaching out for help is the best first step to providing that. Your local music store is a great source for outside assistance. It is important to them that your program is successful because your success is important to their business. They can tap into resources provided by members of NAMM (the National Association of Music Merchants), who can provide your program with resources that are beyond your budget. NAMM has membership from all over the world. These NAMM members include manufacturers, music publishers, music retailers, music product retailers, and recorded music vendors. Many of these groups have educational programs designed to give you unlimited resources.

The design of the book is such that you can read it sequentially or by chapters as a quick reference, depending on your need. Because of this, there will be some overlapping material presented and variations of the same material in multiple locations. This was done so that should you extract a chapter to address particular issues, it is not assumed that you have read the background material needed to fully understand what is being discussed.

In summary, this book is not an answer to every problem you'll face and some of the answers found within will only scratch the surface of what you're looking for because of the complexity of some issues. The book will, however, serve as a compass helping you to plot out the direction you'll need to go in to find more complete and detailed answers. Most issues you'll face in the classroom will be complex enough to have an entire book devoted to them! I just want you to know that you are not alone in this quest to give your students the best music education possible. We can't do what we do alone nor are we expected to. Don't be afraid to reach out to others for help; chances are they sought out help at some point themselves.

Chapter Contents

Chapter 1. So You Want to Be a Band Director!

This chapter is designed to give new band directors an idea of the planning for personal development and the need to have a philosophy of music education. Ideas on how to solicit help from others and how to develop a resource network are discussed.

Chapter 2. Building a Program in Your Current School or a New School

Whether you are a new or veteran teacher building a program in a new school, or a veteran building a program in your current school, you will need advance planning and a clear vision of what you expect to achieve. This chapter gives you some strategies for gaining, maintaining, and retaining students. It also gives pointers on how to engage parents and your administration in the process.

Chapter 3. Creating a Handbook for Band

Having a clear and concise description of how your band program will be managed is important. Everyone should be able to have a clear understanding of what your expectations, requirements, and plans for success are. This chapter is designed to help you put this information in handbook form.

Chapter 4. Developing Lesson Plans

Many band directors make the mistake of thinking that they don't need lesson plans. For every rehearsal, you and your students must be clear on what you expect to achieve during that rehearsal. The lesson plan should state what you want to focus on and achieve but also be flexible enough for you to be able to handle problems that may come up during the rehearsal. Chapter 4 is designed to give you sample lesson plans and ideas on how to write lesson plans.

Chapter 5. A Successful First Performance

The way you and your students feel after your first performance of the school year will have lasting ramifications on the success of your program. This chapter is designed to let you know how important this performance is and provide you with ways to avoid failure. The level of organization you have going into this performance and the standards you establish will mean the difference between success and failure.

Chapter 6. Developing a Support System for your Band Program

If your program is to be successful, you will need the support of your school's administration, parents, alumni, and community. To avoid the "tail-wagging-the-dog" problem some directors have because parents get involved and follow their own agenda, it's important that the director starts a support group and gives its members a clear vision of what they are expected to do. Far too often, parents who think they are helping the program can do it harm by going out on their own without direction or a clear mission.

Chapter 7. Festival Participation and Preparation

Having your program evaluated by trained professionals is an important way to validate the value of your teaching, and also provides you feedback. When used as an educational tool festivals can be quite helpful. Having a panel of judges reinforce what you are teaching will help the quality of your program improve. In your early years of teaching the feedback you get from festivals will help you to see what is effective and what may need tweaking on your part.

Chapter 8. Developing a Budget for Your Band

Band programs require a lot of funding and one of the most overlooked responsibilities of band directors is that of business manager. Business managers are charged with developing and implementing a budget. If your program is going to be successful you must have instruments, equipment, music, uniforms, and other items. In order to purchase or secure these items you must have funding or a cash flow.

Chapter 9. Developing Musicianship in Band Class

Developing musicianship is the first responsibility of every band director. Some band directors forget that they are teachers. Telling students what to do without giving them a clear understanding of why they are doing it is not developing musicianship. Chapter 9 discusses the importance of developing musicianship during rehearsals and classes.

Chapter 10. Classroom Management

The learning environment that you create for your students will affect how they learn. Classroom management is based on how organized and prepared you are and how well prepared to start the learning process your students are. This chapter offers some strategies on organization and planning.

Chapter 11. Improving Your Band's Performance

Preparing for the first performance and establishing standards for future performances lays the groundwork for improving your band's performance level. Once you have provided your students with the tools they will need for individual preparation and performance, it is important that you constantly remind them of these principles and reinforce them. Ways of how to achieve this are included in this chapter.

Chapter 12. Developing an Elementary Band Program

Because some school districts expect band directors to teach elementary, middle, and high school bands, it's important that you know how to establish, schedule, and plan for elementary school and middle school bands. Chapter 12 covers the basics for starting an elementary school program.

Chapter 13. Structuring Your Concert Band, Symphonic Band, and Wind Ensemble Leadership in Band

How you structure and plan for your classical band groups will make a difference on how much your program will grow in quantity and quality. In order for your group to retain students/members, you will need to have groups that they can aspire to and play more challenging music. Chapter 13 discusses the difference between each group and the needed instrumentation and suggests the grade level of music for each.

Chapter 14. Using Small Ensembles to Improve Your Band's Sound

Using small ensembles to improve the overall performance level of your band is a valuable tool for many reasons. The smaller ensemble enables your students to put to use all of the skills required for good band playing. There are some techniques that are more easily taught in a smaller setting than in a larger group. More advanced players' interest can be maintained through more challenging music. This chapter provides strategies for teaching musicianship through smaller ensembles.

Chapter 15. Developing Satellite Groups for Your Band

The main band class listed on your schedule will be a classic band class called Concert Band or Symphonic Band. Students who enroll in this class will also be interested in other styles of music so you can customize your program around a wide range of music styles. Chapter 15 discusses how to develop and organize satellite groups such as marching band, pep band, jazz band, and small ensembles to enhance your program.

Chapter 16. Developing a Marching Band as Part of the Complete Band Program

Of all the satellite groups formed from your major band, marching band will be the largest and most visible. Because of this, very careful planning is required. The first performance seen by the community will be the marching band. Chapter 16 discusses some of the most important points for developing and maintaining a good marching band.

Chapter 17. Developing a Jazz Ensembles as Part of Your Overall Band Program

One of the most advanced satellite groups formed from your classic band class will be a jazz ensemble. Some schools have jazz ensemble as a separate class that students can take for credit. Depending on whether it is an extracurricular class or a "for credit" class, the course description and class organization will be totally different.

Chapter 18. Using Technology and Multimedia in Band Class

Technology has changed the way band programs are developed, managed, and instructed. Besides record keeping and spreadsheets, technology has revolutionized classroom instruction. Band directors can design marching band shows, set up students for computer-assisted instruction and assessment, audio and video record band performances and rehearsals, and undertake many other musical activities. The purpose of this chapter is to explore the many uses of technology by band directors.

Chapter 19. Quick Fixes and Emergency Repairs

Emergencies tend to happen just before concerts and performances. As you're walking to the stage a student comes to you with a pad in one hand and his instrument in the other. Is there a quick fix or does the student miss the performance? There are some simple quick fixes that can help save the performance. A few solutions are found in this chapter.

Chapter 20. Nonmusic Responsibilities of Band Directors

With all of the "hats" a band director wears to effectively do the job as a music teacher/band director, there are also responsibilities the band director has to perform as a faculty member in her school. Nonmusic teaching responsibilities take up a considerable amount of your time and care should be taken to be as organized as possible.

Chapter 21. General Program Management

This chapter deals with strategies for general management such as folder selections, keeping inventory, and other general management procedures. If you are starting a new school there will be an equipment budget for stocking the school that you'll need to develop. Suggestions for doing this are made in this chapter.

Chapter 22. Sample Forms

This chapter furnishes you with sample forms that can be used or modified for use. If you choose not to use these forms, you will need to develop your own or check with your music supervisor to see if any forms exist for your school's program.

PART ONE

1

So You Want to Be a Band Director!

Most people who decide that they want to be a band director want to do the job because of their love of music and a desire to share that love with students. They have good performance skills, good conducting skills, and an overall knowledge of music history and the importance of music as part of an educational system. What most young band directors don't know is what is expected of band directors beyond music teaching.

Unfortunately, most music training programs at colleges and universities don't prepare future band directors for the many other responsibilities they will have. Most college music teacher training programs in the United States prepare students to teach, perform, and conduct music. Very few programs, if any, have band budget development courses; office and staff management courses; public relations training; sales, marketing, and advertising training; or basic administration courses at the undergraduate level. Though not listed in any job descriptions, these skills are needed for you to be a successful band director. Even though they are not listed, you must prepare yourself to be able to perform each of these tasks if you want to be successful—or just survive—in the job.

Very few job descriptions for band director on any level completely describe the actual job band directors do. Middle school and high school band directors are business managers, public relations directors, personnel directors, sales people, travel agents, administrators, and many other things as needed. Before applying for the position of band director, you should talk to a band director personally or participate in an electronic forum to find out what you need to know beyond teaching music in order to be a successful band director. Getting firsthand information for what the job entails beyond teaching music will help you to prepare for what will be expected of you and what you'll need to be able to do.

Recruiting for your band will be one of the first and most important jobs you will do. If you can't sell your program to kids from feeder schools or inside your school, chances of your program growing are slim. That's where being a good sales person comes in. You must "sell" students on the idea of investing their time and talents in your program. If they don't buy into your mission or philosophy, you will not succeed no matter how good your music skills are. In order to teach, you must have students. In order to get students, you must sell and market your program.

Good marketing means getting people to realize the value of what you're selling. Before your band plays a single note you have a real product to sell; you're selling the idea of participating in band. You are selling yourself and your vision. How well you present your ideas and sell your mission will mean attracting students or pushing them away. The variety of the product you want to sell is very important. An ice cream shop that only sells one flavor is not going to be very successful. A band program that only offers one style of music or one band is not going to be successful. Make sure that every class offering and extracurricular band you plan to offer is mentioned every time you speak to future students and parents. If classes you want to teach or are trained to teach are not on the course selection form, have your administration add those classes to the course selections for the first or second semester. Besides offering a variety of classes, this customizes your program to you. In some cases you will be forced to recruit for existing classes but you can still give those classes your personal "spin."

If you have a marching band, you will probably want to bring in some help for your drum line, section coaching, silks/flags, or for show design. This means that you will have to review candidates' qualifications and hire the right personnel. You should interview candidates for each position and make sure that they are willing to follow your vision of what the program should be. This is where your best personnel manager/human resources skills come in.

Once you've hired the personnel for your band and put your student leaders in place, you'll need to manage your staff. This means laying out clear expectations and holding everyone accountable for their job performance (the same will be true for your band students performing their jobs). A good manager is also a good motivator. The effective manager creates an environment where people want to do their best and look forward to coming in to do their jobs. Good management skills are vital for today's band director. Organization is the key to success and very few disorganized band programs survive, which means the director's job security is at risk. The better manager you are, the better band you will have.

Good leaders are good administrators. Good administrators articulate their vision to others and get them to follow their lead. As a band director, you will discover the need to develop a plan (such as a mission statement) that incorporates your goals and your vision and sell that vision/plan to your school's administration, students, and parents. Only after you have put your goals and objectives in place will you be able to articulate those goals to others.

PREPARING YOURSELF FOR YOUR NEW PROFESSION

The transition from college student to professional teacher can be difficult and challenging. Student teaching helps you to see some of the things that will be expected of you but since there is a supervising teacher present, you have a support system in place in case you fail. The first day you stand in front of your class and realize that you are the one in charge with no backup, you will have a range of emotions. You will face the anxiety that every new teacher faces as a normal part of starting their teaching career. Having a classroom full of students looking expectantly toward you for direction is the nature of the job. This is one of the reasons you're called a director, not just a conductor. As the name implies, the class will be looking to you for direction.

So, the question is: How do you prepare yourself for success in your new position? How do you go about transforming yourself from student to teacher? What kind of a support system will you need to help you establish yourself in the position and create a strong band program? "How will I attract students to my new program? Am I prepared?" should be questions you ask of yourself.

In order to answer these questions and go about preparing yourself for the first day you stand in front of your class, you must make extensive plans, which involve self-preparation and devising a strategy for building and maintaining a successful band program. This requires systematic planning, finding external resources, and creating a help system or a resource network. The thing you must remember is that you are not alone and there are organizations and services available to you. Creating a resource network should be a major priority.

Creating a Resource Network

One of the first things you should do as a new director is to join your state music teaching association. This provides you with a network of skilled professionals who will be willing to answer your questions and help to allay your fears. State music associations are affiliates of MENC: The National As-

sociation of Music Education. MENC and its state affiliates have resources
that are designed to provide you with the resources needed to be a successful band director.

By attending in-service conventions/conferences on the state, regional,
and national levels, you will be able to associate with some of the best and
brightest music educators around. State association and the MENC websites
have electronic forums that allow you to post specific questions that will
be answered by mentors who have faced some of the very problems you
are facing or will face. Some sites have mentors who have volunteered to
answer your questions as well as open forums where the general membership can act as mentors. Even though you may be the only instrumental
music teacher in your school, there are others in your state or around the
country who are willing to assist you. They know what you are facing and
faced many of the same problems in their early years. Rather than see you
go through trial and error, they will be willing to offer solutions they've
discovered. The first step in learning is facing up to the fact that there are
things you need to learn. Don't be afraid to admit that there are things you
need assistance with.

Most of the problems new teachers or teachers new to a school face involve organization and advance planning. If you don't formulate a plan to
follow, your program will not have a clear direction. Students, parents, and
members of the school community need to have confidence in your ability
to lead, teach, and provide a good music environment in which students
will develop their music skills. You must have your own personal objectives
in place before you and your students develop goals or a mission statement
(which will be discussed in detail later). This includes writing a description
of your program, developing and implementing your personal five-year
plan, and developing a personal philosophy of music education as well as
your own assessment system. All of these will be discussed in detail later
in the book, but creating a system of checks and balances for your achievements is essential. There are National Standards of Music Education that
have been developed to guide music teachers to help all music students to
develop to their optimum level. The National Standards for Music Education referred to in this book are from the Consortium of National Arts
Education's *National Standards for Arts Education.*[1] Here are those standards:

National Standards for Music Education

1. Singing, alone and with others, a varied repertoire of music.
2. Performing on instruments, alone and with others, a varied repertoire
   of music.
3. Improvising melodies, variations, and accompaniments.
4. Composing and arranging music within specified guidelines.

5. Reading and notating music.
6. Listening to, analyzing, and describing music.
7. Evaluating music and music performances.
8. Understanding relationships between music, the other arts, and disciplines outside the arts.
9. Understanding music in relation to history and culture.

Using these standards as a guide for developing your personal mission statement, philosophy, and teaching goals will help shape what you do as a teacher and what your band program will become. The standards will also help you with developing an objective way of assessing your progress and will help keep you on track with what you hope to achieve. They will also serve as a system to keep you on track to achieve your goals. If there is someone you trust such as a former professor, colleague, or mentor from a state or national music education organization, have that person evaluate your progress based on your prescribed plan. This will require you to be able to handle criticism from others should you discover that you're not following your plan or that your plan is too broad or not specific enough to be effective.

The resource system you've created should be used for feedback before you've gone too far in the process of developing your program's objectives. Waiting for an entire semester to elicit assistance may be too late if there is a problem in your plan, goal, or terminal objective (the objective you hope to achieve by the end of a specified period of time).

Being afraid to reach out to others and accepting their criticism is a reason some band directors fail. You are evaluated every time your band performs. Performances are a reflection of how well you have prepared your students and/or how well they have executed what they've been taught. Having an objective listener evaluate your group will be very useful to you in your early days of teaching. By the time your band performs for judges at a band festival, which is usually held in the second semester, bad habits or poor instruction have already negatively impacted your program. Having experienced teachers evaluate your group's progress early on can help you to avoid having to go back and correct your or your students' mistakes.

MENC and its state affiliates provide a network of individuals, materials, and products that can help you address some of the most challenging aspects of music education. These organizations help guide you to people and resources that cost you nothing or very little. By searching their websites, participating in their forums, and reaching out by e-mail or phone to their membership, you will be able to access resources that would be beyond your budget. There are instructional videos, computer-assisted instruction, video master classes, and clinicians that are available to you by you simply asking for help. Join in with another school in your district or a school within a fifty-mile radius of your school to have a clinician or master teacher come and evaluate and clinic/critique your band if necessary.

Another resource that is available to band directors is the system of performing artists provided by instrument manufacturers, reed and mouthpiece manufacturers, and other companies that create band-related products and services. Many of these artists are orchestral players or recording artists and their fees are covered in part or in full by the companies for whom they endorse. These companies want to see your band succeed and grow because that means more products or services purchased. Most of these companies provide a list of clinicians available by region or nationally and will cover the travel costs involved to get the artists to your school or your school's community. As in the case of MENC affiliates, it may be a good idea to join with another school for a clinic/master class. Some artists will perform along with your band, provide a concert that you can use as a fundraiser (or help defray costs), or just do a master class for a select group of students. Whatever way you decide to utilize this resource you should have a clear understanding of what you hope to achieve.

Using Guest Artists with Your Band

In order to get the most out of a guest artist, you need to consider a few things. First, plan how to best use the expertise of the guest artist. To do this, you must be familiar with the guest artist's area of expertise. You wouldn't want to have a classical artist teach jazz technique unless he is also a jazz performer. True, there are techniques that apply to both areas but when bringing in an expert you want to utilize her best field of knowledge. Secondly, be sure to tell the guest artist exactly what you want him to focus on. This does not mean that you should tell him what to do, as an expert; you want him to work from his strengths, not try to use your techniques. Once you start trying to dictate to him how to do his job, you're no longer using his experience, you will simply have him repeating your instructions (you will probably discover he is saying the same things you've said).

Be as specific as possible when describing what your needs are. If intonation is a problem, describe where in a particular piece intonation concerns are greatest. It may be due to several problems from embouchure, range, or breath support (depending on the instruments that are encountering the problem and the amount of experience the players have). Once the "specialist" knows what kinds of stress players are going through to control intonation, she can key in on the specific problem. Since brass players and woodwind players face different challenges, use artists who have experience on those instruments to work with those sections only. Very few artists play both brass and woodwind instruments professionally. Since you want more than general observations from a guest artist, you should use her main area of expertise for your group. When you want the clinician to rehearse a large group, minimize the number of pieces or sections of a piece you want to concentrate on. If your group is having difficulty with rhythmic precision, choose a section of the piece that has the most rhythmic challenges. Ask the clinician to use some exercises that she uses to count tricky rhythms. Untie the clinician's hands to present the material with a fresh perspective.

Once you have created and utilized your resource network, you will be ready to address building and maintaining a program. What you want to build and what others expect you to build may be very different. There are schools and school systems that want to have strong marching band programs, and others that may want a strong concert band or classical program, and others still that want a strong jazz-band program. Whatever the desire of the community is, you will need to make sure that your skill set applies to what is expected. If not, you should find in-service courses, continuing education courses, or summer school courses that will help you develop those skills you may be weakest in. If you're not comfortable, maybe this particular job is not for you.

If there is a community band that you can perform with, join it so that you will be able to maintain an understanding of what players on the other side of the podium experience. Sometimes after being involved in college music programs you lose touch with how players with limited abilities synthesize instructions from the podium. Participating in a group where the "fun" of being in band is the main motivation for membership will help you to understand why creating the right environment for your students is so important. Your perspective of why you're doing the job will shape the perspectives of your students and the way you implement your plan, while building your program will influence others to support you in your quest to build a strong band program. Of course, in order to provide your students with meaningful instruction, it is important that you as a professional musician keep your performance skills strong. Participating in a community band, small ensemble, or performing as a soloist is very important.

Most band directors don't use a textbook for band classes, so method books and sheet music should be chosen carefully. These materials as well as your personal music knowledge and experiences will help shape the type of instruction you will offer your students.

NOTE

1. Consortium of National Arts Education Associations. *National Standards for Arts Education* (Reston, VA: MENC, 1994).

2

Building a Program in Your Current School or a New School

One of the most daunting tasks faced by a new teacher or a director new to a school is to gain acceptance and prove she's the right person for the job. Before interviewing for the position you should make finding out as much as possible about the position, the school's philosophy, parent expectations, the school community, and student expectations and performance levels a priority. One of the first questions you should expect to have asked is what you think you can offer that no other candidate for the job can offer (or some variation of this question). You may also be asked why you wanted to be a band director. If you are not prepared to answer these questions in some variation or another, you shouldn't be interviewing for the job. A well-articulated and thoughtful answer could make the difference between getting the position and not getting hired.

PREPARING FOR THE INTERVIEW

The current trend now for hiring band directors is to have an interview team made up of parents, students, administrators, and the choral director or other music faculty members. Each of these interviewers will have a different expectation and concern you'll need to address. For a successful interview, you should be sure that you express an understanding for each member of the interview team's interests or concerns.

You should be sure to clearly articulate what your personal philosophy of music education is. Share your vision for the position and the band's future, your expectations of students participating in your program, the fact that it's

11

not just your band but the school's band and the community's band, the educational value you see band as having and anything that is specific to you and your mission. Point out why you are the best person to take charge of this program and what you will do for your students, the school, and the community. If you have taught in another school or schools, bring along programs, a list of accomplishments and/or awards, recommendations or references, and a list of songs your previous band(s) successfully performed.

If you have video or audio recordings of past groups, share them. It will impress the interview team if you have copies of your portfolio in individual folders that you can give the committee to view as you speak. Since you probably won't know how many interviewers will be present, print at least ten copies. It's better to have too many copies than not enough. If you are taking video or audio recordings to the interview, be sure to request audio/video equipment for playing the audio CD, tape, video, or DVD.

As you interview, listen carefully to the questions asked and comments made so that you can customize your answers to this particular position. A lot of schools have their philosophy and goals posted either in the main office or main hall way near the entrance to the school (or on their website's home page). Be aware of what they believe and strive to do in order to best answer their questions. Check the trophy cases to get an idea of the kinds of sports participation there is in the school. One, because these are the sports that your program will be competing with to draw students, and two, it will let you know how dedicated the students are to afterschool and extracurricular activities. If there is very little extracurricular activity in a school in general, there will likely be a lack of participation in band. Athletic team successes will help you to understand the level of accomplishment expected of school activities and teams. If there is a school website, familiarize yourself with your potential colleagues. If you can incorporate something about them in your interview answers it will show how well you'll be able to fit in as a "team member." It also demonstrates how meticulous you are in preparing for important activities.

PERSONAL PHILOSOPHY DEVELOPMENT

Not having a personal philosophy of music education is like trying to navigate without a map or Global Positioning System (GPS). You must be able to articulate to others what your belief system is. How much you value music education helps shape how your students value your class and your program. In your personal philosophy you should clearly state how you view the musical development of students as being a lifelong pursuit. Whether they become professional performers or educated audience members and patrons, your job is to help them develop a strong appreciation of music and what musicians do. Future administrators and decision makers who have had a positive experience in music classes are less likely to cut music programs. A sample of what should be contained in your personal philosophy of music education is provided below.

1. State your belief in the importance of music education in the educa-tion of the "whole" child. This means that aesthetic education (cre-ative courses) helps to round out a person and gives him a means of expressing himself creatively. Explain why it is important for a person to realize herself through creative expression.

2. Explain how music is a lifelong endeavor. Every student may not become a performer but most will become consumers and/or audi-ence members. In order for the arts to survive and for people to enjoy leisure activities involving music, they must be informed consumers and patrons. State how much value music has in the everyday life of people. Include how music relates to an individual's cultural, ethnic, and nationalistic identity. An act such as singing the national anthem requires a fundamental understanding of music.

3. Address how your personal view of music shapes your understand-ing of the importance of music as part of the American educational system.

4. Define what music education is in your opinion and how it applies to your personal philosophy of music education. Speak in specific terms, not broad generalizations.

5. State why music is as important as other subjects in American schools. Marching band is not taught in schools just to support athletic ac-tivities and events. Music is a stand-alone subject with its own weight and importance. The self-discipline learned in music is important to personality development. Music is the first course of study that re-quires young students to do serious independent study at an early age. Art starts at an early age but the principles of art learned by younger students are not necessarily the same principles learned by older and advanced students. Students who learn to read music in elementary school are reading the same music as older students though it may be at a lower level of difficulty.

Demonstrate your personal philosophy by continuing to develop your mu-sicianship. Practice your instrument and provide a model for your students. You may be the only professional musician they know personally. Attend in-service training programs or go to summer school to help sharpen your music skills (performance, conducting, and pedagogy). Discuss with your classes, parents (in parent meetings and at concerts), and administrators what you see as your function as the resident musician in your school. The passion with which you express your philosophy will be contagious and will spread throughout your program. Conversely, your inability to articulate your philosophy will also affect your program but the impact will be negative.

PREPARING TO MEET YOUR STUDENTS

Once you have been hired your next task is to connect with your students. Unless this is a newly established school, many of these students have worked with another director and will be waiting to see how you compare. No matter how successful or unsuccessful a band director was, you will still have to win over his students to make them yours.

As soon as you are named to the new position you should prepare a letter to be sent to the homes of current students, post a letter on the school or music department's web page, and plan a meeting with students and parents. An informal meeting as a get-together is a good idea. This gives you an opportunity to mingle with individuals or small groups of students. A pizza party for the students works well and organizing a potluck dinner or cookout for parents and students also works well. In either case the objective is to give your students and their parents an opportunity to get to know you as a person and it gives you an opportunity to get to know them. It is important that you are as open with the students and parents as possible. Connecting on an informal level gives you an opportunity to express how much you are looking forward to what you and your students can achieve and how much you have to offer your students. If you can passionately express your love for music and band and your enthusiasm for doing the job, it will be contagious and your students will feed off of your enthusiasm and passion.

Solicit help from your students to recruit or reclaim students. Your students will know students who may have taken band previously and are not currently enrolled in band. Encourage each student to try to bring at least one student back into the program. This personal contact from students who have met you and discovered your passion for band may cause students who have left the program to return. Form a committee of students who have the responsibility of introducing you to the student body. Let them decide the best way to achieve this. They may use signs or posters, or come up with an activity that will help. If there is a website or social network page the students use, let them post information about you that other students can access.

The impression you make with your students during your first encounter will rally them to help recruit or cause them to not encourage others to join or return to the program. Assuming that students will want to be in band solely because of their love for music is a mistake. You, as the director, will be the means by which they gain musical knowledge. If you are not a "people person," work hard to develop that characteristic. Developing interpersonal skills will help you recruit and retain students. Sell and market your program.

Recruiting

One of the most important activities for building a band program at any level is recruiting. There are several ways to recruit but the common denominator is creating interest in you and your program. When starting a program it is as important that potential students know about you as much as it is important that they know your program goals.

Before you make contact with any students or parents, it is important that you can articulate verbally and in writing what your program will do for individual students and a collective group of students. On the elementary level music classes are often "pull out" classes, meaning that students are taken away from other class activities to come to band. You must prove to them in some way that your class will be as "fun" for them as competing activities. The best way to do this is to show them their ultimate goal—developing into good players and being a member of a good ensemble. Using videos of good bands or good individual players, or going to youtube.com to show them what they can become is very important. Students will vicariously experience what being in band is like. If there are videos of the programs that you feed into that are impressive, use those. Not only do the students see your standard of excellence, they will see the band that they will eventually be a part of. They may see older siblings, neighbors, or friends in the high school or college band in their community.

Elementary students may expect band to be "fun," which it can be, but you must make it clear to them that "fun" is based on achievement and performance excellence. In all of your recruiting it should be very clear that your goal is to develop a program that will achieve and maintain excellence in performing. You should use signs and handouts that focus on the student being a very important part of what will be going on. Students must know that they are an integral part of your group's success. This will help you once the students get in your program and need to practice and work hard in order to achieve excellence. At this point, "fun" may become cloudy so it will be important that the students have "bought into" your idea of program excellence.

Middle school recruiting must start with the elementary school feeder(s) so it's important for middle school band directors to have contact with the feeders. Because of the number of activities middle school students have to choose from, it is very important that you reach the students before they enter the school. One of the biggest challenges is afterschool athletic activities. These activities generally are seasonal but some have year-round events in preparation for the season (e.g., swimming, diving, and gymnastics). You should meet with coaches or the athletic director to find out their competitive schedules and their practice schedules. Avoiding conflicts with these activities is vital to the survival of your program. Making the student choose between band and an athletic activity is not good. More often than not, peer pressure will push them toward athletics and the appeal of professional sports draws students to sporting activities (they see the glamour of professional sports on TV and live). If you have not "sold" students on the benefits of band in middle school while they are in elementary school, you may lose them. One of the best ways for middle school (and high school) directors to get students interested in their program is to bring students from the feeder school to the new school to perform "side by side" concerts or play with the marching band in the stands. Some schools have a middle school marching band night to which they invite middle school students to rehearse and perform one or two selections with the marching band. This gives the students a chance to get to know current students and feel as though they are part of the higher-level band. The idea of "moving up" a level and associating with students from the higher-level school has major appeal. Understanding the dynamic of peer association is important. The younger students feel as though they are a "step above" their current school peers. This also serves to provide them with a group of students in their new school that they can readily identify with once the new school year begins.

Recruiting for the middle school band and the high school band involves many of the same strategies. Developing a newsletter that highlights your program's success and distributing it to your feeder schools is very important. Using technology such as youtube.com or facebook.com can help. Post your band's successes on youtube.com by posting videos that demonstrate your band's best performances and fun activities. Create a facebook page that allows students to post pictures, videos, or comments about band that will make your program appealing to new students (and keep the interests of current students). Create handmade signs with current students that you can post on walls at your school or the feeder schools that use quotes that are unique to your school or community (low tech still works well). In the newsletters you should include a spotlight section where you emphasize individual student achievements. If you have a student who has excelled in activities other than band it's good to highlight those achievements. This sends the message that you are interested in each student as a person, not just what they do for band. Once parents and students know you care about individuals as well as your group's success they will spread the word about you and your program. Word of mouth is still the best way to advertise your program.

High school recruiting is the most difficult. Besides school activities, high school students are part of the work world, drive, and perform community service. It is less difficult to encourage middle school students to continue in band than it is to reclaim students who have had an interruption in their band activity (i.e., dropping band for a year or more). Athletics and peer pressure become greater challenges than before. There will be a core of students loyal to band who won't need recruiting and will enroll in band activities every year with little or no encouragement. Unfortunately, that is the smallest group of students who sign up for band. The line between recruiting and retaining is blurred. You must try to bring in new students and keep those already enrolled.

Once the students come to your school it is important to check on students the middle school or high school counselors may not have enrolled in your classes. This is where a good relationship with your school's counselors is important. They can allow you to go through student records to find students who took band or orchestra in middle school so that you can contact them and their parents to convince them of the benefits of participating in your program.

During the summer before school starts, work with the high school counselors to schedule students for your band classes. Unless there is a class scheduled for a single period that conflicts with your band class, encourage the counselors to schedule students for your class first. Most schools use computer scheduling and the computer simply uses a formula to match students with classes that are available. Students are placed in classes until classes reach the class size cap. Counselors can go into the scheduling program and manually place students in band and mark band as a priority. The computer then locates classes that do not conflict with band. If a class is not found, the counselor can manually locate a class that doesn't conflict or ask the student if he wishes to sign up for another class. If you have explained the importance of continuity for band to the counselors, they may encourage students not to drop band and look for alternatives in the schedule. Because this is time consuming it is in your best interest to offer assistance to the counselor. In your recruiting campaign you should strive to make band appealing.

Creating the aura that band is the best place for students to "belong" is very important. Most high school students are interested in being where the "cool kids" are. It is important that you make band appear to be a "cool" place to be. This is where social networking Internet sites can help. Posting "cool" pictures of your band on one of these sites emphasizing the social side of band will help. During marching band season, "cool" shots of fun in the stands is a big draw. MENC has a sample release form that you can customize to obtain permission for posting images. Use the following link to view this form: http://www.sagepub.com/upm-data/22997_MENC_Audio_visual_likeness_release_07_08.pdf.

One of the dynamics of high school is that students want to be socially active. This translates to band being a place where students can feel as though they are valued and can relate to others (including you as the director). There is a delicate balance between making band fun and striving for excellence. Parents want their children to enjoy Friday or Saturday night high school activities safely. Since most football games are played on Fridays or Saturdays, parents appreciate the fact that band offers a supervised activity that allows their child to have fun in a safe environment. Your recruiting should emphasize that fact.

Developing an attitude of "Fun through Excellence" is important. Emphasize the point that no one enjoys looking bad in front of others and that a poor performance looks bad, so it is important that your band works toward excellence. This helps to create the balance between the hard work that bands have to do to achieve excellence and the fun that can be had after an excellent (not perfect) performance.

As stated, high school recruiting begins with high school and middle school counselors. Middle school counselors help students decide their five-year plan before their last year of middle school. It is important that you articulate to these counselors the importance of these students participating in your program. The fact that colleges and universities look favorably on students who have participated in band and other extracurricular activities is a major selling point.

The other positive points of individual learning activities, self-discipline, and higher levels of achievement help bolster your presentation for parents and counselors. Students are more interested in knowing that they will be able to be successful in an activity they love than they are interested in the long-term results. Keeping all three of these "stakeholders" engaged is very important. In the last year of middle school counselors from the high school will go to the middle school to register students and guide them through the last four years of their five-year plan. It is important that the high school counselors understand that it is important that students who have participated in band in middle school have continuity in their participation. To assist you, there are studies that show that once continuity is broken students generally will not re-enroll.

Whether you are new to a school or are continuing in the position, your recruiting must be aggressive. Going to the guidance office and scouring through student records to find students who have taken band in middle school or your current school is an important part of the recruiting process. Once you find these students, personal contact from you by phone, e-mail, or letter is important. You are the face of your program and it is important that students know that you are interested in them as individuals. Signs, social networks, and videos are appealing but personal contact from you or your students means more. Form a committee of students who have the responsibility of locating students they knew in middle school and high school band. Let them use contemporary media and TV or movie expressions in their presentations. Their choices will relate to the students on their level and will be much more recognizable to the targeted audience. This group, along with you, is responsible for recruiting, retaining and reclaiming.

Retaining

Whether on the elementary, middle school, or high school level, retaining students currently in your program is of the utmost importance. One of the best ways to achieve this on the high school level is to have your students actively participate in writing a program mission statement or setting terminal objectives. During the first week of school, most high schools have abbreviated schedules. This may mean that you don't have time to have a full rehearsal. This is a perfect time for you to explain where you want the program to go and what you personally hope to achieve. Have the students express what they as individuals expect to achieve through participating in band and then as a group formulate a mission statement and steps needed to achieve that terminal goal.

Once this mission statement is decided upon it should be posted on a wall in the band room so that every student sees it every day and is reminded what you are working toward. In your newsletter or on your web page, state your mission clearly for parents, community members, feeder schools, and potential students to see. Everything you do throughout the year should reflect that you are striving to achieve what has been stated in your mission statement. It is important to periodically return to the supporting goals of the mission statement. These goals should be stated in behavioral objectives. Example: By the end of the first quarter students will perform major scales up to four sharps and four flats with 100 percent accuracy. Band is one of the few activities that students must actively strive for 100 percent perfection that can be measured. There is no "almost" performing the right notes; they are either right or wrong. Mastery of goals is measurable.

There will be students of three levels that will be in every band. These students are usually marginally motivated and marginally successful, motivated and successful, or very motivated and very successful. Retaining the marginally successful and very successful is the most challenging. Students drop out of band most often because the music is too challenging or not challenging enough. Finding a balance between those two groups is important for the success of your program. You as the director must be able to identify students at risk of dropping out. Beginning band students are the most vulnerable but discouragement and disinterest can occur at any level. Peer assistance can bring these students together and keep them in your program. Pairing students of a high level with students of lower levels helps. Section rehearsals that give higher-level students an opportunity to help lower-level students learn their parts can serve to build group bonding. This very important social element helps keep all students engaged. It will take some students longer to master a goal than others so boredom or discouragement can take hold. You as the director can control this dynamic by being as encouraging as possible to the lower-level students and finding ways to engage the higher-level students. This may mean giving higher-level students an opportunity to work on solos or more difficult music in a separate rehearsal room. Whatever you can do to engage students at all levels will help you retain these students.

SCHEDULING BAND CLASSES

One of the most overlooked ways of retention is avoiding scheduling conflicts. Music students tend to be some of the most academically advanced students in most schools. That means that there are chances that music classes will conflict with honors classes or classes designed for higher-level students. Knowing this makes it crucial that you communicate this concern with class schedulers and your administration so that these conflicts can be avoided. As a band director you need to take an active part in your school's scheduling. The first step is to make sure that your administration is aware of the fact that your students are involved in advanced classes. Talking to the counselors and polling your students will help. The counselors know immediately when there is a conflict. If you haven't made it clear to them that continuity in your program is vital, they may not attempt to find an alternate class schedule. By polling your students you can determine beforehand the number of students who may face scheduling problems. Having raw numbers will help you make your point with the counselors and the administration that scheduling considerations need to be made to avoid the loss of any of your students. This may seem to be a lot of work but the survival of your program depends on it. Once this is established, there should not be a problem in subsequent years. If you are on the high school level you must make the middle school counselors aware of the same things you are doing with the high school schedulers and counselors.

DEVELOPING A FIVE-YEAR PLAN

Before you set program goals, you need to develop your own philosophy of teaching. What do YOU want to do as a professional? What do you want your students to gain from working with you? What resources do you need to have to achieve your individual goals? Once you've decided where you want to go personally, you can then decide on what you want to achieve with the program you wish to build. Whenever you set goals, you always start with the end product first and then work your way backward. Simply put, where do you see your program five years in the future? If you can't visualize the finished product you have nothing to strive toward. This shouldn't be vague; you must specifically state your plan: "In five years I'll have the best band program in my district." Once you establish specifically what you hope to achieve with your group you need to work with them to develop a group "mission statement." You can call this statement whatever you want—that's not important. What is important is getting the group to decide on a unified goal to strive toward.

MISSION STATEMENT DEVELOPMENT AT LOWER LEVELS

On the middle school level developing a mission statement will require active participation from you. You should develop choices of a mission statement and let your students vote on or choose the statement that best represents the group's overall goal. The importance of the group taking ownership in the group's mission will be important. The idea is the same as the high school mission statement, engaging students so that they will want to stay in your program. Your rehearsals should reflect parts of your mission statement and supporting behavioral goals. Later in the book there will be specific suggestions on writing lesson plans and stating behavioral objectives. At this point it is important to note that retention is directly related to how engaged your students are and how they feel about coming to your class. Reinforce these ideals and goals every year. Don't assume that your students will remember why you were successful the year before. Write a mission statement every year even if you are restating the same goals. Change the sentence structure to reflect that this is a new year and a new statement.

Elementary school students won't be able to develop a mission statement but the importance of them "buying into" the mission of the program is important. Talking about your goals in class and emphasizing how important achieving your goals is to the life of your program. The goals you set must be understandable and achievable by your students so that you can constantly reference them. For example: "Remember, we said that we want to play this song on our winter concert; well, if we keep working on this section and do it as well as we're doing it now, we'll reach that goal." A sample mission statement could be written and stated in this manner:

It is the Mission of the Atlantis Middle School Band to promote, enhance, and maximize music performance levels of all students of Atlantis Middle School.

This statement is short but succinct and states very clearly what you and your band plan to do during the year.

WRITING A SYLLABUS

The music supervisor for most school districts has a description or syllabus for each type of band class (e.g., Beginning Band, Intermediate Band, Marching Band, Concert Band, Symphonic Band, and Wind Ensemble). If there is a class description or syllabus available, you can customize it to apply to your particular school and classes. The syllabus should clearly state your class expectations, the class description, your grading policy, discipline policy, performance attire, and how the final or semester grades will be determined. You may customize your class syllabus to address your objectives for the grade level of music a particular band will study. Since this is a class, it's wise to use the term "study" to refer to rehearsal pieces so that parents and administrators are aware of the educational value of your class. The misconception of how easy it is to successfully participate in a music class is expelled once your syllabus clearly states that you expect your students to be active learners. Stating your lesson plans in behavioral terms will reinforce this concept.

If there are prerequisites for a class, a limited number of parts, or if the class is by audition only, a description of each of these requirements must be listed and explained in the syllabus. Parents and prospective students may not know the difference between a class listed as Concert Band from a Symphonic Band or Wind Ensemble. If the progression you expect is for students to move from Concert Band to Symphonic Band and then audition for Wind Ensemble, you need to clearly state that. Students may be able to participate in Symphonic Band without participating in Concert Band if your instrumentation needs make that necessary but to avoid looking as though you arbitrarily made the decision, state that in the syllabus. Since Wind Ensemble sometimes only has one player per part it may mean that some advanced students will not get to audition for the group due to instrumentation restrictions. Once again, to avoid looking arbitrary, state those restrictions and any exceptions in the syllabus.

TEACHER–STUDENT RELATIONSHIP

One of the problems a lot of directors have is not connecting with their students on a personal level. This relationship is a key to maintaining a successful program. Knowing the names of each of your students can be an important part of their retention. Calling a student by their name is better than calling them by their part (i.e., 3rd chair 3rd clarinet). If possible, you should stand at the door, greeting each of your students as they enter the classroom. This way you have a chance to say things to them that aren't necessarily related to band. Yes, you're busy; yes, there are other things that could be done; but nothing is more important than connecting with your students.

Because band classes are larger than most other classes it can be difficult to immediately memorize your students' names. Make a seating chart that has the students' names and the parts they play. As time goes on you'll know their names. It also cuts down on taking roll; you have a visual of who is present. Ask the students not to fill in empty seats until you have checked the roll. After you have auditioned students for seating placement you will probably not need to use the seating chart. To give students the message that they are important to you as individuals, you'll need to make every effort to memorize their names.

It is a difficult task to memorize the names of students in larger classes but the same attention you pay to reading scores or memorizing a piece of music should be used to memorize names. Once again, people are more apt to want to be involved in activities in which they feel that they are valued members than to stay in activities in which they feel they are expendable parts. Retention of students involves subtle, nonverbal messages as much as verbally expressed messages. Creating a welcoming environment starts with activities as small as a greeting at the beginning of class.

During that first week, there are many activities that you can use as bonding exercises. One activity is to have each student interview another student and then present their findings to the group. Students will talk one-on-one with more ease than standing in front of the group and talking about themselves. Have a student interview you and share their discoveries about you. Share with them your favorite movies, hobbies, video games, and so on. The more they feel they know about you, the more they'll bond with you. The ultimate goal is team building so that each person feels a connection with others. That's the goal of band when you think about it; a group of individuals forming a connection to face a single goal—an optimum performance. Band is an activity that requires a group of individuals to work together as a single entity. This attitude will cause students to sign up for future classes because they don't want to let their group down.

Reclaiming

Reclaiming former students should be an activity of all stakeholders—current members, parents, staff, and you, the director. As described earlier, stakeholders are all of those who have "bought into" the mission of the band program. This can and should involve your band boosters or parent support group. The simplest acts performed by your boosters' organization can reap major benefits to reclaiming students.

The boosters can hold activities that have great mass appeal to your present and former students. Some of the same activities used for recruiting new students can be used to reclaim students who have left the program. Having students who are currently in the program "reach out" to students you wish to reclaim is very important. Don't underestimate the effectiveness of personal contact. Posting signs on walls or using social networks for mass appeal is good, but there is no personal connection. One-on-one contact shows the targeted students that they as individuals are important. By now, you should recognize that this is a recurring theme for recruiting, retaining, and reclaiming. Nothing you do is as important as appealing to students personally.

At the end of the year as you prepare for your awards and recognition activity, make it a point to let those students who have left the program know that they are missed and you would very much like for them to return. Of course, if there are students who have been disruptive or negative influences, bringing them back into the program may be risky. In these cases you should meet one-on-one with these students and let them know what your expectations are for them if they decide to return. Meeting with them and their parents to review the benefits of the program and how their positive participation affects them and the rest of the band can avoid future problems. There will obviously be some cases where the student and the band will benefit from their nonparticipation.

Developing a plan for reclamation is very important. The following points are important to consider before launching a reclamation drive.

1. Identify the students you want to reclaim. As was stated above, you may not want to reclaim all of the students who left your program.
2. Present a united front. You don't all have to say the same things the same way, but every "recruiter" should have talking points that highlight your goals. Avoid generalizations and be specific as to why you think the student will benefit your program and benefit from your program.
3. List the program's goals and points from the mission statement and how they relate to the student being recruited. Highlight points that specifically apply to the student. If he is a low brass player and you need low brass players, tell him how much his returning to the program will mean to everyone. Tell him how much he can contribute to the group's attaining its goals.
4. Stress how much they are missed. Everybody likes to know that they are needed. Letting these students know that their contributions to the group were significant and that without them participating things are

just not the same. They may or may not have been soloists or leaders but that doesn't mean that their contribution wasn't important to the life of the group. Stress that a group is no stronger than the sum of its parts.

Remember, the important part of reclaiming former students is that it will give your band continuity from year to year. If students don't see band as a four-year commitment you will find yourself rebuilding every year.

The Importance of Praise and Individual Recognition

One of the best ways to retain students is to recognize individual or small-group achievement. This can be done as a student spotlight, player of the week, or section of the week recognition. It can take many forms. Take a picture of the person or group to be recognized and display it on the bulletin board in the band room, post it on the web page, put in on the social network page, announce it from the podium. The esteem of the recipient(s) will rise and this will create the kind of environment individual players will want to remain in. You can leave the recipient's picture displayed for the entire year and have a special recognition for those who get recognized more than once. At the end of the year you can award a section of the year award or most valuable player award. Students who are interested in signing up for band will notice that they can be recognized for their achievements and see that they as individuals will be valued in your program. Don't underestimate how much this means to students of all levels.

If you have a newsletter that is sent to feeder schools or goes home to parents (elementary schools have weekly newsletters that go home to parents), this is a valuable recruiting tool. Parents see that their child will be recognized for their contributions to your program. Middle school band directors and high school band directors can send items to the elementary school to be included in their weekly newsletter. This sense of community helps to reinforce the fact that successful programs on the high school level depend on continuity from elementary school through high school. A lot of middle and high school students have siblings who are still in elementary school and who will see their older siblings' accomplishments and want to achieve the same kind of recognition in the future. This kind of "recruiting from within" helps to insure that you have a system developed to cause younger students to aspire to become a part of your program in the future.

BEYOND THE FIRST ENCOUNTERS

Make sure that the person your students and their parents first met is the same person they see every day and at performances. If your students aren't reminded every day that you have their best interest and success as a priority they won't want to stay with your program. Establishing standards and expectations is the best way to establish what success is for you. Without standards and expectations, your program will not have a sense of direction or purpose. Band students are generally interested in a lot of creative activities and will not want to waste their time in activities that are not fulfilling or challenging.

During the first meeting have your students fill out cards with their name (nickname), instrument, e-mail, phone number, parents' names, parents' emergency phone numbers (cell phone is recommended), grade, and age. Make note of the phonetic pronunciation of difficult names so that you can call their names correctly. After learning your students' names, try to find out their interests outside of band. If you participated in activities besides band when you were in school, share that with your students. It lets them know that you don't expect them to only be a part of band but that you do expect them to give themselves completely to band while they are participating in band activities. High expectations yield high achievement and commitment is a key to success.

In all communications with your students and their parents you should include scheduled performances and rehearsals so that it is clear to all that you expect your students to honor their commitment. If students are not in band for a grade there should be something that holds them accountable to their commitment. Whether it is trip eligibility or awards, there needs to be some motivation and consequence for participation or for not participating. To have consequences without rewards will be counterproductive. Praise and reward your students who demonstrate their dedication to the group by recognizing those who are punctual for rehearsals, have perfect attendance, come prepared for rehearsals and performances, and so on. You can post their names on a bulletin board or hold a special social activity for them once a week (pizza party, video viewing, ice cream or dessert party). Generally, the recognition will suffice. Something as simple as calling out their name in front of the group to give them special recognition goes a long way with young people.

Whatever you choose to do should become a tradition for your program. Incoming students will look forward to being recognized. The reasons for the recognition promote positive actions from your students. You can even recognize the section that has the most people who are punctual, well prepared (having their music, instruments, and equipment), and who have the best attendance overall. This promotes quality participation and will help build group unity as sections strive to work positively together. You'll discover that when you focus on the positive so will your students. This creates a nurturing environment that students will look forward to being a part of. Studies show that team building for groups united by a common goal is very important to the life and success of a group. That's why many businesses hold survival retreats for their employees. These retreats are quite valuable to building the company's morale and confidence in one another. Band camp in the summer can serve as a team-building activity. Besides marching, learning music, and preparing for shows, your summer band camp should include activities designed to reinforce the concept of band being a "one for all, all for one" activity. Remember, the concept of band is based on individual parts working together to create a unified body.

3

Creating a Handbook for Band

PREPARING A COMPREHENSIVE HANDBOOK

One of the first of many tasks you should undertake as a band director is to develop and write a band handbook. This handbook should include your mission statement, a description of your band program, concert attire, fees, festival information, trip information, fundraising information (student expectations and accounts), grading policies, and a clear statement from you as the director concerning your personal goals and expectations. This handbook will be a reference for your students and their parents.

Because there may be students who are not enrolled in band as a class but are participating in band as an extracurricular activity, it is important that the handbook contains a list of expectations for those who are not taking band for credit. This includes the number of rehearsals a student can miss before being excluded from a performance or a trip and their award eligibility. Students who could not take band for credit may be interested in continuing in band as an extracurricular. Should they elect to participate it is important that they know what is expected of them. It is also important that students taking band for credit don't feel that extracurricular members don't have to follow the same rules they have to follow.

If there are fees and expenses associated with participation in band, those fees and expenses should be stated in the handbook with an explanation of how and why they are required. If students will receive financial assistance because of special needs, those requirements for eligibility should be listed along with the process the student must follow (with a timeline) to secure funding. If students are required to provide their own equipment or rent instruments, vendors and prices should be included in the handbook. A list of private instructors and their rates should also be included. The band handbook should be a quick reference with complete information on the requirements, expectations, and needs for band participation.

If your school district has rules for band participation, those rules should be included in the handbook. A copy of the health or medical form that will be used for the year should be included and removed from the handbook to be returned to you to keep on file. Be sure to include a table of contents for quick reference. Parents should not have to read the entire handbook to locate a specific topic (even though you do want them to read the entire handbook at some point).

Make sure that your music supervisor and school's administration receive a copy of the handbook before you distribute it. This will guarantee that the handbook is in compliance with school district and local school requirements. You want to avoid running into difficulty with administrators because a parent takes issue with something in the handbook. Check with other band directors in your district or your music supervisor to make sure that your book covers all expectations and requirements that will help your program to be successful.

Program Description

Your program description should be a clear, unambiguous statement of your expectations of what your program will be. You should make it clear to everyone who reads it what your vision of the program is and what you expect it to become under your leadership. Allow for there to be space for you and your students to develop a mission statement so that they will have a stake in the program's success. This will give them an opportunity to take ownership in the program. This ownership will lead to their having accountability in the success or failure of the program based on a mutual vision.

The program description will be as important as the mission statement. It will be a description of how all components of the band program will work together to achieve the goals and objectives stated in the mission statement. If the mission statement is a general/overall view of the program, the program description should state how you will achieve these goals. As in lesson plans, these goals should be stated in measurable behavioral terms.

Concert Attire

One of the most unifying actions that can be taken is the simple act of everyone being dressed in uniform fashion. This can be in the form of actual band uniforms, concert dresses and suits, tuxedos and formal dresses, or a variety of dress styles. The important thing is that a uniform mindset leads to the achievement of a unified goal. You are not a group of individuals once you take the stage. You are a unified force with a single common goal—an outstanding musical performance. In the handbook you should explain clearly why it is important that your students dress uniformly. It is more than a visual effect; it is a mindset that says we are one, a group of individuals working as one toward a common goal.

Fees

If there are out-of-pocket fees for participating in band they should be explained in the handbook with a clearly stated schedule of when the fees are due. Some schools and school systems have fees built in for participation in extracurricular activities. Since band is a cocurricular activity (graded and nongraded participation), it is very important that you itemize what the fees are for. The range of these fees can be for uniform deposits covering cleaning and maintenance, instrument rental (maintenance and upkeep), and field trip or festival fees (for buses). If your band has needs that aren't listed here, customize your list to meet your program's needs.

Festival Information

Every state music association has a description of the importance of festival participation and a description of festival grades. Include this in your handbook so that your students and parents understand the purpose of the festival. Most local, state, and district festivals are not competitions. There is no winner or loser determined. Bands are graded based on standardized criteria. You may also include your personal view of festival participation and why your students are required to participate. Show the percentage of their grade that is associated with festival participation and that you expect 100 percent participation from your students. Also explain that successful participation (a Superior rating) in local festivals qualifies bands to participate in state festivals. Even though a Superior rating qualifies bands to participate in state festivals, a Superior rating is not the only successful rating. Most state associations have a festival handbook that explains festival ratings and those explanations should be copied exactly as printed and placed into your handbook. Bands in their early stages may not qualify for the state festival but receiving an Excellent or Good rating may demonstrate how far along they have come since first performing the music. For educational value you should explain how your view of your band's growth is not determined just by the final rating but also includes how well your students conducted themselves during the learning process. Judges only see a snapshot of what your band has done and judge the band based on a standard of performances they have witnessed or expect from personal experience. You recognize individual and group growth. If you state this in your handbook before the festival experience it doesn't sound as if you're trying to rationalize a poor performance.

Fundraising Overview

If students can cover part or all of their fees and additional expenses through participating in fundraisers, explain that clearly in the handbook. Determine the percentage of all monies collected that will apply to individual participants. If you have the dates and types of fundraisers that you will be sponsoring, furnish that information in the handbook. State that if you discover the need for more funds to be raised you may need to add more fundraisers. If the number and types of fundraisers will be determined by a committee of parents and yourself, explain how that process will work. You should also meet with the school's financial officer to make sure any statements you make in writing comply with your school's financial policies. Some schools have complete guidelines for fundraisers and require that they be added to the school calendar. Your fundraising activities and dates should be included in the handbook.

Grading Policy

Your grading policy and the percentage of the grade each activity will be averaged on should be spelled out completely. Class participation, tests or quizzes, festival participation, concert and performance participation, special class projects, outside-of-school concert attendance, and individual performance assessments are a few of the items that should be included. This list can be customized based on your expectations or requirements stated by your school district. A lot of school districts have standardized grading policies and expectations, so print those exactly as stated in your handbook. It is important that students and parents understand that students aren't guaranteed an "A" in your class just for being present. You can't argue the academic value of band if you don't value the academic side of your class. Don't be afraid to give outside-of-class assignments. Those assignments can include critiquing a professional or college-level performance, preparing concert notes on one of the pieces you're performing, researching the composer of one of your performance pieces, or many other items you consider important to the musical development of your students.

4

Developing Lesson Plans

DEVELOPING CLEAR LESSON PLANS

A lot of band directors make the mistake of thinking that they don't need lesson plans. For every rehearsal you and your students must be clear on what you expect to achieve during that rehearsal. The lesson plan should state what you hope to focus on and achieve but also be flexible enough for you to be able to handle problems that may come up during the rehearsal. Example: If your lesson plan is based on articulation for a specific section of a piece but you discover that students are having technical difficulties, clear up the technical problems and return to your written plans. If you are being observed by administrators it's important that you explain to them the elasticity of your lesson plan for the day. Since they are not always aware of how band classes are managed and how our goals differ from other classes, it's imperative that you make it clear that letting a problem go unresolved in order to stay "true" to the lesson plan negatively impacts the overall goal for your program. You, your class, and any observers must understand that each lesson is building on a measurable goal of excellence and achievement during performances. Audiences may not be aware of your plan but they will be aware of whether or not your band has achieved its goals.

Be sure to state your goals in measurable objectives. Band is one of the few classes where 100 percent achievement of a goal is realistic. There is no such thing as "almost" playing the correct note. It's either 100 percent correct or 100 percent incorrect.

Before writing daily or weekly lesson plans you should plan your semester or year. This means formulation of an end or terminal objective. This terminal objective states your "destination" and your plans state how you will go about achieving that goal (getting to the destination). You will need to break the objective down into units. Unit plans will be broadly stated plans that will include several specific goals. These goals can include the items you consider to be the most important objectives you wish to achieve by the end of a specified term (a quarter, semester, or full year). Once you have formulated unit plans, you will want to break them down into manageable lessons. These lessons can be divided into weekly or daily lesson plans.

Every part of your rehearsal should be reflected in your lesson plan, from the warm-up to the closing exercise. If you state that you plan to work on intonation, articulation, or attacks and releases, it's important that you describe specifically how you plan to address each during the rehearsal and what exercises you plan to employ in order to achieve your stated goals. If you encounter problems with specific sections or instruments, state in your plans that you will schedule section rehearsals to fine tune things that class time will not allow. Your daily or weekly plans should demonstrate a measureable relationship to your unit plan(s).

Sample Plan #1: Intonation

Getting your band to play in tune with themselves (good intonation throughout the range of their instrument), their section, and the band overall should be a major and ongoing priority. Having your students tune to a tuner helps but should not be the only tuning exercise during the rehearsal. Each rehearsal should have a minimum of ten minutes dedicated specifically to tuning and during the rehearsal intonation problems should be addressed as they happen. Some directors have an electronic tuner set up in the band room and have their students tune up at the beginning of the rehearsal. This is a good pretuning exercise but once the instrument warms up and the student's embouchure warms up, the pretuning will not remain the same. The following is a sample plan to state how you plan to address intonation during your class/rehearsal.

> To achieve pitch accuracy while playing, the class will play a C major scale alternating between singing and playing each note. The students will play notes 1, 3, 5, and 7 with 100 percent pitch accuracy and will sing notes 2, 4, 6, and 8 with 100 percent pitch accuracy. Descending, the students will sing and play the notes in opposite order, playing notes 8, 6, 4, and 2 and singing notes 7, 5, 3, and 1 with 100 percent accuracy. Upon the completion of this warm up, the students will play the Bach chorale found on page 16 in the warm up book of *16 Bach Chorales*: G. SCHIRMER, INC. After playing the chorale, the band will tune to concert pitch F and then concert pitch B-flat.
>
> The group will perform our first rehearsal piece playing each note of section A as whole notes, listening carefully to each note and correcting pitch prob-

lems with 100 percent accuracy. We will then play section A as written and each student will make intonation corrections as we play in "real time." The focus will be on listening to pitches from the bottom up within their section and across the band.

The concept of the Pyramid of Sound will be explained and reinforced during the rehearsal. The Pyramid of Sound is a visual concept showing that the lower voices (bottom) should be the strongest dynamic level, the middle of the pyramid should be the medium volume, and the top (apex) of the pyramid should be the softest (f–mf–p). When tuning, tubas and lower voices will play and tune first, the mid-range instruments will join the lower voices and adjust to the lower voices, and then the upper voices and students playing first parts will be the last group added. Following this, the entire band will play at the same time and make any necessary adjustments. Percussion instruments will not balance from the bottom up (the bass drum or lower timpani can destroy the best efforts at balance if played too loud).

As the band plays, the director will bring attention to the constant need to adjust individual tuning from within each section, listening to the lower parts and lower voices (third parts, second parts, and first parts). This constant reinforcement from the director will increase the awareness of the students to the importance of listening as it relates to playing well in tune.

If possible there should be a digital chromatic tuner near each section so that students can have reinforcement to their "ear" to assist them with tuning adjustments. As time passes during the year, students will depend more on their aural discrimination (ear) than on the mechanical tuner but should still be encouraged to utilize the digital tuners. Directors who make good intonation a priority will discover that besides working on intonation, they are also working on developing cross listening skills. Cross listening will help with balance, identifying where the melody is as it works its way through the band and intonation accuracy. The unit plan for this lesson plan could fall under the general goal of cross listening.

Quick Fixes for Intonation Review

Intonation will be an ongoing concern for most bands. Students have to be made aware of the importance of playing in tune throughout the range of their instrument; playing in tune in their section; and playing in tune across the band. One of the first jobs for you as the band director is to make your students aware of the way to play their instrument in tune. You should address embouchure control; have the students check each note they play with a tuner, and have them sing pitches. Have your students alternate between playing and singing the notes of the major and minor scales during warm-ups. The more they sing, the more conscious they will become of pitch accuracy.

As a band, tune by Concert F and Concert B-flat. Have brass players play pitches a fourth or fifth apart to place stress on the embouchure (trumpet and baritone players should play the first five notes of the key they are tuning to in succession). Have clarinet and alto/baritone saxophone players tune to Concert D because of the short distance the air travels through the cylinder. All other woodwinds (including tenor saxophones) should tune to Concert A. Remember, a lot of bands are very conscious of playing tuning notes in tune but do not transfer that care to other notes. Use minor scales and different modes for full band warm-ups. Some bands tune to Concert C so that trumpets, baritones and tubas have to learn to use the third valve slide to play Concert C in tune.

Sample Plan #2: Tempo Control

One of the problems a lot of bands have is the tendency to rush. There are many reasons why bands rush but more often than not it is because students are not looking up at the director. Building on what was done in Lesson Plan 1, you can use the initial warm-up to drive home the importance of watching the conductor's baton. Instead of giving each note of the scale, chorale, or the rehearsal section fixed rhythmic values, have the students move from note to note based on the movement of the baton. Use an unpredictable dictation (baton movement) so that students have to watch without anticipating your motion. It can be stated in the following manner:

> The class will perform the B-flat major scale based on baton dictation (movement) with 100 percent accuracy. The director will conduct each note and will not change notes until each student attacks with the down beat with 100 percent precision. Students will adjust their stands in such a way that they will be able to see the conductor and the music. During the rehearsal piece, students will look up at the podium every four measures and at each rehearsal mark.
>
> Next, the director will have students close their eyes and play the F major scale on whole notes after the conductor counts out two measures of 4/4 time. Students will count to themselves without tapping their feet. If the director senses that the students are rushing, the director will tap or clap the tempo to get the students to focus on the established tempo. Once students are back on tempo the director will stop tapping or clapping the beat.

Another helpful and fun exercise is to have the students sit someplace in the room other than where they would normally sit and sit beside someone who is playing a part other than the part they are playing. This serves many helpful purposes. First, students can't build up the momentum to rush by gathering fellow rushers. Second, they will hear parts being played by instruments they may not hear normally. When they return to their normal seats you should point out the importance of them listening across the band to hear the part(s) they heard during the "scramble" seating.

From this point you can continue to discuss balance, intonation, and tempo accuracy/rushing in every rehearsal. Also, discourage students from tapping their feet while playing. If they must tap their feet have them tap their heels. When students see the movement of another player's feet, they tend to rush. It is impossible for any player to tap with the same tempo dictated by the baton. The unit plan for this lesson could be cross listening or a unit on rhythmic and tempo accuracy. Since rushing sometimes results from inaccurate rhythms from releasing too soon, tempo accuracy should be paired in a unit on rhythmic accuracy.

Sample Plan #3: Attacks and Releases

One other reason students rush and play out of tune is because of attacks and releases. Most directors don't often think of attacks and releases causing bad intonation, but the tongue placement for attacks and releases can negatively impact on the embouchure. Changes in embouchure while playing will cause intonation problems unless those changes are purposely being made to correct intonation problems. Because some students stop the sound with their tongues, "slap tonguing" will cause most players to play sharp.

The most recognizable problem with attacks and releases is rushing. If notes are started early or released early or late, rushing occurs. Stress the importance of attacks coming precisely on the down beat or exactly where they are to occur on the up beats (after an eighth rest, sixteenth rest, etc.). Notes must be held until the start of the next note or rest (unless a mark such as staccato shortens the note). A whole note must be held until beat one of the next measure. If the note is released early, the start of the next note will be early and rushing will be the result. The exercise used to have students avoid rushing is the same exercise that can be used for accurate attacks and releases. Have the students attack on your down beat and release precisely on your cutoff. The down beat will be important even for those who have a rest on the down beat. They still must watch to accurately come in on time. Have your students cut off notes by stopping the air, not by using the tongue. Not only does this help with tempo accuracy, it sounds better. This can be stated in the following way:

> In order to achieve 100 percent accuracy with attacks and releases, students will start the note (attack) with their tongue and release the note by stopping the air (not by using the tongue). Students will watch the conductor for the start and release of the note. Using the F major scale in 4/4 time, the students will start each quarter note on the beat dictated by the movement of the baton. Upon completing this exercise, we will use the same scale but students will attack each note on the "and" of the beat (eighth notes on the second half of the beat). For both exercises the students will hold the last note until cutoff by the conductor. This will be repeated until completed with 100 percent accuracy.

This exercise may take a long time to complete until the students are watching and adhering to the movement of the baton. Do not stop the exercise because of the amount of time needed to complete it accurately. As has been discussed before, the amount of time devoted to achieving goals with 100 percent accuracy will cut down on problems and time later. Once a goal has been met, periodically revisit the exercise for reinforcement purposes. Incorporate all exercises into your daily warm-up activities throughout the year. While rehearsing, remind your students of the exercises you used to address certain problems and they will start to make the necessary adjustments. The idea of all of these lessons and exercises is to get students to self-correct and be conscious of the necessary remedies to common problems. By reminding your students of the purpose of each lesson, they will take performing the warm-ups with more seriousness and attention to purpose.

Articulation is a key to accurate attacks and releases. It is important that you explain to your students the fundamentals of proper articulation. There are a few quick fixes you can use to explain basic articulations and have your students execute them properly.

Simple Articulation Fixes/Explanations

Staccato: Short and detached.
Tenuto: Note held full value until the start of the next note.
Marcato: An accented short and detached note sometimes referred to as a "bell tone." This can also be thought of as an accented staccato note.
Legato: A slurred note; notes that fall under a slur mark should not be tongued except for the first note under each slur mark.
Accent: A full value note that begins with a heavy attack; the decay is determined by the duration of the note.

Sample Plan #4: Sight Reading

When you introduce any piece of music to your class you should have them sight read a portion of the piece or the entire piece. Sight reading is an important part of a band's success at festivals as well as developing musicianship. The instincts used to develop good sight-reading skills can also be used when learning a piece of music for class and performing pieces that are familiar. The concept of looking ahead when playing carries over from sight reading to playing familiar pieces. As stated in another section of the book, most students don't sight read well because of the fear of sight reading. Once again, if students are aware of the fact that they sight read in daily life with such activities as reading, driving down an unfamiliar street, and carrying on a conversation, the fear of sight reading becomes a less daunting task. As they drive they must look ahead to see street signs and potential dangers and as they converse they must listen in order to contribute or react to a conversation.

The same can be true with sight reading music. They may not know every rhythm in a measure but by working from the familiar to unfamiliar, they can figure out how to play a difficult measure. Sight reading depends on aural recognition of intervals, analyzing rhythms at sight, and looking ahead. Most students think that sight reading is only reading the written notes but you should point out that sight reading includes following dynamics, watching for tempo and meter changes, expression marks, and looking for signs or symbols telling them to repeat or go back to a specific section or part of music (e.g., D.C al Coda, etc.). You should make it a point to sight read music one grade level lower or the same grade level as the music being played in class at least once a week (more is better but at least once every week). You can even have them attempt to sight read a piece that is more difficult than pieces they are currently working on in class.

If your school has block scheduling and your class meets for sixty to ninety minutes, these plans can be expanded. You will be able to spend more time on developing good band skills through having students perform, organize, and describe the points you are covering. Once students articulate the concepts you are working on, they will grasp them much better. Even in shorter class periods you should have students analyze their progress in achieving specific goals and objectives you have been working on. Their insights and observations may surprise you. Peer evaluation is a valuable part of your band's improvement. You should be sure to explain that their observations should not include personal attacks on individual players. If there is a single player on a part, the students should not identify the player by name. They should refer to the specific part even though everyone knows the player's name. Example "In measure 23 the tuba was rushing," rather than, "Ron was rushing in measure 23." This way the player is not defensive and does not disengage from the rehearsal. You don't want any students to feel that they are not valued and therefore elect not to return the next semester. Retention is a process that takes place every day. How you monitor peer assessments affects how students feel about you and your class. Maintaining a positive, nurturing environment should be one of your top priorities.

Sample Plan #5: Phrasing and Expression

One of the key points of a good performance is phrasing and expression. Phrasing and expression give a piece of music life. The more accurate the expression and phrasing, the more interesting the performance will be. Breathing, articulation, fingering accuracy, and dynamics all play major roles in a good performance of a particular piece of music. Phrasing and interpretation come from the podium but depend on the execution by individual performers to be effective. This is also something that starts in the warm-up. Having students play scales or exercises that last for four measures on one breath and using different dynamics on eight measure phrases is transferable to whatever piece or pieces you'll be rehearsing. It can't be stressed enough that there should be a recognizable relationship between the warm-up and the rehearsal pieces. This will also help with classroom management and discipline. After taking their instruments out and taking their seats the students are engaged from the very beginning of class until the end. Chorales are very valuable tools for teaching phrasing and expression. You can apply what you are doing for tone control, breathing, use of dynamics, attacks and releases, intonation, articulation and rhythmic accuracy from chorales to your performance pieces.

To make the point clear you can slow the tempo of a fast piece down to a chorale tempo and give the students an opportunity to hear how the chords line up in ways they may not be aware of at faster tempi. Stated in lesson-plan form you can describe exactly what you are doing and the expected result. Explain clearly to your class the purpose of giving them an opportunity to hear the chord progressions and what you expect them to learn from it. This can be stated in the following way:

> Focusing on phrasing and expression, students will play measures one through sixteen of the rehearsal piece at mm. 60 taking a breath every four measures. They will crescendo from piano to forte during measures one through eight and decrescendo from measures nine through sixteen as dictated by the conductor. This exercise will be repeated with staggered breathing using the same dynamics design. Upon the completion of this exercise the class will perform the piece at the marked tempo and then describe the commonality between the two ways citing specific sections of the piece.

Having the class describe what they heard will enable them to recognize that counter melodies are harmonically related to the block chord progressions and the melody. They will also be able to clearly hear how dynamics affect the overall interpretation of the piece. Active listening and analyzing what they heard will make your students more responsible for their performance within the group and their achieving the group's goals. Once again, active participation assures that your students will stay engaged and will work toward the group's common goal.

The most important part of implementing lesson plans is to make sure that your students thoroughly understand what you're expecting them to achieve. By using behavioral objectives and discussing them, your students will see the importance of the exercises and how they apply to your objectives. Since repetition is an important part of achieving mastery, your students will grasp the concept more quickly once you have explained the need to repeat certain exercises.

Program notes are an important part of lesson plans. These notes furnish information on the composer, the style of music, periodic information and national/cultural/ethnic information. When presenting a piece of music, the more you can share with your students about the piece will give them some insight as to how the piece should be played. Researching the pieces you are presenting will help students understand the educational value of the music. Quite often students become engaged because of the information you share. Many of your students have interests such as history and geography that you can build on to get them actively involved. Remember, there are students in band class who may not be motivated by the intrinsic value of the music. The level of interest and motivation of each student will also determine the pace at which they will learn. While working on a march by John Philip Sousa you can discuss the uniqueness of the American band movement. Students may wonder why European music is dominated by orchestral writing and not band music. The absence of the sousaphone as a classical orchestra instrument can lead to a discussion of the development of the marching band in America. This can also lead to a discussion of how music is linked to national pride and the cultural significance of some styles of music.

GETTING YOUR STUDENTS TO REACT
TO DIFFERENT CONDUCTING PATTERNS

After you have focused on your students reacting to the down beat and cut-off movements of the baton, your next step is to get them to react to long, short, slow, and quick baton movements. As you go through conducting motions, have your students play warm-up exercises and scales on different articulation patterns dictated by conducting motions. Small, short motions should be used for staccato (short and detached) or marcato (short, detached, and accented) notes; long, flowing motions should dictate legato (slurred) notes; and a motion with precise movements between the staccato style and the legato motion should dictate tenuto notes (sometimes described as regular or "normal" attack). The preferred description of a tenuto note is that it is a note that is released at the point of attack of the next note or rest (rests should be thought of as silent notes).

The more experienced your players are, the more likely they will be to respond correctly to your motions. Older players with experience will have enough control over their breathing, stronger embouchures, and discipline in watching and listening that will help them to respond correctly to different conducting patterns. The same type of exercises you used for precision in attacks and releases can be used to get students to react properly to the motions for different articulations. As you go through the conducting motions your students will learn to cooperatively decide the length of each note or phrase based on watching you and listening to other players.

Once you have taught these motions, go immediately to one of your rehearsal pieces to apply the newly learned technique. Every piece for band has these three articulations for some part or parts. Later in the book, there will be a discussion on using an overhead screen to teach the whole band specific patterns (Using Technology). The more creative you are as the conductor/teacher, the more likely your students will be engaged in the learning process.

Of course, the ability to get students to respond to conducting patterns is predicated on your development as a conductor. You should conduct in front of a mirror or videotape yourself conducting so that you can see how well you are communicating with your band. Some conductors forget that their whole body communicates with the band while conducting. Changes in facial expressions, rounding of shoulders, bounce of the body, force of the conducting stroke, and use of the hand that is not holding the baton are some of the ways conductors add emotions and expression to music. Conductor's notes are only important as they relate to phrases and musical periods (complete statements).

Good conductors make the music come to life and serve as the "interpreter" of musical thoughts. Since better and more experienced players will form ideas of how to interpret a phrase or musical line, it's important to have a unifying force. That force is you, the conductor. It is generally a good idea to describe what each of your motions is dictating. Ambiguity will cause a disconnected performance. Every musician will have her way of interpreting a piece of music so your explanation of what your interpretation is will serve as the "tie-breaker" and will unify the presentation. Of course, that means that you must study the score, listen to performances of the piece or pieces in like style, or adhere completely to interpretive markings to make sure that your interpretation is based on the composer's intent.

Score Study

How well you are prepared before a lesson/rehearsal will determine how effective you are. Just because you performed a piece in high school or college doesn't mean you know the piece. Score study enables you to determine what sections of the piece will be most challenging to the group as a whole or selected instrument sections. Work through how you will present and rehearse these difficult or challenging parts. The more organized you are before the lesson, the more organized your rehearsal will be. If you must consult method books or professional players to determine the best way to help different sections of your band, do it.

As a band director, you may not know the pedagogy of each instrument, and many problems are unique to different instruments, so seek out help and assistance. Contact another band director who may have experienced similar problems, contact a former college instructor, or contact a master musician if necessary. The bottom line is that once you have studied the score and determined your personal limitations, you can help your students with theirs. If necessary, rewrite or simplify parts that are beyond the technical reach of your students. Some lower grade pieces may have difficult parts for some instruments and less challenging parts for others. Double parts with instruments of similar sounds (double horn parts with alto saxophones or baritone horn parts with tenor saxophones, etc.).

Make Notes on the Score

The idea that a score must remain pristine gets in the way of score evaluation and score study. Circle sections of the piece that will require special attention. Don't give judges at a festival a copy of your work score because it will provide a guide for them to recognize your group's problems or weaknesses. On your work score, write in the solutions you have prepared to explain the challenges of the piece to your students. An annotated score provides you with a narrative to be used to explain the challenges to your students. You may forget something important if you depend solely on your memory. Score study will also help you to create program notes for concert audiences. The notes that you prepare for audiences should be based on the same narrative you have used to introduce the piece to your students.

PACING YOUR REHEARSAL

Many directors have difficulty determining the pace at which student learning should take place. Because students in your band class will have varying abilities, the pace at which they learn will vary. Determining when to press on with a lesson and when to pull up is difficult. You must gain a sense for when you should step away from your quest for perfection. Some lessons will be immediately grasped by your students and others may take quite a while to be achieved.

One solution for this problem is to break your lessons/rehearsals down to manageable short units. Trying to achieve too much too soon can be discouraging to you and your students. Decide before you introduce a piece to your students exactly what parts of the piece pose the greatest challenges. Aim for what you consider a reasonable amount of time to spend on specific sections of the piece. You can then scale down or up based on the actual pace. For example, the clarinet part of a piece may be extremely challenging and the trumpet parts may not be as challenging. Think ahead of how you will be able to keep the trumpets engaged while you work out problems with the clarinets. Once you discover the challenging part will take longer than the time you allotted, leave it and explain that you will hold a sectional to gain mastery. If you have a practice room and a strong player in the section, allow students to go to the practice room to work on the difficult parts under the direction of the stronger player. If only a few people in the section are having difficulty, allow them to go into the practice room with very clear directions on what to work out and why. This helps you to manage and respect the larger group's time and avoid discipline problems. Using technology to achieve this is discussed later in the book.

Try to recognize by body language when your students are getting bored and/or discouraged. At this point, no matter what you're trying to do, you're being counterproductive. Students don't always have long attention spans and once they've reached their limit you will accomplish very little or nothing at all. Choose exactly what you hope to achieve. If the piece poses technical challenges, work those out. If intonation is a problem, focus on that. If articulation is a problem, work on that. These problems may be present in another piece you're working on. If so, leave the original piece and move to the new piece and focus on the problem they have in common. In your next rehearsal return to the piece that you started with and work to master the problem area.

Once again, be sure to keep a realistic sense of what you can accomplish. This may differ from what you want to accomplish. Through your score study, determine if other sections have the same part that is difficult for the instrument section you were working with the day before. If they have the same part in the same key, have the two sections play the parts together. If they have the same part in another key you can have one section clap the rhythm or sing the part as the other section plays. This serves two purposes: one, it keeps a large portion of the class engaged and two, you will effectively teach the difficult part to two sections at one time. The rest of the band can play along as you teach the difficult part to the two sections keeping the full band engaged. You can also have the entire band clap or sing the difficult part and use this as a special teaching moment. The skills learned by the entire band can be applied later. This prevents discipline problems caused by students becoming bored, plus you have taught the entire class some new skills and kept them engaged. Creative ways of doing this will be discussed in chapter 18, Using Technology.

5

A Successful First Performance

PLANNING FOR A SUCCESSFUL FIRST PERFORMANCE

The success of your students' first performance has long-term ramifications. If elementary school students step away from a good first performance with positive feelings, they will strive to repeat those feelings in subsequent performances. It also determines whether or not they want to remain in band and continue through their school career. At every level these students will strive to recapture the joy of that first experience and measure their enjoyment based on the feeling they had during their first concert.

Much care must be taken to choose literature (at any level) that will be challenging but accessible to your students. If the music is too easy your students won't be motivated to practice or prepare for the performance, and if the music is too challenging they will be discouraged by the lack of individual or group success. In every group there will be students who can play well or who are motivated to practice to master the music you choose. Conversely, there will be students who find it very difficult to master the same piece of music and some who do not like to practice. Finding a "happy median" is a challenge for you. One way to challenge the advanced players is to transcribe parts for missing instruments or underrepresented parts. You can also have the advanced students peer coach students at the lower levels. When having students pair up for peer coaching you must prepare the coaches to be nurturing rather than highly critical of the lower-level players. There can be strong bonds formed between these students and they will be protective and supportive of one another. If not managed correctly, this can have a negative impact on your band. You must closely monitor what's going on in these peer coaching sessions. Once the students return from the peer coaching session you should have them play the parts they worked on for the rest of the band. Praise their accomplishment when they have had an effective session and use nurturing, encouraging words to steer them in the direction that you wish to see them move toward.

Most elementary and middle school groups have very few low brass players and an overabundance of trumpets, alto saxophones, clarinets, and flutes. If you need to rewrite parts to boost the group or represent missing parts, the following substitutions can be used. (You should also encourage some of the better players to switch to one of the needed/missing instruments.) Trumpets and alto saxophones can be used to cover F horn, clarinet, and baritone horn parts. Alto and tenor saxophones can cover F horn, baritone horn, and trombone parts. Flutes and clarinets can cover trumpet parts and the melody no matter what part the melody is written for (they can be doubled by trumpets, alto saxophones, and tenor saxophones). If the melody is written for low brass, saxophones can give you the desired color based on the composer's intent (tenor saxophone can cover a tuba melody much better than a flute). Based on the Fair Use section of the United States Copyright Law, "Printed copies which have been purchased may be edited or simplified provided that the fundamental character of the work is not distorted."[1] In order to maintain the integrity of the piece your rewriting should be done in such a way that the substitutions sound musically logical.

The success of that first performance will depend on how musical your transcriptions are and how well parts are presented. Should you be fortunate enough to have the scored instrumentation, your task is still to make sure that the balances of your group maintain the integrity of the piece. During the rehearsal you need to maintain focus so that students develop cross listening skills that will make them conscious of where the melody is and how it travels through the band. Once students identify the melodic line(s) they will be more sensitive to adjusting the dynamics of the "supporting" parts. After you've made every attempt at balance and part representation then you can work on intonation, articulation, rhythmic accuracy, facility, and many other points that will be constants in subsequent performances.

Every performance you have should build on the success of the first performance. Whatever problems and successes you have in that first performance should be discussed the very next time the group rehearses. If you video or audio tape that performance, have a guided listening session during the next rehearsal. Have the students listen critically to the performance and share their impressions. Then, have them play the sections they discussed and make the corrections that you feel are needed. If a student made the correct observation, credit him and praise his observation and solution. This simple exercise helps reinforce the "ownership" part of the mission statement. This is why participants are called "stakeholders." Stakeholders have a vested interest in the success of the group. Passive participants generally don't care how well or how poorly things go. Most groups will do what they are told to do from the podium but unless they "buy into" the finished product, the group won't be as successful as it should be.

On the high school level, marching band is involved in the first performance. Whether it is for a pep rally, parade, or football game, the success of your program depends on how your students feel walking away from that performance. You should choose literature that will be of interest to your students and the audience. Marching Band/Pep Band should be the only time that the audience's reaction will be the determining factor for your music choice.

A lot of bands participate in competitions during the fall and choose music for the competitions and ignore playing for school activities. This is a mistake. Judges at competitions will award points or trophies; school students will talk about your band's performance in the halls, cafeteria, and stadium stands. The positive feeling your students get from peer acceptance goes a lot farther than having trophies in trophy cases (though trophies have value also). Students who stay in the program stay because their peers reinforce the fact that band is a cool place to be.

Band is only a competitive activity when directors make it a competitive activity. In competitions, there are winners and losers. In band you should nurture individual and group achievements that help students feel good about how well they have done in comparison to what they did previously (irrespective of what place you come in). This is different from how well they do in comparison to other groups. Competitions can help you set a standard for where you want your group to go and what you want to achieve but the reason for participating in competitions should be made clear.

If you choose music for competitions you should also choose songs that will help with school spirit during pep rallies and games. A video from a home football game or a pep rally can go a long way with your recruiting and retention. If students remember how well received they were during their first pep rally or game, their self-/group-esteem will rise. Students who enjoy activities are more likely than not to continue in those activities.

NOTE

1. *The United States Copyright Law: A Guide for Music Educators.* New York: Music Publishers' Association. Revised 2003 Copyright Act, 17 U.S.C., §107 Appendix A. www.menc.org/resources/view/united-states-copyright-law-a-guide-for-music-educators-appendix-a-g#a

6

Developing a Support System for Your Band Program

There are many reasons why it is important to develop a strong support system for your band. Your support system can range from having a pool of chaperones to choose from for trips to having a solid base for fundraisers. Sometimes there are important jobs that can be filled by parents, alumni, and your students. Care should be taken to make sure that everyone who works with your band is interested in seeing you and your program be successful. You do not want to have people who will not help you achieve your goals around your band. Disparaging or negative comments serve no purpose, but constructive criticism can help. This chapter will assist you in developing a strong support system. MENC has a *Music Booster Manual* that outlines its policies on music boosters and music teachers' responsibilities. You can use the following link to access the exact guidelines: http://www. menc.org/resources/view/music-booster-manual-excerpt.

STARTING A BAND BOOSTERS CLUB

One of the first responsibilities you will have is choosing a leadership team for the Parents Group/Band Boosters/Band Supporters (whatever name you choose). The smaller the leadership team, the more effective the organization will be. You should seek out an individual who is able to influence people into action, knows the school community, can organize projects, and can work well with you and others. Their motivation should be to support the band in all activities. Avoid abrasive personalities and/or people who cannot motivate people by positive means. Along with you, this person will be viewed as a face of the band program. You can call the person the organization's "Project Chair" or simply "chairperson." Since it is not an elected position, avoid calling this person the "president."

The second leadership position should be a financial officer. This person will be the liaison between you, the school, and the school district. The financial officer should be someone who has demonstrated an ability to keep accurate records and is bondable if that is required by your school district. The financial officer should not be the only person who has access to funds. It is your responsibility to know the school's financial policies governing fundraising, budget development, and purchase requirements. You must make sure to pass this information on to the chairperson and financial officer. In every school there is a business manager or financial aid secretary who handles all school purchases, purchase orders, and requisitions. You and your financial officer should meet with this person and/or the principal to get all of the school's financial policies. At this time you should ascertain what purchases will be the responsibility of your program and what purchases will be covered or supplemented by the school.

One of the first official acts the leadership team should perform is developing an operating budget. This budget should be based on expected income (from the school district, the school, donations from the community, and fundraising) and expenditures. Be sure to budget your expenses below your expected income. Items that should be included in budget development will be covered in detail later. All budget items should have a direct benefit to your program. In the early years the budget should cover necessities and basics only. As the program grows, so should the budget. This will be discussed in more detail in a section devoted to budget development.

Once you have selected the two people who will share leadership responsibilities with you, you will need to decide on what kinds of support you will need. The problem most directors have with forming support groups is not clearly defining needs and roles. These roles and responsibilities should be outlined and be assigned to specific committees. These committees should also have specific guidelines and must be able to work closely with you as band director. As band director, you will have many responsibilities and the band boosters club should not add extra work for you. The purpose of this organization and its committees should be to assist you in developing a successful band program. Do not micro-manage; take advantage of the expertise of those who volunteer to work.

When forming a boosters group it is important that you establish rules and bylaws. These bylaws and rules should clearly state the purpose and function of the group and the group's administrative limitations. It is important that it is clear that the group must abide by school policy and cannot make decisions concerning your group without your approval.

Here is a sample of how to form your bylaws.

The _____Band Boosters Club is established to offer support to the _____ band. The function of the group is to provide financial support, a pool of chaperones, organize support activities, provide awards and recognition, and perform tasks specified by the band director as needed. A checking account will be established in the name of the _____ Band Boosters and two signatures will be needed to conduct any business or write/ endorse any checks. One of those signatures must always be the band director's. No business or official meetings may be held without the band director's presence or knowledge. This does not include committee meetings as designated by the director or the Band Boosters Club.

These bylaws should be consistent with your school's policies and must be approved by your administration. Some schools have one school-wide boosters' organization so you will need to follow the rules. The boosters can also be a music department boosters group and the instrumental program can have committees specific to its needs. The sample bylaws can be used for a department-wide group. If it is a departmental group, take into account the different financial needs and account set-up. If the department takes a trip together the bank account should be combined for trip payments and fundraisers. Have the band financial committee keep accurate records of all funds that are to be used specifically for band activities. It is recommended that two separate accounts be maintained and a special trip account be established. Trip accounting is best done by keeping records on individual students. This way when trip payments are tallied, you can figure in any percentages from fundraisers that are attributed to individual students (spreadsheets). Remember, parents generally don't like students other than their child benefitting from their hard work. You may believe that they should understand that when the group benefits so does their child. Unfortunately, a lot of band directors discover that this is not how some parents feel. Be sure to establish a percentage of all fundraisers that will benefit the entire group. State that in your bylaws or rules if necessary to avoid problems in the future. Communication is important. When you meet with the parents at Back-to-School night or the first parents meeting, have a printed agenda to outline what you will discuss and expect to achieve. If your group has developed a mission statement make sure you have a copy of that included. Having an agenda demonstrates that you value the parents' time and that you are organized. Include your personal philosophy of music education. You can even include a syllabus for each class for parents to peruse.

Forming Committees

At Back-to-School night or another parent–teacher meeting, pass out a signup sheet for committees that can provide support for you and your

program. This should include yearlong committees as well as seasonal committees. At this meeting, have the parents fill out cards that will have their
name, address, phone number, e-mail address, and the group their child is
a member of. Marching Band, Concert Band, and Jazz Band all will need
support on different levels and all will need fundraising assistance, uniform
or special attire purchase, publicity, and chaperones for trips, and so on.
Some parents have students in more than one band activity and others will
have students who only participate in one. You should encourage parents to
participate in activities their child is not a member of. If they work during
concerts, they will be able to watch their child perform and help the band
as concert ushers or ticket sellers, assist with stage setup between groups,
place props and flowers and/or scenery on stage. This is a great recruiting
tool. When parents see what other groups do, they tend to encourage their
child to join the other group. Sometimes students are reluctant to join a
group outside of their comfort zone but encouragement from you and their
parent(s) may cause them to join. This is growing from within and there is
no better way to grow.

As you form committees, be aware that all parents won't have time to
attend meetings, come to the school during school hours, chaperone, or
transport students. This doesn't mean that they can't still be involved. An
at-home mother may not be able to come to the school to work but she can
make phone calls. There are those who can write for the web page, newsletters, or other outlets.

An engineer can help design props and scenery. A skilled craftsman can
make large signs to advertise concerts, and build scenery and podiums for
the marching band. A computer expert can design and maintain your web
page and social networking pages. Parents would love to be involved in
activities that will give them an opportunity to play an active role in their
child's life so think beyond the school and having everything done in the
band room or on the football field.

Marching Band Committee

Marching band season has special needs, especially if you have a competitive band. If you have equipment that needs to be loaded and unloaded,
moved to and from the field, set up and dismantled, these are jobs that parents and other supporters can do. Parents can also help you secure a truck to
transport equipment to and from away football games and competitions; a
golf cart and trailer to transport equipment to and from the band room to
the football field; and just offer bodies to physically carry large equipment.
Parents with vans, SUVs, station wagons, and other large vehicles should
be encouraged to form a transportation committee. This committee can be
used to transport instruments and sets used for competitions. They can also

be used to transport uniforms to and from the cleaners or transport rain gear to games and/or competitions. Anything you need picked up or delivered can be done by this committee. It is better to use this adult resource than face the liabilities involved in using student drivers. Check your school district for rules and liabilities governing parents transporting students before having them transport any student(s).

Marching bands have expenses that are unique to them. These expenses can range from equipment purchases and repairs to competitive entry fees and transportation costs. This can exhaust the band's resources in the first three months of school. The marching band committee should organize one major fundraiser and have several smaller ones. Major fundraisers can include football game or basketball game concession stand operation, concert program advertising, frozen pizza sales, citrus fruit sales and cheesecake sales, as well as any sales that the committee comes up with that may be unique to your area. Smaller fundraising activities can include such things as car washes, bake sales, spaghetti dinners, pancake breakfasts, and so on. The smaller activities can also include things unique to your area (e.g., leaf raking, snow removal, and grass cutting). Competition entry fees are usually based on the opportunity to sell tickets to the competition and there will be a need for phone calls to be made, signs made to promote the competition, and selling tickets in advance. If your committee develops a phone tree or phone data base this data base or phone tree can be used by other parts of your band program. In fact, all committees should have one central data base from which to pull information. Some special needs unique to marching band are:

- Uniform purchases and fundraising to purchase uniforms
- Uniform cleaning costs (unless students are required to clean them)
- Providing cooling aids for hot weather performances
- Providing rain wear
- Outdoor heaters for cold weather performances
- Providing costumes for special performances
- Securing flags or silks
- Getting footwear
- Paying contest entry fees
- Securing cold weather protection
- Purchasing materials used for building scenery or props
- Setting up scenery or props for performances or competitions
- Transporting instruments and equipment to away-from-school performances

All of these items should be figured in when calculating the marching band budget. Most school districts don't pay for marching bands because of the

overall expenses of the total band program. Uniform purchases alone can
be in the thousands of dollars and some parades require that you have new
uniforms as a requirement for participation. Add to that the costs associated
with transportation to marching band activities (parades, competitions,
etc.), marching band budgets alone can be over ten thousand dollars. Because of the visibility of marching band and the effect it can have on your
band program's recruiting, this part of the budget can be considered maintenance and advertising, and should be a major priority.

Fundraising Committee

Even though every group requires fundraising, there should be only one
fundraising committee with several subcommittees. The financial officer
should head all of the fundraising activities. Having a central location for
fundraising information you and your supporters have an opportunity to
pool resources. You should establish a percentage of funds raised by each
group's subcommittee that will go into the program's main treasury. Parents
generally don't like funds raised for their child's group to be applied to another group so establishing this percentage upfront is very important. This
also helps you to have an amount of funds that can be applied to any group
that may need financial assistance during the year. If you have parents who
are tech savvy, they can maintain a spreadsheet for you to have instant access to the amount of ready cash you have on hand. Canvass your parents
and take advantage of any accountants or financial experts you may have
at your disposal. During the first parent meeting be very clear about the
expertise you will need. You may be surprised by the resources that parents
bring to the table.

Create either an in-school bank account or outside-of-school account.
Have it set up so that checks and withdrawals need two signatures to avoid
any problems with accounting. One of the problems band directors have is
with accounting and balancing the band account. Don't be too proud to ask
for help. When you're focusing on teaching music you may lose a check or
forget to make a deposit. The best way to avoid these problems is to have
someone assist you.

If the checking account requires two signatures, have three names on the
list of authorized signatures. This means that if one of the three is not available you still have access to the money you need. There are times during
marching band season that you may need access to your funds because of
an emergency or to order food for the group, or many other possible sce-
narios. Try to make sure that one of the people who can sign a check with
you is with the band or prearrange the food purchases to avoid a problem
with your payment. If you think that you'll need cash for an emergency,
withdraw an amount of money from the account that will be sufficient to

cover an emergency (e.g., drum heads, lost mouthpieces, lost mallets, etc.). Anticipating a need will help avoid a bad situation that could negatively impact your performance.

Publicity and Public Relations

The importance of publicity as it affects recruiting was touched on earlier but there are other reasons you need a good PR committee. Advertising concerts and performances, acknowledging special awards and accomplishments, and bringing favorable attention to your program are some of the reasons for having a committee dedicated to publicity and public relations. If you or your students have accomplished something that deserves wider attention, the public relations/publicity committee should prepare and disseminate information to local news organizations. Most local newspapers will have a section set up to acknowledge student achievements. This committee can also organize poster-making parties outside of school or sign-making parties to make signs that can be placed on school property to advertise a concert or performance, advertise fundraising activities, build large signs to be placed on school property to advertise concerts, and so on. Find out if there is a parent who writes professionally or who is willing to do the writing of copy for your activities. There are ways of writing and reporting that can engage the reader and bring substantial attention to your progress and achievements. Solicit the help of those who know how to present information in the most engaging ways. Remember, you are marketing your program trying to generate positive attention to what you are doing. One of the overlooked jobs of band directors is that of being a salesman. You must be willing to sell your program, especially in its early years.

Have the school newspaper, newsletter, or web page reserve a space for you to submit information on student or group achievements (or any special recognition you personally receive). The publicity committee should be aware of all submission dates and the format that submissions should be in when prepared for publication or broadcasts. There should not be an information dissemination source that your committee does not submit to and there should never be a publication or broadcast during the year in which your program is not mentioned. When parents and students see that you value their contributions, they will become your best PR sources. Word of mouth and personal testimonials are still the best source of publicity you and your group can have. As mentioned earlier, have tech-savvy parents create a web page or other electronic means of communication for you. Grandparents, relatives, and friends outside of your immediate area can access your accomplishments via the Internet. This also elevates your accomplishments for those outside of your school and school community. You should have a "director's corner" where you articulate your goals and satisfaction with student achievements as well as disseminate any vital information you wish to share. This helps to personalize your program. As was stated before, during the recruiting process and the early years of building your program there is no distinction made between you and your program. Students sometimes join a program or leave a program because of their perception of the director. You should strive to be perceived as a caring, nurturing individual who helps students realize their life goals through participation in band. As people read about you and your goals and hear you praise your students, they come to know more about your program.

Use your final concert as a PR tool. Acknowledge students who have made All-City, All-County, All-District, All-State, and/or All-Regional groups. For recruiting and incentive purposes, acknowledge all students who audition for honors-level groups whether they were chosen or not. Report the results of Solo and Ensemble festivals, band festivals, or competitions, stressing the educational values more than the results. In the early years of your program you may not score the highest scores or win many competitions but the value of your group working toward a common goal will be invaluable to future growth and success. If you've gone from a lower grade of music to a higher grade, acknowledge the successful attainment of a goal or completion of your mission as stated in your mission statement. Record all of the music you did that year in writing so that you can review your success with your students. This will also help you avoid repeating pieces during the four-year span in which your four-year students participate (you hope to retain students for four years).

Awards and Recognition Committee

One of the most important things to students is to have their accomplishments acknowledged. The awards you give out are not as important as is the point you are giving them and publicly acknowledging a job well done. You can acknowledge student achievements from the stage at concerts, print achievements in the concert program(s), or make posters with or without pictures that are placed on stands or walls outside of the auditorium for parents and concert attendees to see. These pictures show that you have "living trophies," not just metal and wooden trophies. The publicity committee can compile a list of achievements and decide how to present the information. The best recognition and awards programs are separate from concerts. The concert will be extended because of the added time and some recognition may be cut as a result. A separate activity devoted just to recognition gives you an opportunity to recognize more students and gives parents and students an opportunity to mingle socially. This "family" environment does much for retention. You can have a potluck dinner, a pizza or ice cream social, or just desserts. It doesn't matter what you do to create a social environment as much as it matters that you are presenting awards and recognition in a family setting. If you want to bring attention to your students, give them band pins or band letters that their schoolmates will see. This gives your students even more recognition and is a tangible way for you to thank them for their service. There are some nationally recognized awards that allow you to add recipients' names every year. These names remain on the band room wall or the school's main hall wall for two decades or more. This kind of recognition provides a visible record of how much you value your students' accomplishments.

PUBLICIZING YOUR GROUP'S SUCCESSES

Probably one of the most overlooked parts of recruiting, retaining, and reclaiming is publicizing your group's successes. Far too often, band is one of the best-kept secrets in your school. With today's technology, there are many ways to let students in your school, your feeder schools, and the school community know about your achievements (individual or group). The best way is a newsletter. Whether you use low-tech newsletters that are printed and distributed by hand; eNewsletters on the band's web page; notes or articles posted on social networks or video broadcasts, you should make sure that word about what you and your students are doing gets notice. Public relations (PR) is a major help for projecting a positive image for your program and making your program a place where students want to be and want to stay once they're there.

No matter how large or small the achievements, people need to know what kinds of things your group is doing. Sometimes excellence and success can be taken for granted and you may assume that everyone knows about how well your group is doing, but that is not necessarily the case. Sometimes your students don't share how well things are going even with their parents. A good newsletter can help start the dialogue you want taking place about your program.

Things That Should Be Included in Your Newsletter/PR Campaign

After you and your group have formulated your mission statement or yearly goal, anything you do that reinforces your mission statement or goals should be publicized. This includes individual and group achievements. When students are recognized for their achievements through media, they feel good about themselves and the program. This also lets recruits know that you consider individual achievement an integral part of your group's success. This creates an environment where students feel they are valued. Students tend to remain involved in programs that they see themselves as an important part of. Family members, teachers, fellow students, and community members help to reinforce this feeling of personal value by recognizing the students by complimenting them or commenting on what they read about them. Even if the student performs at community or church activities musically that are not necessarily related to school, they should still be recognized because your program gives them the training and/or encouragement that helps them be successful in or out of school.

If your marching band or pep band plays at half-time or in the stands, publicize it with comments and/or pictures (live or on social networks). The fun and camaraderie that takes place at games comes through clearly and the social side of band is demonstrated as well as displaying school spirit, showing that band is an important part of the school. This is where a social network page can help. Posting pictures of a football game lets recruits know how much fun they can have in band and reminds current members how much fun they had. Remember, the social dynamic of the "cool" place to be is in play. If it looks "cool" to be out on a game night or afternoon, students want to be in the middle of that fun. Even if you print a hard copy of your newsletter, color copy machines make it possible for you to use pictures and images. You can even blow some of these pictures up as posters and add captions. When it's time for students to go through scheduling, put these posters on walls around the school to keep band on the minds of students as they choose their classes. This works for concerts, car washes, and trips away from school or any activity. Pictures speak for your program much more than listing your goals or sharing the value of your program in writing (even though those things are important also).

There should be a coordinated effort to link your goals and your mission statement to the pictures you post. This is a form of subliminal advertising. Every time students and parents read your mission statement/goals, they should have a visual to go along with it. You can't expect them to make the association themselves. Behavioral objectives and mission statements are somewhat sterile but when you see students in action demonstrating those objectives your program takes on a life of its own. Most social networks allow you to post an unlimited amount of pictures and statements so every year you can add more information. Students can trace their achievements by term and year. Once again, this helps with retention and it also makes recruiting less challenging.

7

Festival Participation and Preparation

Festivals are a good way to assess your band's progress toward your goal. You, your students, and three independent music educators will analyze your execution of two judged pieces and your sight reading ability. Preparing your students for a positive festival experience is important to gaining the most educational value of festival participation.

The mistake a lot of directors make in preparing for a festival is to make the experience all about the rating rather than the group's growth over time. Judges grade and evaluate bands based on how well the band executes/performs the prepared pieces for adjudication. This includes articulation, dynamics, balance, intonation, rhythmic accuracy, and interpretation, among other things. There is a standard that every band must reach in order to receive a high rating. Judges see a snapshot of your band and base their rating on what they hear that particular day.

Based on the expected standard, your group may not receive the highest rating but that does not mean they weren't successful. Only you and your students know how far you have come since the first day you started playing the music you play at a festival. It is important that you hold them to a high standard and have high expectations for them but it is equally important that you acknowledge how far they have come trying to meet that standard. If they have improved and have measurable achievement based on your goals, it is important that you explain to them differences between what the judges expect and what you were able to achieve. Before going to the festival there are a few things you should do.

- Record the band and have them listen critically to evaluate their progress.

- Have students maintain a festival score sheet and grade themselves the way the judges would grade them.
- Fill out a festival grade sheet yourself the day before the festival and grade the band. Seal your sheet in an envelope and share your comments with them, comparing what you said with what the judges said. If the judges said the same things you said, point that out. If the judges said something that you didn't say, use that to prepare your students for the next performance.
- Play the tape of the band's performance without the judges' comments before playing the tapes with their comments. Have your students write their comments on the evaluation form and compare what they heard with what the judges said.

The worst mistake you could make would be to discount or dismiss the judges' comments. This diminishes the festival experience value. Your students don't elevate you when you make disparaging remarks about the judges; they simply dismiss the value of participating in the festival, and preparing for the next festival will be more difficult. The educational value of a festival is based on how well your students have learned to execute the music and how well they presented it. The two cannot be separated and it is important that you openly discuss their success and/or failure. You can't praise the judges for their positive comments or grades at one festival and criticize their comments at another festival.

Logistically, preparing for a festival includes organizing the music, determining concert attire, entering and exiting the staging area, and having parents or supporters present to help with things that come up before, during, or after the performance. The parents who accompany you to the festival can be parents who signed up for the festival committee on Back-to-School Night.

Organizing the music for the festival is an important part of preparation. When you pass out the festival music, be sure to keep a copy of each part so that if someone loses their music or their folder you will have a reference copy on hand. If a parent is accompanying you to the festival you can put all folders in a box or boxes and give the folders out once you enter the warm-up room. The parent can be responsible for supervising this process and should have a checklist. This is a case where you can also use your section leaders. Section leaders should check members of their section to make sure that all section members have everything they need for the performance.

Determining concert attire is another process that should start at the beginning of the school year. In your syllabus or handbook parents and students should be told what is expected. In case students have to purchase clothing or shoes it is important that they know well in advance for proper planning. If you are having concert attire made (skirts or dresses), you should arrange to have a seamstress or tailor present to measure your students.

Permission slips and forms are necessary for taking students out of school and classes for festivals. Most school systems have forms for these out-of-school field trips but if your district does not have system-wide forms, you must write one. These forms should include the date and time of the trip, the location, departure time, return time, transportation vendor and means, any costs for students, and an opportunity for parents to approve or disapprove. If you have not given students concert attire beforehand it should be included on the permission slip. Even if you have given the information out, include it as a reminder. You should have stated in your syllabus or class requirements that festival and concert participation make up a percentage of the student's grade. If parents choose not to allow their child to participate they need to know that their child's grade will be negatively impacted. You can also include a place for teachers whose class will be missed to sign the form acknowledging that they are aware that the student will be absent and that it is an excused absence. This form can help students should the teacher mark them unexcused. Students will be able to present the form with the teacher's signature as proof that they were indeed excused.

Planning for Out-of-State Festivals and Trips

As in the case of local festivals, out-of-state trips or out-of-state festivals require permission slips or travel forms. Before planning any out-of-state trips you should consult your principal to determine school travel policies and system-wide policies. When securing buses for an out-of-town trip, you will have to make a deposit. These deposits are quite often nonrefundable. You don't want to make a deposit and then find out you cannot go on the trip. Get all necessary approvals before planning or announcing the trip. After September 11, 2001, many school systems require out-of-state trips to be approved by the Superintendent of Schools. Once you have secured all approvals that are needed, line up chaperones. Generally, you will need one adult chaperone per fifteen students. Once again, individual schools and school systems set the number of chaperones needed (student-to-adult ratio). On Back-to-School Night have parents sign up for potential trips based on your local and/or state's festival dates. If the out-of-town trip is not for a festival, tell the parents in advance what kind of trips you want to take pending your administration's approval. The following should be done:

- Secure approvals for the trips during the summer before school starts. This way, you can announce definite dates at Back-to-School Night.
- Survey for a parent who is in healthcare. With or without a health worker, you will need a health form for each student. This form should include any allergies or special needs for each student, medications re-

quired by the student, known conditions and permission to administer
life-saving care until a parent can be notified.

- Parents of students who require medications or special services should
  be encouraged to travel with you to care for their child and accept the
  liability. Also include a place for parents to include dietary needs or
  concerns (food allergies, religious diets, etc.).
- Once all permissions have been received and you have completed the
  above, you should follow the same procedures you would for a local
  festival.

Planning for International Festivals and Trips

Planning international trips is quite often a two-year endeavor. Because of
the financial requirements, passport status, security, health concerns, air
travel arrangements, lodging, special permissions, itinerary setup, and supervision, international trips require a lot of advance planning. It is best to
use an educational tour company that can handle most of the logistics. Ideally, you want to be able to handle this trip in the same way you would an
out-of-town trip with the added requirements of passports, visas, and special needs for foreign travel. Travel companies will handle securing airline
tickets, lodging, performance venues or festival sites, tours, and itineraries
for you. A lot of these companies are associated with international festivals
and build your itinerary around festival performances. They also are aware
of any special tariffs or taxes that must be paid. They will also get special
information on baggage requirements and weight requirements for the
airline. They will make arrangements for meals and will take care of special
meal requests for the airline and the trip lodging location. Remember, there
will be times that you will be eating in places other than where the hotel is
located, so you or the tour company must be sure to secure a food venue
that can accommodate large groups.

Chaperone requirements for foreign travel are often different from do-
mestic travel. Check with your school administration about the required
paperwork to request permission for foreign travel. Again, after September
11, 2001, school systems have specific requirements that must be satisfied
before you can start planning a trip. There are also general requirements
that you furnish a complete itinerary including where you will stay, plans
for meals, educational value of the trip, supervision and security, emergency plans for medical care, and overall costs for students including
scholarships and anticipated emergency financial needs. Because the system, the school, and you can be held liable should anything happen to a
student while overseas or in foreign countries, you must have a complete
description of your plans and how you will care for your students. Once
again, most educational tour companies have a checklist and contingency

plans for emergencies that you may customize and adjust specifically for your needs. Your principal is the first stop for approval, who will then forward it up the chain of command. You should have a planning meeting with parents to gather valuable information about trip affordability and fundraising activities to help defray individual student costs and to go over the proposed itinerary. You must also leave complete plans for what will happen to students who are not going on the trip and must attend class in your absence. Larger schools and school systems often have a printed package of requirements for you to complete but if your system does not have one, here are things you should include in your trip proposal and trip planning.

- Travel plans and details should be spelled out completely, leaving nothing to be assumed. These plans must include when you plan to leave, the airport and airline to be used, arrangements for currency exchange, travel arrangements, travel means, travel times, travel costs, meals, medical forms, chaperones, performance venues, and hotel accommodations.
- There are some bands that participate in school exchange programs that have students stay in the host school's family homes. Before planning this type of trip look carefully into student security and safety and your liability. Most foreign countries have no minimum age for alcohol consumption so make sure that if students stay in family homes these families do not allow alcohol consumption.
- Have a special form that explains your school community's policy on underage drinking and/or drug use.
- Include information on available health care in the country you will visit and what plans you have for your students' health care needs.
- Find out what medications students are allowed to have in the host country.
- Remind your students that giving or selling prescribed drugs in a foreign country is considered black market selling and they may be arrested and held.
- It is important that you review the laws of the host country with parents and students and have them sign a form that states that they attended the meeting explaining laws and liabilities.
- Do not allow any student to travel who has not attended meetings reviewing trip policies and expectations.
- Find out the location of the American Embassy or Consulate so that you and your students will know where to go for assistance should you get separated or need diplomatic assistance.
- Dental care is a health care that may need to be arranged by contacting the embassy or consulate. Dental care in some foreign countries may

be less than what you desire but most embassies and consulates have doctors and dentists on their staff or who they use in the host country.

- Secure passports at least ten months prior to the trip.
- Fundraising should be done to help defray individual costs, offer scholarships, and cover unexpected costs due to price changes or special tariffs.
- A first aid kit, student health forms, and emergency telephone numbers should be in your possession or with one of your chaperones at all times.
- If the group separates into smaller groups, each chaperone should have the emergency information and health forms for each member of his group.
- All chaperones should have information concerning you and other chaperones in case something happens and they or you cannot speak for yourselves.
- Notify the middle school of your intent to travel abroad if you plan to allow incoming students to travel.
- Contact the State Department to find out about any special requirements that may be in effect for large groups traveling to the country you plan to visit.
- Make arrangements to secure large instruments in the country you're visiting. An educational travel company will normally have vendors in foreign countries that it can secure stands and large instruments from.
- If your marching band is going, make arrangements for your marching percussion, sousaphones, and other large instruments shipped with their arrival a day after you arrive unless you can arrange for a secure storage place at your hotel. Shipping by an international shipping company will be less expensive than trying to pay to have the larger instruments loaded onto a commercial aircraft. If you have enough students to charter a complete flight the large instruments can be loaded on your plane unless the weight limit is exceeded.

Assign your chaperones to specific tasks and maintain a checklist to make sure that nothing is overlooked. Once you have established dietary needs for meals, assign a chaperone to monitor the meals to make sure students are getting the meals that meet their special needs. Establish a committee to check rooms to make sure students are in their rooms according to any curfews you establish. Make arrangements with the hotel to have males and females placed on separate floors if possible. This makes room checks and security concerns less difficult to manage. Prior to the trip allow students to sign up for rooms or make room assignments, and furnish the chaperones with a list of room occupants. Tour companies generally require you to furnish them with a rooming list to give to the hotel prior to your arrival.

In this case room keys will have the names of each occupant on the key envelope. Make it very clear that males and females should not be in rooms together with doors closed. Even if parents allow their children to entertain the opposite sex in their room at home you should make it clear that it won't be allowed on the trip.

8

Developing a Budget for Your Band

One of the major responsibilities of a band director that is sometimes overlooked during teacher training is the management side of being a band director. Band directors are personnel managers, decision makers, and business managers. Large sums of money pass through the band director's hands during a school year. Whether it is money for trips and festivals, uniform purchases, instrument purchases and repairs, classroom material purchases, or other purchases, thousands of dollars must be managed and accounted for. As mentioned in the section on band boosters, if the director can solicit help from parents with business expertise, this will be quite helpful. With or without the help of parents, it's the responsibility of the director to develop a working budget.

In order to effectively establish a working budget, it is important that you list expected income and expenditures. There are standing expenditures that will go from year to year. Some of these expenses include uniform cleaning, instrument maintenance and repairs, festival and/or competition registration fees, bus rentals, and music purchasing.

Most schools provide funds for classroom materials such as chalk, tape, pencils, markers, and so on but band classes have material needs that are unique to band. Because band is extracurricular (noncredit) and cocurricular (for credit), there is a thin line between what is a classroom need and what is a performance need. It is very difficult to separate classroom needs from performance needs since band is a performance class. It is for this reason that your budget will contain some items that are provided by the school (paper, copying costs, pencils, etc.). Band classes tend to be larger than most classes and school budget allotments are decided upon based on the class size cap each school district has. MENC provides a statement on fundraising and budgets that can be reviewed by going to http://www. menc.org/about/view/menc-position-statements.

Here is a sample of the kinds of items that your budget should include. Because every school district is unique, you may have to add or subtract items. This is not an absolute budget; it is only designed to provide you with an outline of expected expenditures so that you may calculate the income needed to maintain your program. Some directors use a two-year budget.

Supplies and Materials: photocopy paper, audio tapes and/or recordable compact discs, football field lining materials, simple repair kit materials, music notation pads and/or workbooks, pencils, markers, and music notation software

Maintenance: piano tuning, instrument repairs, drum heads and marching band equipment needs, office equipment repairs and maintenance, audio-visual equipment maintenance and repairs, stand repairs or replacements

Festival and Competition: bus rental, festival fees, solo and ensemble fees, festival music purchases, extra scores for judges

Equipment Replacement/Purchases: inventory replacement needs, uniform purchases, mouthpieces, mallets and sticks, music stand purchases, sound equipment for recording, sound equipment for playback and classroom use, chairs, music cabinets, instrument storage cages, television monitors, DVD or video tape machine, CD player/recorder, video camera or recording equipment, marching band flags, flag poles, and so on

Travel Expenses: transportation costs, meals, lodging, shipping costs

Once you have listed ongoing budgetary expenses, start listing expenses that will be unique to the current school year. After taking an inventory of school-owned instruments and equipment, take an inventory of uniforms to see whether replacements of equipment or uniforms will be needed. You should not plan your budget to cover known and anticipated expenses only. There must be contingency plans for emergency or unexpected needs. Consult past budgets to gain a feel for the total amount of funds needed. If you are opening a new school your budget will be less than what existing schools' budgets will be. You should still operate your fundraising activities as if you have a need for common budget items. Consult other band directors personally or in forums to determine what a normal year's budget would be for ongoing programs. Within two years of existence, new schools will have the same expenses that other schools incur. The life and growth of your program will depend on how well you develop your operating budget.

If you are new to a school system be sure to consult the music supervisor to determine what financial contributions to your budget you can expect from the school district, your local school, and any other outside source. After reviewing the funds that come from these sources you can accurately calculate what you will need to raise through fundraising activities.

9

Developing Musicianship in Band Class

One of the most important things to remember about band is that it is a class. Students must be challenged and engaged at all times. A lot of directors feel that teaching comprehensive musicianship in class takes away from practice time. It is time-consuming and involves preparing conductor's notes on the music you're rehearsing, but in the long run your rehearsals will be a lot more productive. Once students understand the periodic style of a piece, the composer's intent, the nationalistic background, and so on, the more interested they may become in their individual preparation. Every band student is not just interested in music; some like history and receiving information on different cultures. As you discuss these points you appeal to a group of students you may not keep engaged with just discussing musical terms and performance techniques. Your question may be, "Isn't this a band class and isn't that what I'm supposed to do?" Yes, it is to an extent but you must keep in mind every band student will not pursue music beyond high school. Keeping nonmusic majors engaged will help the overall performance level of your group.

When writing lesson plans for comprehensive musicianship you should include specific comments on the musical style. If you are rehearsing a British March explain the difference between the tempo of a British March and an American March. The function of the British March is different and your students will be aware of how the nationality of the march affects the presentation. Provide information on the composer. This tends to humanize the composer to your students. Have your students do some outside-of-class reading about the composer and the period in which the music you're playing was written. A number of teachers don't realize the importance of students going through the discovery process. During the period between the warm-up and rehearsing the piece, ask one or two students to share what they have found out about the composer and the piece. Students who take band are generally academically motivated and will embrace the academic challenge. Other students will enjoy hearing about the culture surrounding the music and the composer.

Band classes should include multicultural awareness. Choosing music that represents different nationalities, ethnic groups, and cultures will help your band to present a welcoming environment for students of different cultural or ethnic backgrounds. It will also help your students learn about cultures that are different from theirs. Performing music that is not based on Western scales will be less difficult if you have introduced folk songs of different cultures. Learning Korean folk songs, Japanese folk songs, or Middle Eastern folk songs will open up a new level of classic band literature in the higher grades (grade 5 and grade 6). Once students become acclimated to these new scales they will gain facility on their instruments beyond major and minor tonalities.

THE IMPORTANCE OF SIGHT READING IN BAND

Sight reading is an important part of developing individual musicianship. Most students don't sight read well because of the fear of sight reading. If you explain to your band that every time they read a book or newspaper, they are sight reading, it helps them to face the fear and overcome it. As they read they may not know the meaning of every word but they can figure out the meaning by putting the word in context with the words they know. The same can be true with sight reading music. Students may not know every rhythm in a measure but by working from the familiar to unfamiliar, they can figure out how to play a difficult measure. The important thing for them to do is keep playing. It's okay to miss one or two beats in a measure and keep going on to the next measure rather than stopping and trying to restart and catch up. It is very unlikely that if a student stops playing that he will find the correct spot to re-enter. This can cause a domino effect in the band. When one student stops it very often affects the confidence of the other students around. If there is a measure a student just can't figure out have him convert that measure into a measure rest. That way he knows where beat one will fall and he can come back in on time. By counting the rest he is still engaged and has not stopped.

As the students are looking over the music they will sight read, talk them through the process of elimination of patterns they don't know. Some students may be thrown off by a difficult pattern in a measure but if they look ahead they may discover that they know some rhythms in a measure.

If you direct them to convert the pattern that they don't know into a rest or a simplified pattern (multiple notes on one beat into a single note that gets one beat) they will soon overcome the fear of sight reading.

How you as the conductor explain the score to your students determines how they will approach challenging patterns. Your first responsibility when you get the opportunity to view the score of a sight reading piece is to seek out difficult rhythmic patterns and explain them. You can sing, clap, or speak the rhythmic patterns that are challenging and then have your students clap and sing the pattern. Your demeanor while viewing and explaining the score will create either an air of confidence or one of discouragement. Your students will watch you closely as you go through the sight-reading process and they will take your nonverbal cues.

If you have gone through the process of sight reading in class the anxiety of the sight reading process will be less intimidating for your students. The mistake made by some directors is to put more value on the prepared pieces for a festival than on the sight-reading aspect of the festival experience. If you have taught your students to be analytical music readers, sight reading will be one of the better festival experiences. The prepared pieces demonstrate how well you have taught and your students have followed your lead but sight reading demonstrates how well your students can use techniques they have learned and execute those techniques almost instantly. The gratification your students will get from successfully sight reading a piece will last for quite a while and if you capitalize on those feelings their attitudes about band will become more positive.

GUIDED LISTENING IN BAND

Some directors miss out on the importance of their students listening to model bands. There are very few radio stations that play band music. Jazz students can listen to jazz outside of class on the radio and television, orchestra students can hear model orchestras on the radio and television, but band students rarely have an opportunity to hear model bands on radio or television. Fortunately, there are videos on www.youtube.com that your students can access on their time but the quality of the groups on video varies and may not be the kinds of model groups you wish to use as good examples. This means that if you want your students to hear model groups you must select examples for them and present them in class. Since the recording quality of even some good groups varies, be sure to screen all of the videos that you list for your students to view.

Every band room needs to have a sound system with adequate speakers for listening. When the band room is designed, if you have input, have the system built into the walls or placed on wall shelves where it cannot be tampered with by unwanted hands. Most new band rooms have the components (CD player, tape player, turntable) placed inside the band director's office or a storage room where only the director or authorized personnel can access it.

If you are concerned that if your students hear the piece they are working on and rather than learning it by reading their parts learning it by rote, play a piece in a similar style or another piece by the composer for them to hear. This way you can focus on style and not the exact piece. According to your lesson plan, point out articulations, dynamics, balance, intonation, and other nuances that create a model performance. If you play the piece you're working on, have the students follow their parts note for note. You can address the points in specific terms while the students follow the score closely. Most publishers provide a recording of the piece you're playing either on an accompanying CD or an mp3 on their website. A lot of these recordings are made with the composer present at the recording session so the composer's intent can be heard.

Record your group as they play the piece(s) you're working on. This serves several purposes. Students can trace their progress by listening to how they sound between recordings, you can point out the positive and negative points of their performance, and they have an opportunity to self-evaluate. It's generally a good practice to have them evaluate their performance before you provide them with your critique. Very often, their evaluation will be a lot tougher than yours. If they are too hard on themselves you can smooth over their self-criticism and be encouraging, acknowledging the progress they have made. Don't allow them to be critical of individual performances or individuals; have them focus on the group's overall sound and how the group can improve. Human nature will cause each individual to listen for their sound and self-evaluate. Allow this to be an individual process and allow them to maintain anonymity. Once they discover what they need to improve on you will see an improvement in them as individuals and the group overall.

Listening activities work on all levels and elementary students are more astute than most teachers give them credit for being. For younger students or beginning-level groups, the listening activity can be made into a fun activity. Focus their attention on a specific part of the piece you're working on. It can be a particular rhythm or a short motif. By having them listen for one thing specifically, they will listen more closely to the whole piece. You can even create an award for "Best Listener of the Week." Capitalize on the eagerness to learn and the competitive nature of young students to be the first to make a discovery. This lets them know the importance of being good listeners in band and they will continue to apply this even when you're not playing it as a game.

10

Classroom Management

In your efforts to maintain students in your program the classroom environment plays a major role. As was stated earlier, students lose interest in programs where they feel their time is being wasted. Lesson plans give you an outline to follow that will keep you and your students focused on immediate goals. Most disciplinary problems occur in an environment that is disorganized. If students get bored or feel that their time is not valued, they tend to act out. This acting out can manifest in many ways—from harmless talking in small groups to arguments and fights. When discipline gets out of control you'll be forced to take immediate action. How you react can escalate the situation or diffuse it. Of course, the best situation is to avoid the need to take action altogether.

Your level of organization will directly affect the level of discipline in the classroom. Effective teachers are organized and know how to manage time. Efficient use of time is important in keeping your students engaged and productive. The time you take to present an organized, well-planned rehearsal will reap great benefits.

When choosing literature for your band, you must be mindful of your instrumentation and your students' playing ability. Start the rehearsal by telling your students how much time you expect them to take getting their instruments out, getting their music and taking their seats prepared to start the warm-up. Once you've established the time constraints, stick with them. Start your rehearsal immediately after the prescribed time limit has passed. Students will realize that they must be in place, ready to play by the end of the prescribed time. Starting the rehearsal immediately reinforces the importance of being in place.

The more organized you are, the better the rehearsal environment will be. The key to this is writing clear lesson plans. Of course, if you expect them to be in place and ready to rehearse, you must be ready to start the rehearsal once they are. If you start your rehearsals at the time you have established as the class start time, your students will gather their materials and instruments in a time efficient way. From the start of the rehearsal until the end time of the rehearsal before the bell, your students should have a clear focus on the objectives you have established for that day's lesson.

MANAGING DISCIPLINE

Discipline in band rehearsals is a challenge for new teachers and experienced teachers alike. You don't want the classroom environment to be such that it stifles creativity or inhibits students' performance, or so loose that students' unrest distracts other students. Every time the director has to stop the rehearsal to handle a discipline problem, time is taken away from constructive work time. Discipline is based on the director's rapport with the class and the amount of respect students have for the director and their classmates. The simple act of stating clear directions of what you expect to accomplish during a class period can head off some behavior problems. It is easier to loosen up on a structured class than it is to tighten up a poorly structured class. Your remedies to disciplinary problems should be clearly stated and included in your handbook.

Self-discipline is the most important factor to avoiding class discipline problems. If students can manage their behavior, there won't be discipline problems that require the director's attention. Problems generally start from small infractions that go unchecked. If the director permits an undercurrent of talking to go on unchecked, that talking will get increasingly louder and involve more students.

The best way to handle disciplinary problems in band rehearsals is to remove the causes of those problems or avoid them completely. Time management problems and a disorganized rehearsal lead to most problems. Boredom and lack of focus by students cause other problems. When students know that they will be held accountable, they will very seldom cause problems.

One strategy is that while working with one group of students, remind the other students that you will come to their section next or ask them to evaluate how well the section you're working with has followed your instructions. This simple act serves to keep them engaged and focused. If they don't see how the work you're doing with one section applies to them, they'll become disengaged. Assign a specific amount of time you're going to spend on a problem and have a student in another section be your timekeeper to make sure you don't run over the allotted time. This gives the students the message that you respect their time and that they are expected to achieve results in a reasonable amount of time. If students feel that they don't have a limited time to resolve an issue, they may not focus fully on resolving the problem.

If you want your students to be organized and efficient in their practice time, you must model that behavior. If you're not focused on what you expect to achieve, they won't be either. The importance of having lesson plans has been discussed but using those plans as a road map for your rehearsal is of the utmost importance. Skipping from one problem to the next without resolution of a problem will be counterproductive. Your students won't see the need to focus fully because you have not focused fully. Some directors create problems and then become frustrated when those problems manifest. If students are allowed to continue to make the same mistakes in a rehearsal the message they receive is that you have low standards. Very few directors willingly lower their standards but many unwittingly do by not addressing and correcting noticeable mistakes. Open-ended comments such as "we'll fix that later" are frustrating to students if during the next rehearsal those same problems go unchecked. Some disciplinary problems stem from lack of confidence that the director has the best interests of the group at heart (a loss of respect). Students incorrectly interpret a lack of action as a lack of caring. This leads to a lack of caring by the students and feeds disciplinary problems.

As soon as a disciplinary problem occurs it is important that it is addressed. Stop the rehearsal and remind the class that the distractions being caused by the discipline problems are hurting the band's progress. Remind them that they are an important part of the group's success and that you are depending on them to focus so that the musical problems you're trying to correct can be completely corrected. Try the positive approach first. If the positive approach fails, ask the offending student to see you after class and try to resolve the problem with them individually. Trying to handle a problem one on one in front of the class generally leads to a confrontation that won't end well for you or the student. Meeting with the student individually gives you a chance to make a personal appeal to them to modify their behavior. A swift resolution of the problem is very important. It establishes with the offending student and other students observing that negative behavior will not be tolerated.

If the individual approach fails, you'll need to follow your school's policies on classroom disruptions. Contact the student's parents by phone or e-mail to let them know that their child is a disruption in your class. Parents will generally help you rectify problems before they become more of a problem. If there is a detention hall that students are referred to, write a referral. Of course, most schools allow teachers to deduct from a student's grade based on class attendance and classroom decorum but that should be included and explained in your syllabus or band handbook.

If punitive measures are not what you want to use, contact the school's counseling office to set up a parent–teacher conference to discuss the problem. Parents generally don't appreciate having to come to the school because of their child's behavior. They will usually talk to their child about modifying their behavior in class before coming to the conference. They will ask their child what led up to their misbehaving. If the student says that she was bored or that she felt her time was being wasted the parents will mention this in the conference. Being able to demonstrate that your class is organized and managed properly will help your case. If the class is disorganized and several students are acting out in class parents will want to know about your learning environment. If your lack of planning or lack of organization is the problem you will lose credibility. Before you make the call to the student's parents make sure that you have provided your students with clear directives of how you expect them to carry themselves in class, performances, and on trips. If you haven't made it clear what your expectations of good behavior are and what the consequences for poor behavior are, your administration may not back your actions. You do not want to be viewed as the source of the problem. Much of what you want to establish for classroom management should be established during the first week of classes. These procedures should be presented the same way you would present music to the class.

During the first week of school you should:

- Establish your expectation for entering the classroom.
- Describe the procedure for getting instruments out and pretuning.
- Describe how to get music folders from the music shelves.
- Establish that when you are on the podium, all talking and playing stops.
- Establish consequences for not following the rules.
- Describe how to return music to the shelves and instruments to storage areas.
- Establish that the bell does not dismiss class—you dismiss class.

11

Improving Your Band's Performance

Preparing for the first performance and establishing standards for future performances lay the groundwork for improving your band's performance level. Once you have provided your students with the tools they will need for individual preparation and performance, it is important that you constantly remind them of these principles and reinforce them.

After every performance, you'll need to set aside time in the next rehearsal to evaluate and discuss the strengths and weaknesses of the performance. It's important that you stress that the evaluation is for recognizing the good qualities of the performance as well as using constructive criticism to help improve future performances. As the moderator, you should strive to focus on the positive rather than the negative. If your students point out a few problems with attacks and releases, have them listen further to determine if there were places where the attacks and releases were better than they had been in rehearsals leading up to the performance. This stresses the point that even though they may have fallen short of the objective, there was still improvement on the group's part. Do not allow the discussion to become personal; refer to sections or parts only, not individual players even if there is only one player per part. Stress that audiences don't hear individuals, they hear a band.

VIDEO AND AUDIO TAPE PERFORMANCES

It is difficult to critique the band based on memories of the performance. Everyone will have a different perspective based on where they sit in the band. An audio tape or a video tape will give everyone an opportunity to listen objectively and focus on the group as a whole, not section by section or part by part. Video tapes give the added visual effects that audiences have during the performance. If there are visual distractions that cause problems in the performance, the video will give you and your students an opportunity to see them. Foot tapping, besides being a visual distraction, will also cause rushing. As you watch the tape, you as the director can make a point about the relationship between rushing in a particular section of the piece and the foot tapping or other visual distractions that caused the band to rush. Peripheral vision causes players to see things that will distract their attention from the podium. If the group misses entrance cues or expression cues because they weren't looking at the podium due to a visual distraction, point out the importance of being focused on the conducting and listening to what's going on around them musically.

Audio tapes provide you and your students with an opportunity to listen to the performance without being distracted by visuals. If you have an audio and video tape of the performance it is wise to listen to the audio tape first. Have your students follow their music as they listen to the tape. Once the tape has been played, use a guided activity to have them state their observations. An example of this would be to ask the students how well they followed the expression marks in the music for a specific section of the piece. Another example would be to have the students identify where the melodic line was obscured by the balance being improperly executed. All of the principles of a good performance that you have outlined previously should be touched on. This will cause your students to listen more discriminately and hopefully it will cause them to self-correct going into the next performance.

The evaluation of a performance must involve active student participation. You standing at the podium telling them what they did wrong will serve no positive purpose. Students often react to this as a put-down and will assume that they just can't please you. If they are actively involved, they can hear for themselves the problems you would identify and they generally will act to take corrective measures. If there are points you want brought out, rather than tell them they didn't do something correctly, ask them to listen to a particular section to see if there was something that needed improvement. If they still don't hear the problem or are sensitive about pointing it out, ask them to listen for a specific item. Example: "At measure 39, was our attack the way we worked on it?" This causes them to hear an absolute—the attack was either correct or not. The difference between them hearing it and you telling them will be the difference between whether or not it is corrected for the next performance.

If there are players more advanced than others, elicit their assistance in helping others listen discriminately. This serves a few purposes: one, it helps them to be more engaged in the listening activity and two; it helps reinforce the team element of band participation. Band is a collection of individuals working toward a common goal and this concept is easily achieved when students work together despite different ability levels.

EVALUATIONS BEFORE A COMPETITION OR FESTIVAL

One of the best ways of combining recruiting with improving band performance is to have a feeder school concert before a festival or competition. Involve the elementary school feeders, middle school feeder(s), and high school band in a concert that consists of the pieces that will be performed for adjudication. Have all of the groups listen carefully to one another and have them critique what they hear. Elementary students can write a short essay describing their experience. It is important that you point out that there are no incorrect answers because you want to know what they observed. Middle school and high school students can use an actual adjudication form to critique each group's performance. After the concert, during the next class each group should share their observations of the other groups they heard and then listen to recordings or view video tapes of their own performance and critique themselves. This may seem time-consuming but the educational value cannot be underestimated. Hopefully, as students listen critically to other groups they will become more aware of their group's strengths and weaknesses. The time that is spent on evaluating past performances usually cuts down on the time it takes to prepare for the next performance.

Another benefit of the evaluation of a festival preparation concert is that the students involved gain a better understanding of the festival experience and what adjudicators do. Their comments and observations may not be as advanced as the judges but if they hear some of the same things the judges heard, they will realize how much they are learning and how much they can help improve their group's performance.

MAINTAINING A STANDARD OF EXCELLENCE

One of the most difficult things you will face is maintaining a standard of excellence. In the quest for excellence, early improvements are easily seen by your students. After a while, incremental improvements will be less obvious. This is where audio and video taping rehearsals can help. Even though students may not hear improvement on a day-to-day basis, if you tape the group once a week and listen to the recording or view the video tape, those subtle, incremental improvements will be noticeable to your students. If your students don't understand why you continue to work on sections of a particular piece, they may not be as fastidious about working out minor details and problems as they should be. Having them actively listen critically to themselves and evaluate their rehearsals will cause them to understand the importance of repetition. It will also cause them to make the subtle changes they need to make in order to improve their individual and group performance level. Constant drilling on points is counterproductive but repetition and pointing out why repetition is necessary yields benefits.

MEASURING GROWTH AND IMPROVEMENT

It is important that you establish different ways of evaluating your group's progress. You can use techniques as simple as evaluating sections of a piece as you rehearse by stopping the rehearsal to discuss what the students hear and observe or as sophisticated as having students evaluate each piece in writing at the completion of the rehearsal or a week of rehearsals. The maturity and musical abilities of your group will help you decide the best way. For younger students or students of lower ability levels, you may decide to evaluate the group by playing a musical game. Incorporate television game shows or fun children's games into a music activity that brings out what you want the students to focus on. Let the students choose and customize the game. Section Feud can be a music version of the show Family Feud and each section can choose your top ten solutions to performance problems.

USING SMALL ENSEMBLES TO IMPROVE YOUR BAND'S SOUND

Using small ensembles to improve the overall performance level of your band is a valuable tool for many reasons. The smaller ensemble enables your students to put to use all of the skills required for good band playing. Being able to hear things in a smaller setting is the most valuable aspect of small ensemble playing. Students can focus on intonation, attacks and releases, balance, rhythmic accuracy, and many other skills needed for accurate large ensemble playing. Not having the distractions of several instruments playing and being able to concentrate on a small group of instruments allows your students to apply the skills you've taught in the larger group and implement those skills with a high degree of accuracy. They can then apply these skills acquired in small ensemble playing to the larger ensemble. The subtle ways they are learning these techniques enable them to internalize them and apply them naturally and almost effortlessly.

Small ensemble playing is not limited to homogenous instruments. There are several pieces written for small ensembles that use many different instrumental combinations. Pieces that are now played by larger ensembles, such as Bach's Brandenburg Concerti, were written for the instrumentation available to Bach at the time he wrote the pieces. Most state solo lists contain a section of works written for small ensembles that you can use to locate pieces that will enable you to match instrumentation that will suit your needs. You don't have to match players of equal performance skills in many of these ensemble pieces. A lot of the pieces have parts written at different levels of difficulty that will allow you to place advanced players and intermediate players in the same small ensemble. Most music publishers send scores to your school or post them on their websites for you to peruse. As you look at these scores, check to see if they are suitable for the level of players in your small group. If one or two parts need to be simplified to make them accessible to your group, then you may rearrange them or customize them to your group.

The idea of selecting music that will be stimulating and challenging is the goal. You want to be able to keep these students engaged and not allow them to become discouraged. The teamwork and camaraderie that is developed in these small groups will be transferred to your larger group. As with your soloists, if the group is not needed for part of your rehearsal while you work on difficult parts with other students, release them to a practice area to work on the small ensemble music. Give the soloists or small ensemble an opportunity to perform their piece(s) in a concert or in an activity such as a solo or ensemble activity.

Almost every school district and/or state sponsors a Solo and Ensemble Festival. The purpose of these festivals is to allow students who may desire more of a musical experience than individual bands can offer to develop their skills to a higher level. There are always students who are able to play music that is more challenging to them than what the band literature offers. These students have an opportunity through Solo and Ensemble Festival participation to play solos or in ensembles or to do both.

Bands that may not have the best instrumentation for a band festival can form one or more ensembles and have soloists participate in the Solo and Ensemble Festival to receive feedback on their musical growth. Solo and Ensemble Festivals are not competitive but do offer students an opportunity to be rated by an adjudicator based on how well they perform according to universal criteria. Many of the same things bands are judged on are the things found on a solo or ensemble adjudication sheet. Soloists may perform with or without accompaniment. When they play with accompaniment they must play to achieve ensemble with the accompanying instrument.

Criteria such as intonation, rhythmic accuracy, accurate attacks and releases, adherence to dynamics, breath control, tone quality, and articulation will be judged. Becoming aware of the importance of each of these skills is important to ensemble playing, large or small. Learning how to listen for cues and listening to other players is essential to playing with others and can be transferred by the soloists to non-solo settings. Ensembles are like miniature bands. The same principles of good band performance are expected in small ensemble performance. The adjudication form used for small ensemble performances is usually the same as the form used for bands. The ratings for soloists and ensembles are the same as for bands— Superior (I), Excellent (II), Good (III), Fair (IV), and Poor (V). These were designed for band directors to use as teaching tools to demonstrate to students that the qualities expected for good musicianship apply to individual performance and group performance.

Soloists participating in the Solo and Ensemble Festival have an opportunity to develop their individual performance level to their highest degree. They are not restricted by how well others are playing and can often play music grade levels higher than the music being covered in band class. This helps to keep them from losing interest in band because of lack of challenge from the music. As with the small ensemble, if they are not rehearsing problem areas in the band music, you can release them to a practice area to work on their solo (there is computer software available to help with this). By honing their individual playing skills they can help students around them develop theirs. You can use this to help improve playing in various sections of your band. These soloists also help you to present a higher level of performance expectations by displaying to other students the level of some of their peers. They will have an example of what you're saying is possible through practice and hard work by knowing that their fellow students are working hard to develop into high-level players.

Solo playing also gives your students an opportunity to take private lessons or coaching. There will be things about individual instruments and individual performance techniques that you will not be able to help some of your higher-level students with. At the beginning of the school year, you should have provided your students and their parents with a list of private teachers and coaches located within a reasonable distance of your school. You can also ask the private teachers to give their rates for thirty minutes, forty-five minutes, and one or two hours so that parents can formulate a budget. Students should be encouraged to study once a week or once every two weeks based on the cost, length of the lesson, and/or location of the private teacher.

If having the students go to a private teacher is not practical because of distance, have the teacher come to your school to teach several students on the same day or have them coach an entire section. Your parent organization may help you to defray the costs of travel by the private teacher and the cost of group coaching. Having several students take lessons on the same day may be incentive for the teacher to lower the cost of each lesson. If you have a homogenous small ensemble, each student can pay a small fee for one or two hours of coaching a week. This will save them money and give the coach an opportunity to be compensated for time and travel. Example: If the teacher charges fifty dollars an hour for a private lesson and you get three students to pay twenty dollars for coaching, the students save thirty dollars and the private coach gets compensated for the lesson and for travel. You can adjust the cost per student based on the number of students being coached and the teacher's cost per lesson.

Depending on your fundraising efforts, you may include the cost of coaching in your annual budget. Because the skills acquired in the group lessons will be transferred into large ensemble performance, this is a justifiable cost. Some schools engage adjunct faculty members for coaching during marching band season, concert band season, and for jazz ensembles. Once again, since most band directors are not proficient at a performance level on all band instruments, having a specialist come in will elevate the performance level of the entire group, not just the section receiving the coaching. Students tend to share information they have acquired with others so sections not receiving coaching can benefit from sections who are receiving coaching. This sharing of information strengthens the bonds within your band. Anything you can do to raise the standard of members of your group helps to raise the standard of your entire group.

In the smaller setting of a trio, quartet, quintet, septet, or octet, students can make eye contact with other players as they prepare for entrances. This eye contact reinforces the need to watch for visual cues (such as those provided by a conductor) in order to enter at the right time. These attacks must be precise and can be easily heard if they are not. This may not be as evident in a larger group as it is in a smaller setting but by hearing it in a smaller setting your students learn to realize how important accurate attacks and releases are. A sloppy or late attack can negatively impact on the small ensemble immediately. Students will hear how important an accurate attack is and how a late attack spreads through a larger group because others are dependent on someone else's attack. Hearing this for themselves in a small ensemble has a greater impact than you trying to describe it in the abstract. As stated earlier, this kind of learning by discovery is invaluable.

THE IMPORTANCE OF PRAISE
AND INDIVIDUAL RECOGNITION

One of the best ways to retain students is to recognize individual or small group achievement. This can be done as a student spotlight, player of the week, or section of the week recognition. It can take many forms. Take a picture of the person or group to be recognized and display it on the bulletin board in the band room, post it on the web page, put in on the social network page, announce it from the podium. The esteem of the recipient(s) will rise and this will create the kind of environment in which individual players will want to remain. You can leave the recipient's picture displayed for the entire year and have a special recognition for those who receive more than one. At the end of the year you can award a Section of the Year award or Most Valuable Player award. Students who are interested in signing up for band will notice that they can be recognized for their achievements and see that they as individuals will be valued in your program. Don't underestimate how much this means to students of all levels.

If you have a newsletter that is sent to feeder schools or goes home to parents (elementary schools have weekly newsletters that go home to parents), this is a valuable recruiting tool. Parents see that their child will be recognized for their contributions to your program. Middle school band directors and high school band directors can send items to the elementary school to be included in their weekly newsletter. This sense of community helps to reinforce the fact that successful programs on the high school level depend on continuity from elementary school through high school.

Just recognizing students who have obvious accomplishments will not help your band grow or maintain. You should have an award for students who contribute to your program but are not the most talented. Students in "supporting roles" can get an "unsung hero" type of award. Soloists can only sound good if everyone in the band is fulfilling their role. The top players will always return to your program, the players you want to retain are those who may not be the best players but are loyal, contributing members. Some of these students are searching for somewhere to "belong" in high school and it's important for you to attract them and retain them once they join.

Once again, the more you are aware of the human dynamic involved, the more you will succeed. Recognition is equated with value. The recognition can be as simple as you want it to be. Intangible recognition is of equal value to tangible recognition. Trophies, pins, and certificates will eventually wear out and tarnish but a special "thank you" said publicly never fades from your students' memories. A pizza party or ice cream social once a month for Most Valuable People (MVP awards) will serve many purposes from the social aspect of band to raising individual and group esteem.

When students talk about the fun they had while being recognized, this serves as a great recruiting/retention tool. Students can be involved in peer recognition. You can have a special recognition once a semester or once a year that you recognize MVPs who are selected by peers. Most Helpful, Most Encouraging, Most Likely to Practice, and Most Dedicated are a few peer recognition awards. There are a lot of things students do for one another behind the scenes that you may not be aware of. Giving them as stakeholders an opportunity to say thank you to one another is very important in retaining students. This also helps to balance with some of the negative things students may say to one another. You will need this balance to prevent students from being discouraged by peer criticism. Not feeling valued in a group is a major reason students elect not to return. Counter this with as much positive activity as possible.

12

Developing an Elementary Band Program

Some school districts with small budgets assign one instrumental music teacher to multiple schools. Many of these teachers have very little experience or knowledge of developing a band program at the elementary level. Unlike middle school or high school, elementary band classes are usually "pull-out" classes, meaning that students are pulled out of their classroom to go to band for thirty or forty-five minutes. Because art, band, orchestra, and some physical education classes are all pull-out classes, careful planning must be done. Another problem arises when teachers are assigned to more than one school. The schedule must be based on when the teacher is in the school. If classes are in two schools on the same day, travel time has to be considered.

Some music supervisors plan the days and times each elementary teacher is assigned to a school but in smaller districts the teacher and principals of each school must agree on a schedule. If the teacher is also assigned to a middle school and/or high school, this further complicates the problem.

One of the first priorities for developing an elementary school schedule is to determine the number of students in each school. This will determine class size and groupings (all brass in one class, all woodwinds, all percussion, or mixed instrumentation).

RECRUITING FOR BEGINNING BAND

One of the most important jobs of an elementary or middle school band director is developing a strong beginning band. This is the lifeline of the feeder system. Helping students choose instruments to play and encouraging them to participate in band for years to come is a significant responsibility.

Before meeting with students and parents to pitch your program, there are a few very important steps that need to be taken. First, you will need to take an inventory of school-owned instruments and make sure that they are in working condition. You should meet with the local music store(s) to find out about rental agreements and the cost of renting instruments. Gather information on costs associated with each instrument (e.g., reeds, valve oil, slide oil, etc.).

Choose the method book(s) that will be used for band class or individual instrument instruction. There are many methods to choose from but you should choose the one(s) that best serves your terminal objective. Some elementary band programs are designed to develop individual playing skills while others are designed to develop good band techniques. The method book(s) you choose should be used for homogenous instruments or heterogeneous instruments.

Discuss the budget and operating costs associated with a beginning band program with the school's administration to determine the amount of support you can expect. Since many of the instruments students will start on are "jump off" instruments (instruments that will allow students to easily switch to another instrument), make sure that the school has or can purchase large or expensive instruments such as tubas, baritones, tenor and baritone saxophones, percussion instruments (other than snare drums).

Devise a schedule for classes so that students will know how often and for how long classes will be held. Find out if there are college students or private teachers who are available to give private lessons to your students and the cost of the lessons. Technology today allows you to use interactive video such as skype.com or oovoo.com to access professional instructors to offer instruction on embouchure, sound, breathing, and so on. There are many colleges and universities that offer Skype or interactive video instruction. SmartMusic.com offers school registration that allows teachers and student to register for interactive software for students of all levels to play along with.

CHOOSING INSTRUMENTS

Once you have taken care of the logistics required to make a complete presentation to students and parents, decide on the best way to introduce the instruments to the students. The best way to do this is by having actual players come to the school and perform for the students. If the beginning band is on the elementary level, bringing in a middle school group or individuals can serve you well. The elementary students may recognize that some of the students attended their school and/or they may have siblings who still attend the school. Middle school beginners can be impressed by advanced middle school players or high school players coming to the school.

If there are instruments that you want students to begin on, make those instruments look the most appealing. If a large group is used for the presentation, assign a solo to the desired instrument(s). If you're not the director, tell the group's director what you want highlighted on the presentation. Students will not want to play an instrument they view as boring. On the elementary and middle school level, the fun element must be highlighted.

Another way of highlighting instruments is to use recordings like *Peter and the Wolf*. This should be the last choice because students won't have an opportunity to interact with the players. Having an opportunity to ask players why they chose to play a particular instrument or how difficult it is to play an instrument will help students decide whether they want to choose an instrument. Of course, if there are instruments you're proficient on, you can do the presentation. If you only have a minimal proficiency level, don't play the instrument. Your poor performance will make the instrument seem more difficult to play and it will be a less desirable choice. There's an old joke passed on by band directors that if there are instruments they don't want students to choose, they play those instruments badly during the presentation. This should not be your plan; you can always switch students to other instruments later. By allowing students to freely choose their instrument, you can capitalize on their interest and enthusiasm.

MAKING THE PRESENTATION TO STUDENTS AND PARENTS

The next thing you must decide is where and when to make the presentation to students and parents. Your location choice will be dependent on the size of the demographic you're appealing to. If you're new to the school or there was not a program in the school before, you may want to present to the entire grade level you'll be drawing from. Most school districts now start band instruments in fifth grade and orchestra strings in grade 4. If the school has an auditorium or multipurpose room, bring a large group from the middle school or high school in to perform two or three selections and have selected instruments demonstrate what they sound like and how they are played. Some school districts have "Articulation Days" where they bring in an entire grade level to the higher-level school to familiarize the students with the school they will be attending in the next few years. Most middle schools in the United States are arranged in grades 6 through 8 (some districts have grades 5 through 8) although there are still a few grade 7 through 9 junior high schools in existence.

Another choice for the presentation could be to take smaller groups or players of different instruments to each class on the grade level you're appealing to. This can be done over the course of several days or in one day. The smaller group presentation gives students a better chance to interact with the players you've brought in. Elementary students generally don't feel comfortable asking questions in large groups. Those students who will speak up in large groups should be immediately signed up for band! Risk takers make good music students because they are not afraid to take chances on new things.

Having parents attend an evening presentation along with their child gives you an opportunity to answer questions about the economic effect of band class. Parents will want to know how much it will cost them to have their child involved in band. If there will be special attire required, whether the child will have to purchase an instrument, how much maintenance costs are associated with particular instruments, how much private lessons will cost, and how much of a time commitment is involved are a few of the questions parents will have that students won't ask. It is important as stated earlier that you have these answers available for the presentation. If you have a presentation for students only, you will be dependent on students to answer these questions.

To avoid problems, should you have a presentation for students only, give each student a packet that contains the answers to the questions posed above. If the school has a weekly newsletter or web page, put all pertinent information about band participation on the site or in the newsletter. Since some students will be moving to other instruments from the "jump off" instruments, be sure to explain that process to parents. This is the reason students should rent instruments rather than purchase outright. It is also why having an inventory of low brass, low woodwind, and percussion instruments is so important.

If the beginning band is on the middle school level the students you choose from can come from all grade levels. Since middle school students change classes they are not restricted to team-teaching blocks like elementary schools. Even though there may be some team teaching taking place in the school, students still make class selections with their counselors and will start to formulate their five-year plan. Getting students started on band instruments before grade 8 or when they're in grade 8 helps them to include band classes on the high school level.

The presentation process and the information needed for beginning band students and their parents is the same as it is for elementary school beginners. Middle schools generally have larger budgets than elementary schools so that means you will probably be able to have more school-owned instruments. Here are some of the instruments you will need to provide for students along with the "jump off" instruments:

Student Rental or Purchased Instruments

Starting instruments—Trumpets or cornets, B-flat clarinets, flutes, alto saxophones, trombones, snare drum, baritone horn, or tuba

School-Provided Instruments

Instruments to change to—French horn, oboe, bassoon, bass clarinet, alto clarinet, timpani, xylophone, tenor saxophone, baritone saxophone and contra-bass clarinet, tuba (if not used as a starter instrument)

Some teachers wait until students are older before starting them on or switching them to double reed instruments. This is entirely up to the director's discretion. If there is a qualified double reed private teacher available you may decide to start beginners on double reeds if the instruments are available. Otherwise, it is best to wait until they have played clarinet or flute before making the switch. Once again, the availability of private instruction and the musical aptitude of the student will help you to decide when to introduce double reed instruments. The grade the beginner is in and the needs of the middle school or high school band for balanced instrumentation will also weigh in on the decision.

School-Owned Instrument Use

If students are going to be using a school-owned instrument, there should be a school use-agreement form for the student and parent to fill out (one can be found in the Sample Forms section). Some school districts have a form that has been developed for use in every school in their district so that liabilities and expectations will be universal throughout the district. Each student using a school-owned instrument must provide their own mouthpiece (reeds, valve oil, key oil, etc.).

In some cases, more than one student will be using a school-owned instrument and the liability for damages can be difficult to determine. Unless the student admits to damaging the instrument (unlikely) or you witness the damage (also unlikely) it will be difficult to hold one person responsible and financially liable for repairs. Because of this, some directors have a school rental/repair fee that they charge each student who uses a school-owned instrument (these fees go into a fund used for repairs). This charge is usually lower than what it would cost the student to rent the instrument from a vendor. Instruments commonly owned by the school are baritone horns, tuba, bassoon, baritone saxophone, tenor saxophones, bass clarinet, oboes, French horns, double basses, and large percussion (which normally don't go home with students). Other school-owned instruments will be discussed in chapter 17 for jazz ensemble equipment needs.

If students use a school-owned instrument and take it home or use the instrument during the summer it should be very clearly stated on the school instrument-use form that any loss or damage to the instrument while in the student's possession is the student's responsibility. This should be made clear during the first meeting with parents and clearly stated and explained on the agreement form. This means that you are responsible for making sure that the instrument you provide for the student is in good working order and that you have inspected the instrument for dings and dents.

When students request to use a school-owned instrument on a loan basis, there should be an understanding stated in an agreement or on a form. However you decide to handle it, the following points need to be addressed:

- Is there a specified time for student use of an instrument (semester, year, summer)?
- Is the instrument in good playing order and what is the physical appearance (scratches, dents, dings, etc.)?
- Will the student be responsible for damages and/or repairs? If so, is there a limit on the amount the student is responsible for?
- If the instrument is used during the summer while other school-owned instruments are receiving general maintenance, is the student responsible for having the instrument serviced?
- If more than one student is using a school-owned instrument, how will you decide who gets to borrow it for the summer?

Student loaner forms must be distributed to parents and students at the beginning of the school year so that students are aware of costs involved in band participation. The form should have all vital contact information on it—student's name, address, telephone number, and e-mail address. It must have all pertinent instrument information (serial number, condition of the instrument) and the date of the loan (and length of the loan). Since minors cannot enter into contracts in most states a parent must sign the form accepting the listed liabilities.

The importance of keeping accurate records cannot be overstated. Monitoring the "comings and goings" and condition of these instruments is of the utmost importance. Should a student decide to rent an instrument from a music store, the loan instrument should be returned to the school in good working order. If you have not kept a record of the "return condition," the school will be responsible for any needed repairs. Once the instrument is placed back on the shelf you are acknowledging that the terms of the contract have been fulfilled by the student if not otherwise noted.

In case there are two or more students using one instrument during the summer, you will need to check the instrument back in and then check it out to the second student. You will need to note any damages or the condition of the instrument when checked in and make sure that it is still in good working order. The second student must have the same opportunity to play an instrument in good working order as the first student. When you establish a rental fee you need to structure it for semester use, yearly use, and summer use. The amount for each rental period should be based on the cost of routine maintenance. Funds for loaner instruments should not be used for anything other than maintenance and repairs. You will want to have funds available for repairs. Once the loan period ends, you'll need to inspect the instrument and check it back into the inventory, noting any cosmetic information or problems with the instrument. Since general maintenance costs are the responsibility of the student, some teachers waive the summer fee once the student has the instrument serviced. Allowances should be made for students with financial difficulties (schools with Title One or Free Lunch students generally waive all student-use fees).

Maintaining a good-quality inventory used by beginners is very important; you don't want students having difficulty learning to play an instrument because of mechanical problems with the instrument. Of course, if you have a number of school-owned instruments, you will want to periodically check those instruments to determine which instruments need to be replaced.

SELECTING METHODS FOR BEGINNING BAND

As stated before, when selecting methods for beginning band students, there are a few considerations that must be addressed. The first consideration is the kind of method(s) that will be used. There are methods for single instruments, methods for homogeneous instruments, methods for heterogeneous instruments, and class methods. The second consideration is what you hope to achieve through the use of the method. Can different methods be used to complement one another? Do you plan to develop individual players and the group simultaneously or separately? Thirdly, can the method's material and organization be applied or related to music being used by the entire band class?

If you decide to use a method for heterogeneous instruments, does the score give you, the director, an indication of what each instrument is playing? Does the method address good posture needed for breathing and breath control? Does the method address embouchure development for winds and proper stroking positions for percussion instruments?

There are methods that have accompanying DVDs that have professional players modeling the correct embouchure formation and proper stick or mallet grips. Most band director training programs require their students to learn how to produce sound on every band instrument. Before introducing any method to your band you should make sure that you can model embouchure and stick grip positions.

Method books should also demonstrate (with or without a DVD) proper posture, finger position, and the proper way to hold the instrument, sticks, or mallets. All method books used for wind instruments should include a fingering chart which includes trills, mordents, and appoggiaturas. The better method books include a table of notes, a glossary of terms, and rhythmic counting guides. The layout of the book should be logical and should progress at a pace that is not too fast or too slow to maintain students' interest.

There are some methods that are designed to be used with accompanying materials, for solos, for full band, and for ensemble groupings and include some music theory. These books will also have a means of testing and measuring students' progress either by having playing or written assessments. Before players can progress to the next unit they must demonstrate mastery of the previous material.

Some methods for individual instruments will provide an age-appropriate history of the instrument. This will help you to build on the character of each instrument later as your students progress. Individual methods should address putting the instrument together, tone production with the mouthpiece, or head joint for wind instruments. Place a reed on clarinet and saxophone mouthpieces and have the students create a buzz sound. Get brass players to make a buzz sound by taut lips contacting the mouthpiece. Have flutes get a sound by blowing across the sound hole. Try to get double reed players to "croak" an "A" clearly and evenly. Once again, if there is a DVD that comes with the method book, use it to demonstrate these techniques to the players. Once this has been achieved, have the student attach the mouthpiece to the instrument. For woodwind players who use single or double reeds, discuss the care that needs to be taken with reeds to avoid cracks or chips.

After you have addressed each group of instruments individually or in a small-group setting you'll be ready to start with band concepts. You can teach all of the instruments how to identify notes on the staff (give them the names of the lines and spaces even before individual notes are introduced). Then you can work on clefs, basic note values and how they are counted, and bar lines and their function. These items are generally introduced in individual instrument or group methods.

Teaching students how to count basic rhythms will generally come after whole notes have been introduced. Whole notes are introduced first for two reasons. First, they provide a way to control long tones when students are learning to produce sound and second, they give you an opportunity to introduce the concept of counting four beats at a time. Common time or 4/4 time is the first time signature introduced in most beginning methods. Even though a whole note is a long tone, students must learn to count it in groups of four beats per measure. You can then teach the division of beats into four parts. By having the students tap their legs, you can help them learn to internalize the beat count once they are using both hands to hold their instrument (or sticks/mallets).

As students count by tapping their leg, their hands go down and up so you can use this to teach the down beat and up beat concept later. By having the students count one, two, three, four, you can later introduce eighth note counting as one and two and three and four and. Over time, as more note and rest values are introduced you can build on the basic four beats and down and up beat counting. Later when sixteenth notes are introduced you can divide the beat into four equal parts as one-ee-and-uh. This will help you to have a uniform way of counting the beat and partials of the beat from the podium in such a way that everyone will be able to understand. This will remain constant throughout the band experience.

RECOMMENDED BEGINNING BAND METHODS

Accent on Band books 1 and 2	Alfred Publishing
Band Expressions books 1 and 2	Alfred Publishing
Belwin 21st Century Band Method books 1, 2, and 3	Alfred Publishing
Best in Class books 1 and 2	Neil Kjos Music Company
Ed Sueta Band Method books 1, 2, and 3	Ed Sueta Music Publications
Essential Elements 2000 books 1 and 2	Hal Leonard Corporation
First Division Band Method books 1 and 2	Alfred Publishing
Measures of Success	FJH Music Company
Sound Innovations #1 Band	Alfred Music Publishing
Standards of Excellence 1, 2, and 3	Neil Kjos Music Company
Tradition of Excellence	Neil Kjos Music Company
Yamaha Advantage Book 1 and 2	Playintime Publishing
Yamaha Advantage Primer	Playintime Publishing

13

Structuring Your Concert Band, Symphonic Band, and Wind Ensemble Leadership in Band

LEADERSHIP IN BAND

One of the most overlooked positive aspects of marching band is student leadership. Besides drum majors and student directors, marching band has field captains (squad leaders), line captains, section leaders, and rank guides (guide right or guide left). There are camps, seminars, and other summer activities devoted to student leadership. Interestingly enough, there are few if any leadership camps devoted to concert band leadership. Since marching band is a major part of your band program and those students also participate in your concert program, this is a resource you can tap into.

During marching band season, your student leaders manage rehearsals, teach routines, coach sections on their music, and function as part of a leadership team that assists you. Once marching band season is over you don't want to let these skills lie dormant until the next marching band season. As you develop large performance ensembles, find ways to get student leaders involved. These leaders will take building the band program as a personal responsibility and their actions will demonstrate to you and others their feeling of ownership.

LARGE INSTRUMENTAL PERFORMANCE GROUPS

When going into a new school it is your hope that you will have the instrumentation that you need to form a band that is able to perform music that is scored for concert band. Unfortunately, when building a band program you will probably not have ideal instrumentation. If this is the case, you have two options: one, you can adjust the score to match the instrumentation that you have or two, you can choose to have small mixed or homogenous ensembles.

Should you decide the latter, there is literature written for mixed instruments that can be performed at ensemble festivals, not band festivals. If your band is under thirty members, you may wish to teach band literature in class but prepare small-ensemble literature for ensemble festivals. This may require more work on your part but having model groups in your program to present publicly will help with building your program by quality and quantity. Getting enough instrumentation to form a concert band is a major priority for the new director. You need to have at least one band in your school that performs classic band literature.

Bands that perform classic band literature and classical music can be called by different names at different schools but most school districts have course descriptions that describe Concert Band, Symphonic Band, and Wind Ensemble as different courses. The term "concert band" is used to describe all three of these bands, without distinction. Depending on the size of your band program's enrollment, your band may be called Concert Band or Symphonic Band; Wind Ensemble is generally reserved to describe an elite band group.

When describing Concert Band in school districts, the distinction is made that Concert Band is the lowest-level band class in a school. This is the class that incoming freshman students are automatically enrolled in when they sign up for band. Unfortunately, if there are only a few students enrolled in your band program, securing ideal balance on parts will be difficult. Students coming into high school directly from middle school or middle school directly from elementary school will probably be playing flute, clarinet, trumpet, or alto saxophone (the most popular and manageable instruments for younger players). Having oboes, trombones, bassoons, bass clarinets, alto clarinets, French horns, English horns, and contra-bass clarinets in most middle school bands or elementary school bands is rare. Considering this, you will probably have to convert some of your students to a new instrument in order to achieve good balance and meet the instrument requirements of most scores.

Because of the size of lower pitched instruments and elementary school students, some instruments are not practical for them to play. There are however instrument holders and braces for larger instruments that you can purchase for your school so that smaller students won't have to struggle holding larger instruments as they play. Should you desire to start students on tuba or baritone saxophone, you should secure these braces and holders to allow students to have the option of playing these instruments irrespective of their size. The success of a group performing classic band literature will depend on the balance of woodwinds, brass, and percussion. If you have a large number of percussion instruments that will cause imbalances in instrumentation you should consider forming a percussion ensemble as a class or extracurricular ensemble. You want your percussion players to learn and develop good performance habits and become well-rounded musicians.

The woodwind choir should be balanced enough to provide warmth and sonority to the group. In an ideal situation, your band will have more wood- wind players than brass players but if you don't, you'll need to consider ways to prevent the band from having a harsh, brassy sound. You may be able to get experienced brass players to play with sensitivity and not play over wood- wind players but it is more likely that you will need to use muted brasses to cover missing or limited woodwind parts. Should this be the case you will want your trumpet players to listen to the piece so that they can hear the nu- ances in the music based on the clarinet or woodwind players' sound.

Concert Band

Since elementary and middle school bands are generally referred to as concert band, the description of concert band here will refer to high school bands where there will possibly be more than one band. Concert band, as stated before, is the entry-level band for most high school programs and will therefore have the least experienced players. This will require special considerations on your part to make sure that you can achieve a balance of instrumentation that will maintain the integrity of a score and will give your students a meaningful band experience. Since it is likely that you won't turn any students anyway from concert band unless they are beginners with no band experience, you will need to make sure that missing parts are covered.

Using flutes or muted trumpets to cover missing oboe parts for example keeps chords intact and offers the listener a sound that will not be incon- sistent with the composer's intent. This will also help prevent you from having an unbalanced trumpet sound because of too many players. Most concert band music is written for trumpet and cornet parts so that will help you to avoid some balance problems. For inexperienced bands that have nine trumpets or nine clarinets, it is better to have a larger number of second and third players than first players. That means simply that you can have four students playing third parts, three students playing second parts, and two players playing first parts rather than having three players per part. If you put your best players on first parts, the lower parts will have great difficulty balancing. If you decide to audition students for parts, designate your top three players as principal first, second, and third. This way you will be assured of hearing all chord voices represented. The ideal concert band instrumentation would be as follows:

Flute	6
Piccolo	1
E-flat Clarinet	1
B-flat Clarinet	12
Alto Clarinet	2
Bass Clarinet	2
Contra Bass Clarinet	1
Oboe	1
English Horn	1
Bassoon	2
Alto Saxophone	2
Tenor Saxophone	1
Baritone Saxophone	1
Cornet	6
Trumpet	2
French Horn	4
Trombone	4
Bass Trombone	1
Euphonium	3
Tuba	2
Percussion	6

Of course, the likelihood of achieving ideal instrumentation in most schools is slim, but this can serve as a guide for you to use when determining how to substitute parts or rearrange a score. The most important thing to remember is that you want all scored parts covered, and you don't want your band to be top-heavy. Every band director is aware of the need for low brass and low woodwinds, but some overlook the importance of covering second and third parts. The balance of your group depends as much on all chord voices being represented as it does to have lower voiced instruments. You may have to convince your students of this importance because most young players identify playing first parts as identifying the best players. This is where designating principal players is important. You can use orchestral seating as an example of principal seating. Principal players irrespective of part are identified as the top players in an orchestra or band. You should also point out the importance of having all parts covered to get the most from a score. If you tape your band, they will recognize whether or not they are achieving balance if all parts aren't covered or if stronger players are not on second and third parts.

The concert band experience that your students have will affect whether or not your program grows to a point that will allow you to establish another band. Should you decide to develop a symphonic band in your school, you can use concert band as the training ground for less experienced players.

Symphonic Band

In some schools symphonic band is described as advanced band. This simply designates that this band is designed to perform music that is more difficult than the music concert band plays. Most schools use symphonic band as the main source for marching band since the players are more experienced. It is difficult for lower level players to control their tone quality while marching because of embouchure and breath control. Ideally, marching bands project well but also maintain a controlled, refined sound. Marching bands are typically brass and percussion heavy and have a large number of players. Symphonic bands are generally larger than concert bands and therefore give more students an opportunity to perform classic band literature. Your biggest concern should be to make sure that when marching band season is completed, you can convert some students to instruments that aren't usually used outside (bassoon, English horn, oboe and contra-bass clarinet). The ideal instrumentation for Symphonic Band is as follows (though not limited to):

Flute	10
Piccolo	1
E-flat Clarinet	1
B-flat Clarinet	24
Alto Clarinet	4
Bass Clarinet	2 or 4
Contra Bass Clarinet	1 or 2
Oboe	1
English Horn	1
Bassoon	2 or 4
Alto Saxophone	4
Tenor Saxophone	2
Baritone Saxophone	1
Cornet	9
Trumpet	4
French Horn	8
Trombone	6
Bass Trombone	2
Euphonium	4
Tuba	4
Percussion	6 to 10 (maximum)
String Bass	1

As in the case of concert band, you may have more players than you need for balanced instrumentation. If symphonic band is the highest level band in your school, it is advisable to have an unbalanced instrumentation in concert band rather than symphonic band. Training a larger number of inexperienced players is better than lowering the performance level of your symphonic band. Every band program needs to have a band or ensemble that students aspire to grow to. If you have a large number of inexperienced players in symphonic band and concert band, you may wish to consider forming a wind ensemble. The main consideration for this is whether or not you have enough experienced players to form a high-level group that has limited instrumentation. Students in your school and students you are recruiting from middle school need to hear and see a model group. Excellence breeds excellence and conversely, mediocrity breeds mediocrity. If you can't get enough instrumentation to form a full band, you may wish to form small ensembles that can perform high-quality literature. This will enable you to have model performance groups that are at a higher level than your concert band or symphonic band.

Wind Ensemble

Up until recently, wind ensembles were rare at the high school level but now since some music programs have expanded even at a time when others are declining, wind ensembles are being established. Whether there are three bands in the school that perform classic band literature or two, having a top-level band that can perform difficult band literature is important. Wind ensembles are generally smaller than symphonic bands so you can take the top players from symphonic band by audition or director's choice based on instrumentation needs and form a high-quality band group. Colleges and universities have wind ensembles that are designed for music majors and high-level nonmusic majors who can perform the highest level music written for bands. On the high school level, wind ensembles can be used as the group that students aspire to.

The more experienced players can be challenged musically by wind ensemble literature. This will assist you with recruiting and retaining since wind ensemble players are usually the most motivated and most disciplined players in a band program. Some of the discipline problems that are experienced because of students not being focused are not problems with motivated players who are generally associated with wind ensemble. These students generally don't need external motivation from you, the director, because they are motivated by the challenges imposed by the music. Ideal wind ensemble instrumentation would be as follows:

Flute   2
Piccolo   1
E-flat Clarinet 1

B-flat Clarinet	6
Alto Clarinet	1
Bass Clarinet	1
Contra Bass Clarinet	1
Oboe	1
English Horn	1
Bassoon	2
Alto Saxophone	2
Tenor Saxophone	1
Baritone Saxophone	1
Cornet	4
Trumpet	2
French Horn	4
Trombone	2
Bass Trombone	1
Euphonium	2
Tuba	1 or 2
Percussion	6 to 8 (maximum)

Wind ensemble should be used as your main recruiting group if there is one in your school. Since most wind ensemble players will have progressed through your band program, the group is an example of what your program has achieved, the importance of students remaining in your program, and the standard of excellence for which your program strives. The size of the group will make it a manageable group for traveling to the feeder school(s) and having future students meet students who can speak firsthand about participating in concert band, symphonic band, wind ensemble, and marching band is invaluable. No matter how well you write course descriptions, syllabi, and other written materials to promote your program, they pale in comparison to student testimonials.

Whether you are working with concert band, symphonic band, or wind ensemble, there are musical elements that will be presented, discussed, and performed by all three groups. Articulation, intonation, rhythmic accuracy, tone quality, phrasing, attacks and releases, will simply be refined by the higher level groups and should be worked on during daily rehearsal. The maturity of the students in the higher level groups means that you will be able to help them be more analytical during the process. All bands should learn/play a concert march, chorales, and pieces in multiple movements.

Based on the grading system used by most states, concert band on the high school level should perform Grade Four pieces or higher (based on ability levels). In the early years of developing a concert band it may be necessary to perform Grade Three pieces and introduce Grade Four as the band progresses. Symphonic Bands should perform Grade Four minimum but depending on their collective performance level can perform grades four through six. If wind ensemble is your highest level group, it should perform Grade Five and Grade Six (the most challenging grades). Each grade of music has a range within the grade that will be less difficult or more difficult than the grade indicates. Before choosing a grade of music for your group you should study or peruse the score. Focus on the range of brass parts, the technical challenges of clarinet and flute parts, and rhythmic challenges and instrumentation for percussion parts.

Since marching band has more percussion players than you will need for concert or symphonic band, you should have a plan for keeping all of your marching band players involved in band. There are a few ways to achieve this. Obviously, you want to use as many of them as you need to cover the concert literature being performed by the other bands but you may also consider forming a percussion ensemble or even including a percussion class for your program.

Many schools have percussion classes as a course offering. Giving your percussion players an opportunity to develop their musical skills will help your band program. Rather than striking percussion instruments without consideration to the band's overall balance, your students will learn the importance they have to sound shading and balance. You will also be able to teach them the importance of melody and harmony through the use of mallet instruments. Give each student an opportunity to learn all of the percussion instruments rather than specialize in snare drum or bass drum, and so on. Music written for band requires parts beyond the snare drum, bass drum, cymbals, and timpani. Most scores now include parts for xylophone, marimba, gong, chimes, celeste, piano, glockenspiel, and various Latin instruments. Percussion sections now need to have at least six players to cover all scored parts.

The most important consideration for directors of bands that play in concert style is to have all scored parts covered either by the instruments scored or by other instruments that can provide adequate sound substitutions. Good performance habits need to be taught and reviewed constantly and as groups progress from concert band to wind ensemble, there should be measurable improvement to fundamental sound. When teaching the concert band sound, directors have to depend on their aural abilities to identify it and describe it to their students. Characteristics of good concert band sound include (but are not limited to) accurate attacks and releases, good sonority, balance, shaping and shadings, phrase accuracy (connected phrases), good intonation, rhythmic and tempo accuracy, articulation that is consistent to style of music being performed, and interpretation. Listening to how good bands perform classic band literature will help you and your students shape your conception of what a good concert band sound is and should be.

Whether you give your students a visual such as a triangle to think of to understand that bottom instruments and instruments playing lower parts (second and third parts), it's important that they realize that good sound starts from the bottom and works its way up. Earlier, this was referred to as the pyramid effect or the pyramid of sound. At the bottom of the triangle or pyramid the lower voices: tubas, contra bassoon, contra bass clarinet, baritone saxophone, bass trombone, bass clarinet, and bassoon will play at a higher volume level or dynamic than the voices above them. The next level (lower middle level) will contain: euphoniums, tenor saxophones, alto clarinet, and French horns. The upper middle level will contain: B-flat clarinets, cornets, and flugel horns. The final level (the apex) will consist of: trumpets, alto saxophones, flutes, oboes, E-flat clarinets, and piccolo. Within this pyramid there will be other pyramids starting from third to second to first parts. It is the second pyramid that is most often overlooked.

Some of the things you want your bands to be able to do are as follows:

1. Play in tune with themselves and others
2. Listen across the band to trace melodic lines
3. Follow expression markings accurately
4. Adhere to phrase markings
5. Play with rhythmic accuracy
6. Play in the correct style using articulation that complements that style
7. Control dynamic ranges
8. Play with good tone control and note shadings
9. Balance within the section and through the entire band
10. Develop good breathing techniques and breath control

Once you have been able to shape the sound of your concert band, symphonic band, and wind ensemble, these skills can be refined and shaped by smaller performance groups.

WORKING ON INTONATION FOR BAND CLASSES

Intonation is one of the most important elements of good musicianship and good band performances. Standing in front of your band and having them play a given tuning note and telling each student if he or she is sharp, flat, or in tune serves no real purpose. It tells them that the mechanical device you are holding says that they are or are not in tune but does little to help them understand how to hear it for themselves.

One of the best ways to train your students on how important tuning is will be to set up a tuner in the instrument storage room and let the students pretune before taking their seats. Once they have been seated and have warmed up, tune them starting from the lower instruments upward. It's best to tune to two different pitches, Concert B-flat and Concert F. After playing the first rehearsal piece, have your first chair clarinet play a tuning pitch and fine tune the band once more. This lets your students know that tuning is an ongoing process and is a constant concern for bands.

A mistake a lot of players make is to push a tuning slide, mouthpiece, head joint double reed, or bocal all the way in before tuning. Doing this will generally cause a distorted tuning outcome because instruments aren't designed to be tuned in that manner. Saxophone mouthpieces should be place initially halfway down the cork on the neck so that they can be pushed in or pulled out without distorting the sound or tone quality. Flutes should have the lower portion of the head joint a quarter in from the marked tuning area at the base of the head joint. This provides room to adjust the length of the head joint to go from flat to sharp giving the student flexibility to reach the proper spot for tuning. Brass tuning slides (including the first and third valve tuning slides) should not be pushed completely in. Just as with the flute, a quarter of the way in should be sufficient to give the player flexibility in tuning.

There are some directors who only focus on tuning before performances and festivals and are surprised to discover that their students can't achieve a good tonal center. Adjudicators can instantly tell groups who have made tuning a priority from those who have not. There is a saying among adjudicators that states a band is only as good as the director's and students' ears. This statement is true and accurate. If the director doesn't stop to immediately address intonation problems as they occur and students don't make adjustments as they play, the performance will be marred by poor intonation. Most players can hear whether or not they are playing in tune but may not be able to tell whether they are sharp or flat.

In order to help students discriminate whether a pitch is sharp or flat have one player provide a source note and have a second student play a note attempting to match the pitch. If the students hear a slow strobe sound, the second student is flat. If they hear a fast strobe sound, the second student is sharp. This corresponds with the visual students see when playing into a tuner. As they play in large and small ensembles they can focus on the strobe sound that results between them and the tuning sources of the ensemble. Once the students learn how to focus and adjust while playing in their section and expand it to the choir in which they belong (brass or woodwind), the overall intonation of the band will improve.

ADJUSTING THE SCORE FOR
YOUR BAND'S INSTRUMENTATION

It is very unlikely that in the early years of building a band program that you will have the scored instrumentation. This does not mean that you can't perform good literature for band. If you study a score before introducing a piece to your band, you can determine if there is a need to replace missing parts with the instrumentation you have at hand.

Some composers of band music are aware of the need to double parts that may not be covered in some bands. These composers write cues for parts that are missing for parts that you will likely have. You can use their guide for doubling or replacing parts for your band. Common cued or doubled parts are tenor sax/baritone horns; alto saxophone/F horn; flute/oboe; B-flat clarinet/oboe; baritone saxophone/bass clarinet; baritone saxophone or bass clarinet/tuba. Trumpets, clarinets, flutes, and alto saxophones can be used to cover missing melodic lines.

Sometimes you may need to simplify complex rhythm parts for inexperienced players even if the part is doubled by another instrument. If you must simplify parts, make sure to maintain the integrity of the piece. In order to prepare players for the future, you must allow them to play their parts and grow in ability and confidence. Taking out trills, converting triplets to two eighth-note patterns, and limiting syncopations are a few ways of simplifying the score while maintaining the character of the piece. Only after you have studied the score and listened to a recording of the piece will you be able to determine what adjustments can or should be made for your band.

Several music publishers have become aware of the fact that bands have difficulty playing a piece with the scored instrumentation and have included alternate parts or alternate scoring. The alternate scores are usually placed within the ability level of lower level players. This means that tenor saxophones and baritone saxophones carry the low parts and clarinets, flutes, trumpets, or alto saxophones carry the melody. Should you decide to rewrite the score or simplify parts, you may wish to use notation software. Choosing and using notation software is discussed extensively in another chapter but the benefit of using software is that you can view and hear all parts at one time. This allows you to instantly discover whether or not your adjustments work. Because most notation software uses voices that sound like the instruments being scored for, you can experiment with the voices that you think will maintain the integrity of the piece.

Most young bands and inexperienced bands are deficient in the area of low brass or trumpet players with a limited range. This means that you will need to "shrink" the range of the piece by using voices that are not as low as needed and trumpet parts that are not as high as desired. If you are writing parts manually, you will need to experiment with the voices you have in your band. You may need to double low voices to reinforce the bottom quality of the sound and substitute flute or clarinet parts for the upper register. If you double flutes or clarinets with the trumpet parts an octave higher, the sound illusion will be that the trumpet parts are being played higher. Once again, if you have notation software you'll hear this as you make adjustments.

CONCERT BAND CHOIRS

Whether it's concert band, symphonic band, or wind ensemble, teaching blend and balance begins inside two wind choirs (brass and woodwind) and the percussion section "skin" instruments and "nonskin" instruments (membranophones and nonmembranophones). The two wind choirs may also be divided into smaller choirs (clarinet choir, flute choir, etc.) If balance and blend are successfully achieved in these smaller choirs, the overall blend and balance of the full band will be improved.

It is easier to get your students to concentrate their focus on like or similar instruments than it is to get them to listen across the band to unlike instruments. Cross listening is going to be a constant focus on your part and that of your students but initially, it is a difficult concept for your students to understand. Having worked on tone quality, your students should be able to recognize the sound of like instruments or similar voiced instruments (instruments carrying the melody or their part). It is less difficult for players to hear their part or the melody being played by other instruments than it is to listen for an instrument or part with which they are not familiar.

The concept of second and third parts playing stronger than first parts is less difficult to achieve inside choirs than it is listening to the full band. Achieving the best balance will depend on the director being able to balance more and less sound. Players should be given sound parameters and the director should "tweak" those levels to achieve an overall balance. Lower voices should be dissuaded from overblowing to achieve balance (clarinets and trumpets especially). This overblowing will result in harsh uncontrolled sounds that will negatively impact tone quality, balance, and blend. Players trying to balance across the band by playing loud enough for others to hear them do more harm to the band than help.

The director can help with cross listening for balance purposes by isolating each line of music they want their students to listen for. If there are block chords being played by low woodwinds and low brasses, those parts should be played. This helps to reinforce intonation, balance, blend, and the theory side of chord structures. If done with consistency, intersectional and intra-sectional listening exercises will yield major benefits for your band.

Inexperience and limited range cause most balance and blend problems for developing bands. If this is the case with your band, the warm-up you use can be customized to minimize the effects of these problems. Embouchure development and teaching good breathing skills for tone support will help. Sometimes you have to lower trumpet, flute, or horn parts to keep the players from encountering problems that will cause or exacerbate other problems. Students sometimes become more concerned about sound production in the upper range than they are with blending and balancing. Intonation is the first casualty because of the pinched sound that results from forcing the sound. This is where the concept of listening from the bottom up helps. If students are taught that the lower notes are the most important notes to achieve good balance, the self-prescribed pressure to play the high notes will be lessened. Your ability as the director to continue to reinforce this is important.

Once you have gotten your students to balance within sections to a satisfactory level you can begin enforcing your expectations to be achieved by the larger ensemble. You can start the process by having the low brasses and low woodwinds think of themselves as a low voice choir. As they listen for one another and play together as a choir, the concept of the bottom of the triangle/pyramid being broader than other parts of the band can be worked on. Up until this point in your rehearsals your main focus should have been mostly intersectional. By having all low voices identify themselves as the low voice choir, you have begun the intra-sectional process which will help in achieving large group balance. You can also use this intra-sectional listening to reinforce good intonation (balance and intonation are based on the same pyramid principle).

Of course, the "wild card" in this process is the use of percussion instruments. Hopefully, in the early developmental stages, percussionists have been taught how important it is for them not to just bang on their instruments. Percussion instruments used in music composed after 1980 (or just before) have been expanded. Now besides the snare drum, cymbals, bass drum, toms, tam-tam, tympani, and mallet instruments, Latin percussion instruments have been added. The Latin percussion family of instruments includes bongos, congas, timbales, claves, castanets, and guiros. Modern composers have utilized each of these instruments (and more) to add color to their compositions. Each of these instruments requires playing with subtle nuances that are complementary to the music rather than becoming a distraction to players and listeners.

If you are able to get your percussion players to understand that things like cymbal crashes and bass drum strikes can either be complementary or distracting, you have achieved a major part of what you're trying to achieve in group balance. Of course, this is an ongoing challenge for bands and should be presented as such. Bands have to make balance and blend a priority and you, the director, must make this a priority daily or weekly. Most judges at festivals can easily recognize whether balance and blend have been priorities for you and your students.

SELECTED PUBLISHERS FOR CONCERT BAND

Alfred Music Publishing
Boosey & Hawkes
Bourne Music
C. L. Barnhouse
Carl Fischer
Curnow Music
Edition Andel
Editions Marc Reift
Editions Robert Martin
Edwin F. Kalmus
Hal Leonard
Ludwig Music Publishing Co.
Molenaar Edition
Neil A. Kjos Music Company
Queenwood Publications
Southern Music Company
The FJH Music Company Inc.
Tierolff Muziekcentrale
TRN Music Publisher
Wingert-Jones Publications

SELECTED COMPOSERS FOR CONCERT BAND

Alfred Reed
Anne McGinty
Arnold Schoenberg
Carl Orff
Charles Finney
Clare Grundman
Claude T. Smith
Clifton Williams
David Shaffer
Ed Huckeby
Elliott Del Borgo
Francis McBeth
Frank Erickson
Frank Tichelli
Giuseppe Verdi
Gordon Jacob
Gustav Holst

Howard Hanson
James Barnes Chance
James D. Ployhar
James Swearingen
Jared Spears
John Edmondson
John Kinyon
John O'Reilly
John Philip Sousa
Joseph Willcox Jenkins
Karel Husa
Mark Williams
Malcolm Arnold
Morton Gould
Norman Dello Joio
Paul Hindemith
Percy Grainger
Peter Menin
Ralph Vaughan Williams
Robert Russell Bennett
Robert Jager
Robert Sheldon
Robert W. Smith
Roger Nixon
Sandra Dukow
Vaclav Nelhybel
Vittorio Giannini

SUGGESTED ARRANGERS FOR CONCERT BAND

Andrew Balent
David Marlatt
Douglas E. Wagner
Jack Bullock
James Curnow
James Swearingen
Jay Bocook
Jerome Naulais
Jerry Brubaker
Johan De Meij
John G. Mortimer
John Kinyon

John Moss
John O'Reilly
Larry Clark
Mark Williams
Michael Story
Michael Sweeney
Robert Longfield

14

Using Small Ensembles to Improve Your Band's Sound

Using small ensembles to improve the overall performance level of your band is a valuable tool for many reasons. The smaller ensemble enables your students to put to use all of the skills required for good band playing. Being able to hear things in a smaller setting is the most valuable aspect of small ensemble playing. Students can focus on intonation, attacks and releases, balance, rhythmic accuracy, and many other skills needed for accurate large ensemble playing. Not having the distractions of several instruments and being able to concentrate on a small group of instruments allows your students to apply the skills you've taught in the larger group and implement those skills with a high degree of accuracy. They can then apply these skills acquired in small ensemble playing to the larger ensemble. The subtle ways they are learning these techniques enable them to internalize them and apply them naturally and almost effortlessly.

Small-ensemble playing is not limited to homogenous instruments. There are several pieces written for small ensembles that use many different instrumental combinations. Pieces that are now played by larger ensembles, such as Bach's Brandenburg Concerti, were written for the instrumentation available to Bach at the time he wrote the pieces. Most state solo lists contain a section of works written for small ensembles that you can use to locate pieces that will enable you to match instrumentation that will suit your needs.

You don't have to match players of equal performance skills in many of these ensemble pieces. A lot of the pieces have parts written at different levels of difficulty that will allow you to place advanced players and intermediate players in the same small ensemble. Most music publishers send scores to your school or post them on their websites for you to peruse. As you look at these scores, check to see if they are suitable for the level of players in your small group. If one or two parts need to be simplified to make them accessible to your group, then you may rearrange them or customize them to your group.

The idea of selecting music that will be stimulating and challenging is the goal. You want to be able to keep these students engaged and not allow them to become discouraged. The teamwork and camaraderie that is developed in these small groups will be transferred to your larger group. As with your soloists, if the group is not needed for part of your rehearsal while you work on difficult parts with other students, release them to a practice area to work on the small ensemble music. Give the soloists or small ensemble an opportunity to perform their piece(s) in a concert or in a solo or ensemble activity.

Almost every school district and/or state sponsors a Solo and Ensemble Festival. The purpose of these festivals is to allow students who may desire more of a musical experience than individual bands can offer to develop their skills to a higher level. There are always students who are able to play music that is more challenging to them than what the band literature offers. These students have an opportunity through Solo and Ensemble Festival participation to play solos or in ensembles or to do both. Bands that may not have the best instrumentation for a band festival can form one or more ensembles and have soloists participate in the Solo and Ensemble Festival to receive feedback on their musical growth. Solo and Ensemble Festivals are not competitive but do offer students an opportunity to be rated by an adjudicator based on how well they perform using universal criteria. Many of the same items bands are judged on are the things found on a solo or ensemble adjudication sheet. Soloists may perform with or without accompaniment. When students play with accompaniment they must play to achieve ensemble with the accompanying instrument. Criteria such as intonation, rhythmic accuracy, accurate attacks and releases, adherence to dynamics, breath control, tone quality and articulation will be judged. Becoming aware of the importance of each of these skills is important to ensemble playing, large or small. Learning how to listen for cues and listening to other players is essential to playing with others and can be transferred by the soloists to nonsolo settings.

Ensembles are like miniature bands. The same principles of good band performance are expected in small ensemble performance. The adjudication form used for small ensemble performances is usually the same as the form used for bands. The ratings for soloists and ensembles are the same as for bands—Superior (I), Excellent (II), Good (III), Fair (IV), and Poor (V). These were designed for band directors to use as teaching tools to demonstrate to students that the qualities expected for good musicianship apply to individual performance and group performance.

Soloists participating in the Solo and Ensemble Festival have an opportunity to develop their individual performance level to their highest degree. They are not restricted by how well others are playing and they can often play music grade levels higher than the music being covered in band class. This helps to keep them from losing interest in band because of a lack of challenge from the band music. As with the small ensemble, if they are not rehearsing problem areas in the band music, you can release them to a practice area to work on their solo. By honing their individual playing skills they can help students around them develop theirs. You can use this to help improve playing in various sections of your band. These soloists also help you to present a higher level of performance expectations by displaying to other students the level of some of their peers. They will have an example that what you're saying is possible through practice and hard work by knowing that their fellow students are working hard to develop into high-level players.

Solo playing also gives your students an opportunity to take private lessons or coaching. There will be things about individual instruments and individual performance techniques that you will not be able to help some of your higher-level students with. At the beginning of the school year, you should have provided your students and their parents with a list of private teachers and coaches located within a reasonable distance of your school. You can also ask the private teachers to give their rates for thirty minutes, forty-five minutes, and one or two hours so that parents can formulate a budget.

Students should be encouraged to study once a week or once every two weeks based on the cost, length of the lesson, and/or location of the private teacher. If having the students go to a private teacher is not practical because of distance, have the teacher come to your school to teach several students on the same day or have them coach an entire section. Your parent organization may help you to defray the costs of travel by the private teacher and the cost of group coaching. Having several students take lessons on the same day may be incentive for the teacher to lower the cost of each lesson. If you have a homogenous small ensemble, each student can pay a small fee for one or two hours coaching a week. This will save them money and give the coach an opportunity to be compensated for time and travel. Example: If the teacher charges fifty dollars an hour for a private lesson and you get three students to pay twenty dollars for coaching, the students save thirty dollars and the private coach gets compensated for the lesson and for travel. You can adjust the cost per student based on the number of students being coached and the teacher's cost per lesson.

Depending on your fundraising efforts, you may include the cost of coaching in your annual budget. Because the skills acquired in the group lessons will be transferred into large ensemble performance, this is a justifiable cost. Some schools engage adjunct faculty members for coaching during marching band season, concert band season, and for jazz ensembles.

Once again, since most band directors are not proficient at a performance level on all band instruments, having a specialist come in will elevate the performance level of the entire group, not just the section receiving the coaching. Students tend to share information they have acquired with others so sections not receiving coaching can benefit from sections who are receiving coaching. This sharing of information strengthens the bonds within your band. Anything you can do to raise the standard of members of your group helps to raise the standard of your entire group.

In the smaller setting of a trio, quartet, quintet, septet, or octet, students can make eye contact with other players as they prepare for entrances. This eye contact reinforces the need to watch for visual cues (such as those provided by a conductor) in order to enter at the right time. These attacks must be precise and can be easily heard if they are not. This may not be as evident in a larger group as it is in a smaller setting but by hearing it in a smaller setting your students learn how important accurate attacks and releases are. A sloppy or late attack can negatively impact on the small ensemble immediately. Students will hear how important an accurate attack is and how a late attack spreads through a larger group because others are dependent on someone else's attack. Hearing this for themselves in a small ensemble has a greater impact than you trying to describe it in the abstract. As stated earlier, this kind of learning by discovery is invaluable.

Because there is no conductor in small ensembles, students have to listen carefully for sound prompts and cues and look up at one another often. Hopefully, this will transfer to their large ensemble playing, and they will discover that they don't have to stare at the music and not look up for expression cues and conducting patterns. Overall, the musicianship developed in small ensemble playing will help the performance level of the larger ensembles these students perform in almost immediately.

ALL-STATE, ALL-CITY, ALL-COUNTY AUDITIONS AND SOLO/ENSEMBLE

The music selected for honor band auditions will usually challenge your students to a greater degree than most of the music you are working on within band. The obvious benefit of having your students play this music is that they will have to put in a lot of practice time. Some directors have all of their students practice the audition music whether they plan to audition or not. Other directors use the music for their band's seating auditions. The idea is that if their best players have to practice this music for their school seating audition, they will learn it well enough for an honor band audition.

In the early years of your program, giving your advanced players an opportunity to audition for an honor band or play in small ensembles will help them to keep their skills sharp and develop their musicianship to a higher level. As was said before, keeping the better players in your band challenged and giving them an opportunity to perform in quality groups will help you to retain these students. If there is another school in your district that has advanced students who would also benefit from playing in small ensembles, make arrangements to form an ensemble that includes students from both schools. Most states allow students from different schools to participate in Solo and Ensemble.

If your band does not have the instrumentation for a full band to participate in a band festival, form one or two small ensembles to be adjudicated at the Solo and Ensemble festival. Ensembles with up to ten people can participate in most state festivals and the items ensembles are judged on are the same items bands are judged on. As your group develops and gains enough members to participate in a band festival they will have developed skills required for good musicianship.

Sometimes directors confuse the problem of achieving balance with poor blend. Before instruments can achieve balance across the band, they should develop balance within instrument families. This effort to achieve balance within families can be expanded to larger choirs, such as brass choirs and woodwind choirs. The use of small ensembles to become proficient in balance and blend can help you and your students greatly.

Brass Ensembles

Brass ensembles of various sizes can help your band's sound improve greatly. As mentioned earlier, being able to focus listening in a small group helps with cross listening and focused listening in band. The main benefit, however, is that brass players get an opportunity to discover the true character of brass instruments. This, of course, will improve the sound of the brass choir in your band.

Some of the qualities of brass sound your students can acquire through playing in a brass ensemble are: being able to control their tone quality in louder dynamics; control attacks and releases; blend within the brass choir; control their sound/tone quality at lower dynamic levels; and learn breath control needed to support a full, rich sound. As students become aware of the characteristics of brass instruments' sound, you can help them shape those individual sounds into a unified brass choir sound.

Have your brass ensemble tune to Concert C as well as F and B-flat. This gives them an opportunity to learn how to use their third valve slide for tuning. Most young brass players are not taught to use their first or third valve slides for tuning. Since playing concert C causes them to use their first and third valve to play their "D," it is very important that they know how to adjust the note to be able to play in tune with others. When playing in the brass ensemble students have to tune to others who are making the same adjustments they are making. Concert C is also a challenge to trombone players so listening and adjusting to an instrument with a different tone color makes students have to listen more closely in order to match pitches.

Woodwind Ensembles

Woodwind ensembles create some of the greatest challenges faced by young players. Because of the wide range of woodwind instruments found in the woodwind choir or your band, there are many combinations used for small ensembles. Unlike brass ensembles where sound is produced with taut lips on different size mouthpieces, woodwinds range from single reed, double reed, to no reed or mouthpiece (flutes). Because of the difference in sound produced by single reeds and double reeds, intonation is one of the major challenges. Since each woodwind instrument has a different timbre, blending is difficult for young players. Listening in small ensembles helps the players hear and recognize each instrument's distinct sound. This sound recognition will transfer from the small ensemble to the larger woodwind choir in your band as well as blending with the brass choir. Since flutes, oboes, E-flat clarinets, and B-flat clarinets all play in the same general range, it is important that players are able to distinguish sounds of each different instrument. French horns are grouped with the woodwind choir to help with balance and reinforcing the mid-range sounds of the woodwind choir. Small woodwind ensembles can be all part of one family (clarinet, flute, saxophone) or can be mixed to include oboes, English horns, bassoons, and French horns. Each kind of small ensemble instrumentation serves a useful purpose and function.

To help clarinets to develop a good characteristic clarinet sound, there are small ensembles made up of B-flat clarinets, alto clarinet, bass clarinet, and contra bass clarinet. Using this grouping, tone quality and intonation can be addressed with a small group of students rather than taking up band rehearsal time. Once the students have an opportunity to recognize the requirements to create a good sound on the clarinet, that full, rich tone can be used to get a better blend and balance within the larger group. Clarinet choirs can have as many as eighteen players using E-flat, B-flat, alto, bass, and contra-bass clarinets. The more players, the more challenging the blend, balance, tone control, and intonation will be. All clarinets regardless of size use the same fingering and similar or same playing technique. Being able to address these problems in a controlled setting will help you and your students discover the true character of the clarinet family. When clarinets are used in other small ensembles or the larger band unit these concepts will be transferred by your students and you have a frame of reference that can be addressed.

Flute choirs and flute ensembles of various sizes can be very helpful with tone quality and supported sound for flutes. Since flute sections are large in most bands, it is very important that sound production, breathing, and tone quality can be addressed. Intonation problems for flutes generally occur because flute players don't know how to correct intonation problems by rolling the flute in or out. It's important that students are aware of the fact that even though they may have made the correct adjustment with the head joint, there will still be times as they play that they will need to make small adjustments. Being able to adjust their intonation within the flute section is the first step for improving flute intonation with the entire band. Flute players generally find intonation difficult to control as they move from one register to the next. Going sharp on high notes and going flat on low notes commonly occurs because of inconsistent air flow. When playing with other flutes, players must provide enough air support to match sounds. Sometimes when playing in the larger group the flute sound is obscured and it is difficult for players to hear whether or not their tone quality has changed (especially in the lower register). When teaching flutes in a small ensemble setting takes place, you can concentrate on breath support and sound projection and how they affect intonation, blend, and balance.

There are chorales written specifically for flute quartets and octets that will help flute players hear how there parts fit into harmonization in music. Since most band music has first and second flute parts only, flute players generally don't find themselves playing in the lower register too often. Because of this, students may not understand what it takes to fully support and adjust low notes. There are techniques that students will be able to develop when playing in a flute ensemble that cannot always be developed in a larger band setting. Once again, this is generally because they cannot hear the character of their instrument over brass instruments and other woodwind instruments.

Double reed instruments can be the most challenging instruments to play in tune and to achieve blend in the woodwind choir. Because of the difficulty in choosing and adjusting reeds, breath support for a rich tone, and intonation, double reeds need to refine their playing skills in a smaller setting whenever possible. The double reed sound is unique and difficult to create with a good, sustained quality and the more students are challenged to blend and balance, the better they will become at accomplishing it. Since most groups don't have more than two oboes, it is best to place them in small ensembles that include clarinets, flutes, and bassoons. Being able to find their place in the woodwind choir greatly influences how well they will understand their role in the larger group. Works such as R. Vaughan Williams' First and Second Suite (in F and E-flat) require oboes to be able to play solos with full, rich sounds. Some directors will have a muted trumpet double the oboe part in order to achieve balance but if the oboist has a chance to develop his sound, this should not be needed. Learning how to project and balance in a smaller setting can really help an oboe player to discover the oboe's characteristic sound. Because no other band instrument has the same sound and only the English horn and bassoon have similar sound qualities, it may be difficult in a large setting for oboist to know what the oboe is capable of.

When playing in a small ensemble with a flute, the oboe may be relegated to playing harmonies found between the flute and clarinet parts. Having to project for balance will help the player to discover when too much or too little air is being used. Determining the amount of air needed for good tone quality will directly impact the ability to effectively blend and balance. The air flow will also affect the ability to play in tune. If the reed does not vibrate enough to support good tone quality, oboes will generally play flat. Too much air being forced through the reed will cause the player to pinch the sound which generally leads to playing sharp. In a large ensemble, it is tempting for the player to overblow to try to achieve balance. When playing with a small ensemble, the player through trial and error will discover how much air is too much and how much air is too little.

The bassoon, like the oboe, does not always have another instrument of its type with which to blend. Some larger ensembles can have as many as four bassoonists but most bands are fortunate to have one. Unlike the oboe, the bassoon is quite often written to be reinforcement for the bass line in concert band music (unlike the solo role that it generally has in orchestras). Because some composers of band music consider the bassoon an exotic instrument, most literature for high school concert bands does not have exposed bassoon parts. The bass trombone, bass clarinet, or contra-bass clarinet (and sometimes tuba) quite often double bassoon parts or are cued as replacements for missing bassoon parts. Sometimes the only opportunity for bassoonists to explore and realize the quality of the bassoon is through small ensemble playing experience. In most small ensemble literature, even with the bass clarinet included, the bassoon carries independent lines. As in the case of the oboe, having to discover and maintain the character of the instrument forces the player to experiment and develop a full, rich sound. Recordings such as *Peter and the Wolf* are helpful to get students to hear and identify the quality of the bassoon but nothing is better than playing with other members of the woodwind choir to help develop good technique and good tone quality. Having to blend and balance in a smaller setting gives the bassoonist an opportunity to listen to the quality of his sound and listen to how that sound can be adjusted for good blend and balance.

In the larger ensemble bassoonists play a major role that is sometimes overlooked. The colors that the bassoon creates cannot be duplicated by any other low woodwind or brass instrument. When played properly the bassoon has a distinct, full sound. It is one of the most versatile instruments in the band with few instruments having a range like it from high to low. When bassoonists play with other woodwinds in small ensembles they become aware of what is required of them to play in tune over the complete range of the instrument. In the lower range they must blend with bass clarinet and contra-bass clarinet and throughout the complete range they must match pitches and blend with clarinets. Having to develop this flexibility in small ensembles will help players gain confidence in applying these techniques in the larger group.

Percussion Ensembles

A mistake a lot of band directors and percussion players make is to assume that tone and sound quality on percussion instruments cannot be controlled. Band directors sometimes accept pounding and banging on the drum heads of some percussion. The stroke is the key to membraneophones (skins) having a good sound along with the tuning of the head and the placement of the stick on the head.

If possible, you should bring in a trained or professional percussionist to model if you aren't a percussionist. There are techniques for playing membraneophones that a nonpercussionist can't demonstrate. The stroke without the proper rebound (commonly incorrectly referred to as bounce) setting up the next stroke or rest will negatively affect the sound. Care should be taken to assure that the student understands and executes the proper stroke and rebound.

Percussionists differ on whether it is best to have percussion players use matched or unmatched grasp on the drum stick. Proponents of the matched grasp (holding the stick facing straight out with both hands) contend that it makes it less difficult to move to mallet instruments. Proponents of unmatched position (holding the stick in the left hand horizontally rather than straight out) feel that the snare drum and tom tom strokes are better controlled than matched stroking. In both cases the position should be a forty-five-degree angle with both drum stick tips meeting at the point of contact with the head.

Whether it is a matched or unmatched stroke, the stroke should be as relaxed as possible. Some percussionists refer to this as a "relaxed motion." Trained percussionists can look at the position of the player's arms, shoulders, and upper body and diagnose stroking problems. They can see tightness that will lead to the banging problem a lot of percussionists have. Just as a tight embouchure for wind players produces a pinched sound that affects the tone quality and intonation of wind players, tension in arms and shoulders negatively impacts drum strokes.

Tightness in the arms will affect the fluidity of movement, which will affect the contact with the drum head. This incorrect contact will affect the sound and tone quality of the drum (snare, tom, timbales, etc.). If there is no trained percussionist or professional player available for your students to model, there are videos available that will show your students the importance of using their wrists rather than their forearms to initiate the stroke. Students who use their forearms will suffer fatigue that will cause them to attempt to "pound" the drum by throwing their upper body into the stroke. This strained stroke will lead to improper contact with the drum head. This stroke affects the snare and toms but is much more noticeable on timpani.

Having your students go through rudiments on drums or drum pads will help them begin to master wrist strokes and strengthen the wrist muscles. Once students have spent a sufficient amount of time using sticks or mallets doing rudiments they will be ready to apply those techniques to playing parts found in band music or percussion ensemble. The importance of preparation cannot be overstated. If you expect your students to be able to blend in percussion ensemble or band, they must have the proper technique for good sound production.

Blend is not something a lot of band directors think about when working with percussion ensembles or working with percussion players in band. The concept of "touch" is a concept some percussion teachers use to help their students understand the importance of blend. An example commonly used to explain touch to percussionists is to use the analogy of piano players playing the same piano. Piano players get different sounds from the same instrument because of their touch. The strings on the piano have the same tension but how the hammers hit the strings is caused by the pianist's touch. Some players "hammer" the strings by putting a lot of pressure on the keys very much like a lot of percussionists put a lot of pressure on the drum head with their stroke. Adjusting the stroke adjusts the sound or touch.

When playing in a small ensemble, percussionists have to be more conscious of blend because there are fewer instruments to mask the sound they are creating. Focusing on how their sound relates to and blends with the sounds of other percussion instruments will cause them to experiment with their playing technique. They also will become more aware of supporting the melody (being played by mallet instruments in the ensemble). Being aware of the melody causes them to become aware of how their part complements what is being played by other instruments. This awareness will hopefully transfer to their playing in the larger group.

As the director you should choose percussion ensemble music that requires your percussionists to develop skills that will benefit your band's performance level. Far too often percussionists are an afterthought for band music selection. In fact, as early as beginning band, some percussionists are assigned percussion parts because they are not musical enough to play wind instruments. Needless to say, this is a major mistake and leads to discipline problems (as discussed earlier), and creates a problem with the band's overall sound quality.

Each member of your percussion section should be required to have some percussion ensemble experience. You can use some wind players to supplement the missing parts (preferably on mallet instruments). The members of the percussion ensemble should also be required to learn multiple instruments. Having membraneophone players play mallet instruments helps them to understand their role in blending with melodic and harmonic instruments. Getting them to understand that they are harmonic instruments and melodic instruments makes them conscious of blend and sonority, something that a lot of percussionists don't consider as they play. Trained listeners can tell when percussionists are aware of their part in blending with the rest of the band. Too many performances are ruined by percussion sections that don't make dynamic adjustments or play in such a way that their sound is complementary to the overall band sound. The better the percussion section is, the better the band will be.

SELECTED PUBLISHERS FOR SMALL ENSEMBLE

Advance Music
Alfred Music Publishing
Alphonse Leduc
BrassWorks4
Breitkopf and Haertel
C. Alan Publications
Cimarron Music Press
Doblinger Music Publishers
Edition Peters
Editions Henry Lemoine
Editions Marc Reift
Eighth Note Publications
Hal Leonard
Kendor Music Inc.
Masters Music Publications Inc.
Schott Music
Sound the Trumpets
Southern Music Company
Theodore Presser Company
Universal Edition

SELECTED COMPOSERS FOR SMALL ENSEMBLE

Wolfgang Amadeus Mozart

Johann Sebastian Bach
Franz Joseph Haydn
Ludwig van Beethoven
George Frideric Handel
Franz Schubert
Johannes Brahms
Felix Bartholdy Mendelssohn
Peter Ilyich Tchaikovsky
Claude Debussy
Robert Schumann
Antonin Dvorak
Scott Joplin
Edvard Grieg
George Gershwin
Johann Strauss, Jr.
Henry Purcell
Dmitri Shostakovich
Antonio Vivaldi

SELECTED ARRANGERS FOR SMALL ENSEMBLE

David Marlatt
Jerome Naulais
Carlo Martelli
Lennie Niehaus
Daniel Kelley
Frank Halferty
Arthur Frackenpohl
Deborah Greenblatt
James Christensen
Mary Elizabeth Clark
Bryan Doughty
John Beyrent
Lloyd Conley
William Ryden
Lynne Latham
Himie Voxman
Robert D. Vandall
Albert Andraud
Red McLeod

15

Developing Satellite Groups for Your Band

Every successful band program offers musical opportunities for its students that vary from solo performances, small-ensemble performances, marching band, pep band, and jazz ensemble. Each of these satellite groups offers a different way of musical expression for your students. In order for your band program to grow you should make every effort to attract students with a wide range of musical interests. Most students don't just want to participate in only one style of music; they have a desire to explore as many styles as are available to them.

Before you start offering classes or extracurricular groups for your students to participate in, you should make sure that you will be able to provide the best participation experience possible. This means making sure that each group maintains the integrity of the style of music they perform. If you do not perform a particular style of music that's being offered it is your responsibility to learn as much about that style as possible or bring in someone who can assist you. Poor instruction leads to poor performance levels and poor performances will do your program harm.

During football and basketball season, pep band is a smaller group formed from the marching band. The music used for marching band is generally the same music used for pep band. The purpose of pep band is exactly what the name implies—to provide pep and enthusiasm to support the team or lift the spirits of the audience.

PEP BAND

When establishing a pep band, your main concern is to select players to cover the instrumentation required by the score and students who will bring pep to school activities. If you cannot get the instrumentation needed for the score then you must write an arrangement substituting for the missing parts (this will be discussed in more detail in the section on technology and notation software).

If the pep band is performing outside during football games, brass instruments and saxophones should be used to carry the melody. Sound projection is the most important element of what instruments should be used. Since flutes and clarinets don't carry well outside, they should be used to double the melody not carry it alone. For performances inside, flutes and clarinets can be used to carry any melody that is underrepresented by instrumentation. Since gymnasiums are the sites of pep band performances during basketball season, you should limit the number of brasses used. Even though many band directors use marching band arrangements for pep band, there are many published pep band scores. There are music books that are written specifically for pep band. Rather than having to purchase individual songs for use by pep band, select books that have several songs in them. Some of these books specialize in music of specific styles and periods (e.g., '70s, show tunes, etc.)

Pep band is one of the groups that will fulfill the need to offer a well-rounded band program that includes performing popular music. Since some students are interested in performing music other than classical music, pep band will be an outlet for these students to learn popular styles. Pep band is also one of the satellite groups that provide a recreation side of your program. The camaraderie of the group and performing for sports activities makes the appeal even greater. To help your program grow, you can use participating in concert or marching band as a condition to participating in pep band.

When establishing a pep band, you want to be sure that it maintains the standards of your program as stated in your mission statement. The "Fun through Excellence" motto should be first and foremost a concern. The same principles of music you teach in band class should be used in pep band. Pep band should not be a low-quality group because of the type of music being performed or the kinds of activities at which it is performed. The mistake a lot of directors make is to forget that more people will see the pep band than will attend concerts. Football games, basketball games, soccer games, and other sporting activities have hundreds of people in attendance. Because of this, the group should perform at the same standard that you expect from your classical groups. The principles of good articulation, intonation, rhythmic accuracy, breath control, and precision must be taken as seriously by you and your students as they are when you prepare your other classes and groups.

Pep band players should be players that can project their sound and carry their part alone. Since a lot of pep band performances will be inside, it will be important to have a small number of students in the group. As stated earlier, the number of brass and percussion players should be limited due to volume and balance concerns. Some bands use electronic instruments to supplement the instrumentation and give the popular music authenticity and audience appeal.

Managing pep band rehearsals is an important part of developing a successful pep band. The problem some directors have is that they assign pep band rehearsals to student directors who are not prepared to correct problems that may occur. Having student leaders for pep band can benefit your program if used correctly. Potential students viewing student leaders in action may envision themselves doing what the student leaders are doing and join your program so that they can be a leader one day.

The typical pep band instrumentation will be twenty to thirty-six members in size, but there is no maximum size. The minimum size would depend on the minimum instrumentation on the score (one player per part). Smaller groups are generally used for indoor performances (basketball games and volleyball games). Most pep bands use three (3) to six (6) trumpets; two (2) to four (4) alto saxophones, one (1) or two (2) tenor saxophones; one (1) baritone saxophone; six (6) clarinets; four (4) to eight (8) flutes; one (1) piccolo; one (1) baritone horn; two (2) French horns; three (3) trombones; one (1) tuba; one (1) drum set or one (1) snare drum, one (1) bass drum, and one (1) cymbal. The positioning for playing should have woodwinds in the front rows; trumpets and horns on the next row; trombones, baritone, and tuba on the last row. If you use a drum set, it will be placed on the floor (best at the corner of the band, not in front). If you use a snare, bass, and cymbals, they should stand behind the last row or in the side corner beside the band. Remember, sound inside will be amplified by acoustics so you don't want percussion instruments and brasses in the front. Since one of the things you're going to work with your band on is sound projection, you don't want to create balance problems by your set-up. If the band plays outside at football games you want to use a larger number of players. The following model should be used to prepare pep bands for performances.

At the beginning of your rehearsal you want to work on sound projection and tone quality. Start with scale exercises on long tones. Have the brasses lift the instruments in a similar manner as marching band, playing to the box (playing toward the press box on the football field) so that they will use good posture to produce good tone and use good breathing techniques for producing round sounds. Have the band hold each note for full value and attack and release together.

After the band has played the warm-up exercises have them begin work on the first performance piece. If you are using a student conductor, you still must be present and listen to the group. When rhythmic problems, intonation, or articulation problems occur it is important that you or the student director stop the band and work on the problem until it is corrected. Even though most of the pep band repertoire will be popular music, you must still work toward perfection and proper musical technique. Anything that is unacceptable for classical groups should be unacceptable for popular music groups.

Since whistles are not usually used for pep bands, don't use whistles in pep band rehearsals. The rehearsal should mimic a performance even though you may be continuously stopping to correct mistakes.

One of the most important items to work on during pep band is tempo accuracy. Because of echoes and "bounce back" (the sound coming back at the band after bouncing off the walls), you'll need to work on having the group watch the conductor. Have the conductor start the group and arbitrarily stop at unexpected points in the song. If students aren't watching the conductor they will continue to play even though the conducting has stopped. Do not allow this to go uncorrected. During a basketball game some schools allow playing only during timeouts. If this is the case at your games, referees can call a technical foul on your team if the band's playing delays the game. That means that besides being an important part to the music, this is an important part of your team's success and the group's adding to the school spirit during the game (you won't be popular if you cause your team to lose points).

JAZZ ENSEMBLES

Developing a jazz ensemble as a satellite group will be discussed in detail later in the book but for the purpose of this chapter, jazz ensemble is an important addition to the entire band program. Jazz ensemble will appeal to some of the same students who are drawn to pep band and marching band because it performs more popular styles of music. Jazz ensemble will be smaller than pep band and will use more electronic instruments (electric guitar, electric bass, electric piano, and vibraphones).

Jazz ensemble also gives students an opportunity to develop their creative skills through improvisation. It will be the only part of your band program where your students will be expected to put their music theory to use actively during performances and rehearsals. Much of what is expected of jazz students involves spontaneous composition (improvisation), which involves them creating melodic lines of music over a given harmonic structure. Because of this, jazz ensemble will appeal to your most advanced band students.

SMALL ENSEMBLES

Small ensembles as satellite groups can help you teach all of the principles of classical performance in a smaller setting. There is a wealth of literature available for small groups, from duos to double octets. Groups can be formed from homogeneous groups to heterogeneous groups. You can form these small ensembles based on your needs or the number of advanced students you have. There are also some groups formed to remediate students and help them to "catch up" with the large group by focusing on basic skills needed for large ensemble playing. This is also discussed in more detail in the chapter on small ensembles.

MARCHING BAND

The next chapter will give detailed descriptions on how to establish and maintain a good marching program. As a satellite group, marching band will be your most visible group. There will be students interested in participating in your total program because of the appeal of your marching band. Marching bands are generally seen by audiences who will never attend a concert so it is important that everything you want known about the quality of your program can be seen through your marching unit's performance.

16

Developing a Marching Band as Part of the Complete Band Program

Developing a marching band as part of your band program can be tricky. In most schools, the marching band is the most visible component of the complete band program and the entire band program is judged by its success or failure. Since this is the case, you'll want to make sure that the principles of a good band program are used in the development of the marching band.

During football season, more people will see your marching band at one game than will see any other component of your program during the entire year. Marching bands are viewed by audiences as entertainment but most music educators view them as educational activities. Because of the balance required to have the band be an educational tool for music students and entertainment for audiences, the band director must choose music, show designs, and marching styles that provide both.

One of the decisions the band director must make is what style marching band she will have. The two most popular marching band styles fall into two categories—show style, also known as high step, and corps style, known as heel to toe. Each style is unique and requires knowledge of language that is specific to that style. These terms will be described in detail later in this chapter. Choosing which style to use for your marching band should be decided upon by the makeup of your band and the appeal to your community and the style of music you plan to perform. You should develop knowledge of both styles so that you will not force your group or community to adjust to a style that they won't enjoy. This may not seem practical but remember, this will be your first recruiting tool and the way the community reacts to your band will determine how much support you will receive. Show bands generally choose music from top 40 radio or basic pop tunes. The tendency for corps style bands is to choose thematic shows based on current musicals. Corps style shows will require some props and the percussion section is stationary in front of the band in an area referred to as a pit.

A more detailed description of the two styles of marching band will come later, but here is a brief description of the two. Show style or high step is just as the name implies. Bands lift their feet high off the ground at a ninety-degree angle (twenty-two and a half inches). They will take eight steps for every five yards marched. As the audience looks at the band they are generally impressed by the uniformity in the lifting of the legs to a common level. Viewed from an angle parallel lines can be seen when the group is stepping together. Corps style marching is generally distinguished by a heel to toe rolling motion while marching when the band is moving from set to set (position to position). The "glide" motion of corps style bands is impressive as the audience watches the group move from point to point. The common denominator for both is that music is adjusted to suit the overall show. In show style whole songs are used generally, and dancers, twirlers, flags (silks), and drum majors are part of the show. For corps style, snippets of songs are used, and the purpose of each song is to help the group move effortlessly from each component of the show to another. Drum majors in corps style will usually conduct from a podium while the group is maneuvering. Corps style now generally incorporates visual effects and an elaborate script.

TEACHING MUSICIANSHIP DURING MARCHING BAND

All of the musical components of band that will be taught throughout the year need to be introduced during marching band. Because marching band season starts at the beginning of the school year this means that everything you want to cover in a year must be compressed into two or three weeks before the first performance. Many band directors will hold band camps at an actual overnight campsite so that they can have eight-hour band days that combine teaching and recreational activities. Other band directors choose to hold band camps at the school in two four-hour sessions during the day. In either case, band directors are focused on compressing many principles of music into a very short period of time.

In order to teach musical skills during marching band, the band director must decide on what skills need to be taught. Those skills will be the same skills that will be needed for good band performance for concert band and other inside instrumental performance groups. Students in all bands need to be able to:

1. play in tune with themselves and others;
2. play with rhythmic accuracy;
3. play in the correct style using articulation that complements that style;
4. control dynamic ranges even though projection outside is important;
5. play with good tone even when projecting sound outside;
6. develop good breathing techniques and breath control; and
7. have accurate attacks and releases.

These skills need to be taught and reinforced from the first rehearsal until the end of the year. Even though the reality is that marching band has been preparing in a relatively short amount of time, they will be judged as if they have practiced a complete year before their first performance. This may not seem fair but it is a reality. Explaining this to your band will help you to keep them focused.

Teaching Intonation in Marching Band

A lot of band directors make the mistake of thinking that because marching bands perform outside, intonation is not a major concern. Intonation in all bands is very important. Daily tuning for marching band is as important as tuning any indoor instrumental ensemble. Temperatures outside will constantly affect the pitch, especially cold temperatures. Doing a regular tuning and warm-up activity is very important for the life of any band and contrary to common belief, especially marching band.

Marching band presents a unique challenge to intonation because of movement and the shifting of the embouchure because of body movement. Warm-up activities before tuning and during tuning should include marching activities. Having the group march down field while playing a scale or other warm-up will help give them an opportunity to experience the stress associated with an actual performance. This will help them recognize what needs to be done in order to make the adjustments to play in tune. Playing in tune while seated is a totally different experience from playing with a shifting embouchure. The more your students march and play the better able they will become at playing in tune.

Rhythmic Accuracy

Playing with rhythmic accuracy is one of the less difficult tasks to teach during marching band. Marching with two or four basic beats per measure can assist students with subdivision and counting basic time. The concept of downbeats and upbeats is easily taught when the feet are going up and down based on two or four beats per measure. It is almost impossible for marching bands to rush if everyone steps to the rhythm of a drum cadence.

Teaching students how to play rhythmic patterns based on the beat is less difficult to do when students are relating the beat to physical steps. Breaking the beat into partials (that students can recognize and relate to) makes the process of teaching divisions of the beat less challenging.

Tone Quality and Tone Control

One of the most difficult adjustments wind players have to make when playing while marching is the shifting of the embouchure and mouthpiece placement while marching. As the mouthpiece shifts, tone quality can suffer. Some band directors accept the fact that marching bands will have bad tone quality because of the challenges of embouchure control while marching. This is not the case. Students should not be encouraged to project their sound beyond the point that they can control it. If students are taught not to expect a good tone while marching they won't attempt to control the tone or produce a controlled sound. These marching bands have difficulty making the transition from marching band to concert band because the tone production process has to be learned after having been ignored during marching band season.

Just as a good warm-up is important for concert band, it is important for marching band. Having the marching band play scales on long tones while marching allows the students to make the necessary adjustments for good tone production. Marching bands must be taught with the same attention to musical skill development as any other part of the band program and it all begins with the sound.

Recording and video taping of the marching band is as important as it is during concert band. Once students hear the difference between blasting and refined sound, they will choose refined sound. You as the teacher must capitalize on every opportunity to teach basic band skills during marching band rehearsals and performances. No matter what size the band is they should not be encouraged to play beyond the level at which they can control their tone. Individual tones will shape the overall sound of your band. Harsh, cutting sounds are not appealing to audiences or your students.

PLANNING A MARCHING BAND SHOW

Even though marching band is not usually a class, it still needs to have concrete plans so that rehearsals are organized and constructive. Technology has greatly changed the way marching band shows are planned and plotted out but some directors who don't have access to computers or expensive software due to low budgets use Patterns in Motion (PIM) graph paper. PIM planning uses a system of Xs and dots to plot out movements, formations, and field positions of individual players.

Charting out a show using the PIM graph requires the use of a compass, protractor, rulers, divider, and pencils. These shows are designed by hand and require meticulous measurements and plotting the movement of each individual player. In order to effectively plan the show, the designer must keep in mind the dimensions of the football field, the area that most viewers will be watching the show from (generally between the two twenty-yard lines), and the amount of time it will take to move from set to set.

There are books devoted to show designs and space here does not permit a complete show-design description. There are also drills that are sold with marching band music that are prepackaged and require simple customizing on your part. The end of this chapter includes a list of music publishers for marching band, and you should seek out those that sell "packaged shows" if your budget doesn't support the purchase of marching band software.

Computer software for marching band show designs is the best way to design a show using a limited amount of time. All calculations can be done by the computer once you input the design of the formation you want, the number of people in your band, the number of measures you want to use from a given piece of music, and the length of your show. Good software will give you the meter marking needed to perform the song to get from set to set. If you are using plotting or graphing paper, you must use a stopwatch to calculate these factors. The software figures will be precise but if you are using a timer and designing by hand, you will need to add a few seconds for each maneuver to make sure you allot enough time to get from point A to point B. Drill construction can be frustrating for the novice designer. If you have not taken a course in show design, it is best to purchase a prepackaged show. There are marching band camps that teach design as well as helping to prepare your student leaders. If your program can afford it, you should pay to send your drum major(s) to a camp and you should attend one.

Once the design has been done you must decide which direction the show will face. For home games this is a simple decision. For away games you may wish to perform toward the visitors' side for your fans and toward the home team's fans. As you choose the music to be performed, you will need to decide on music that will complement your show's theme or have entertainment value. Some bands choose two performance pieces and use the school song as the closer. Others use three songs that are based on a show theme or are designed to lift the crowd's spirit (*Phantom of the Opera* was one of the most popular themes of half-time shows). Generally, music that you would use for a competition is not entertaining for football crowds. The reason for this is that judges at competitions are judging you on many aspects of your performance and football audiences are judging you on entertainment value and appeal.

As you are working on the music for the show, tape the band so that you can hear whether the melody and harmonic parts are being carried by the instrumentation the piece is scored for and/or the instrumentation you have on the field. If there is a need to double or rewrite parts, try to make those changes early on in the process so that the band can hear the results of their projection toward the audience. This will help with balance and help avoid overblowing resulting in poor tone quality.

Types of Physical Movement

Football audiences have watched two quarters of movement on the football field before the halftime show and are generally interested in seeing the band move while playing. Even listening to the most musical performance can become boring after having watched action for two quarters. This doesn't mean that you have to move nonstop during your show but you should move from formation to formation.

If you have a small band, you may choose to use simple geometric designs such as circles moving within circles, diamonds, or squares. Having the group countermarch using step two spacing (two steps between marchers) with lines moving between lines is a simple maneuver with a good visual effect. These kinds of maneuvers can be done without assigning marchers numbers or positions. More difficult shows with larger groups depend on each player being assigned a spot and position. This means each player will be required to get to a specified point at a specified time. The drawback with this kind of a show is that if someone is missing for a performance there will be a "hole" in your formation or set.

Before you present your show concept to your students, you should visualize the entire show in your mind (if you use a software design program, you will be able to watch it step by step). When planning movements, be sure to consider numerical balance in the formation. On the computer smaller numbers may seem to work, but once you consider the size of your band and visualize how they will look on the field, you'll know whether adjustments will need to be made. Remember, the program will not tell you how your band will sound, just how they will look, so once the band plays you may need to make small changes.

When presenting the show to your students, you should break it down into teachable units. During band camp it is wise to teach basic marching skills and maneuvers that you can reference later during show design. In the section "Marching Band Terminology" you will see some of the most common terms used during show design and teaching. Distribute these terms and visuals of simple formations to your students so that they may become familiar with them before you use them to describe your show.

Structuring Your Marching Band for Parades

There is no standard marching band lineup used by American marching bands. The basic consideration is lining up your parade band in such a way that sound is projected forward for several city blocks. A lot of bands march with five-, seven-, or nine-man fronts (ranks). The term "five-man front" is gender neutral since marching units are male and female units. Irrespective of the number of players in each rank, most bands start off with trombones, horns, trumpets, baritones, saxophones (alto, tenor and baritone), sousaphones, percussion, clarinets, and flutes. Having the drum line and sousaphones in the center of the band helps with outside balance and avoids tempo problems caused by a delay in sound or echo.

The type of music your band performs and the size of the band will help you to determine the lineup you should use. Bands generally don't put flutes and/or clarinets in the front ranks because of their limited ability to project well outside. Also, visually, having the shiny brass of trombones up front builds the excitement of watching a band march forward during a parade.

NONRESIDENTIAL MARCHING BAND SUMMER CAMP

Structuring the rehearsal day for nonresidential band camps varies from school to school based on the range of temperatures during summer days where the camp is located. In areas where the temperature is very hot during the day, band directors have a split day rehearsal with four-hour rehearsals before noon and four-hour rehearsals after 6:00 p.m. Some schools rehearse music inside during the hottest part of the day and then do field drills during the cooler part of the day. This may be a negligible temperature difference but the sun will not be shining directly down. Sufficient rest and water breaks should be used. An eight-hour rehearsal day could be as follows:

8:00 a.m.–12:00 noon
Physical warm-up: Students will do jumping jacks, run around the track, and/or do other cardiovascular exercises to prepare themselves for rigorous marching and set/show preparation. Once the students have done cardiovascular exercises without their instruments, they will play scales or short musical pieces to adjust to movement and playing. It is best to use long tones for this exercise to aid in embouchure development and diaphragmatic breathing.

Upon the completion of physical and musical exercises students will go to the field and assume their positions for the first set (show position) or wait to be placed in their opening positions. The drum major(s), section leaders, or the director will place students or check to see if students are

in the correct places based on the field plot (this is based on copies having been printed out for everyone to see each set of the show). If students
have been given a show printout, and each has been given a number,
each student will walk through each position without instruments. Once
you have had the students walk through the entire plot, have them return
to position one and move to the next position using a clicked meter on
one drum or having the percussion play a cadence (having to follow a
cadence will help the band develop a good sense of time and step size).
12 noon–12:30 p.m.
Lunch with sections: Students will eat based on their sections for team
building.
12:30 p.m.–1:00 p.m.
Review with the entire group what was accomplished during the morning
session. Specific problems and achievements will be noted and corrective
actions will be outlined and discussed.
1:00 p.m.–3:00 p.m.
Music warm-up inside: Students will play scales and work on tone production while standing in place. The director will introduce the concept
of projection with their instruments raised (to the press box position).
The concept of pointing toward the press box in the stadium will help
students to visualize how high they need to hold some brass instruments
for best projection purposes.
The group will then work on the music to be used for the show(s). If
an entire song is not to be used, the director or drum major will have
the group mark their parts for start and stop points. If the music is to be
memorized the director will rehearse manageable sections of music and
help the students begin the memorization process. The students should
play the sections repeatedly with and without the music. As the music
is being rehearsed, the director will make the association between show
marching positions and where in the music each maneuver will start/
stop. Flags, silks, and pom-poms will work inside with recorded music
for the show or to learn basic routines and maneuvers. If the temperature
permits, flags and silks can rehearse outside but care should be taken to
make sure students don't overheat.
3:00 p.m.–4:00 p.m.
Students will assemble based on the section in which they belong. The
purpose of the sectional is to work in small groups to master the music.
Section leaders will conduct these smaller rehearsals and the director will
move from section to section to offer assistance and correct any problem
areas in the music. Students will be dismissed from the section rehearsals.

Using the eight-hour rehearsal model works for some directors, and non-
residential camps usually last for two or three weeks (first week for new

and incoming students). Adequate rest and water breaks must be used for student safety (avoiding heat exhaustion and heat stroke). Another non-residential model utilizes a split eight-hour day. This model has a morning session and a late afternoon session to avoid rehearsing outside during the hottest part of the day. The daily structure of the split day model could be done as follows:

Session 1
8:00 a.m.–10:00 a.m.
To build up endurance, students will do jumping jacks, run around the track, and/or do other cardiovascular exercises to prepare themselves for rigorous marching and set/show preparation. Once the students have done cardiovascular exercises without their instruments, they will play scales or short musical pieces to adjust to movement and playing. It is best to use long tones for this exercise to aid in embouchure development and diaphragmatic breathing. Playing while moving will require students to adjust to the feel of the mouthpiece shifting and help them develop marching band embouchures.

Once they have completed physical and musical exercises, students will go to the field and assume their positions for the first set (show position) or wait to be placed in their opening positions. The drum major(s), section leaders, or the director will place students or check to see if students are in the correct places based on the field plot (this is based on copies having been printed out for everyone to see each set of the show). If students have been given a show printout, and each has been given a number, they will walk through each position without their instruments. Once you have had the students walk through the entire plot, have them return to position one and move to the next position using a clicked meter on one drum or having the percussion section play a cadence (having to follow a cadence will help the band develop a good sense of time and step size). Breaks should be added as needed.

10:00 a.m.–12 noon
Students will assemble in the band room to work on the music that will be used in the field show(s). Music warm-up: Students will play scales and work on tone production while standing in place. The director will introduce the concept of projection with their instruments raised (to the press box position). The concept of pointing toward the press box in the stadium will help students to visualize how high they need to hold some brass instruments for best projection purposes.

The group will assemble in the band room and work on the music to be used for the show(s). If an entire song is not to be used, the director or drum major will have the group mark their parts for start and stop points. If the music is to be memorized, the director will rehearse manageable sections of music and help the students begin the memorization process. The students should play the sections repeatedly with and without the music. As the music is being rehearsed, the director will make the association between show marching positions and where in the music each maneuver will start/stop. Flags, silks, and pom-poms will work inside with recorded music for the show or to learn basic routines and maneuvers. If the temperature permits, flags and silks can rehearse outside but care should be taken to make sure students don't overheat. Breaks should be scheduled as needed.

Session 2

4:00 p.m.–5:00 p.m.

Students will assemble in the band room for a briefing on what is expected to be accomplished during session 2. Sections will break out for section rehearsals to rehearse the music taught/presented during the morning session. Section leaders and/or section coaches (paid professionals) will rehearse the music to be used with emphasis on memorization. The leaders will break the music down into small, manageable units that students can play from memory. The musical snippets will be associated with places in the show where those music segments will be used. It is important that those associations be made at the time the music is being learned so that the students will know exactly where and how the music is to be used during the performance.

5:00 p.m.–7:00 p.m.

The entire band and auxiliaries will meet on the field or large parking lot to learn show positions. If the show has been plotted by computer, the students should follow their assigned number position through the section of the show you're working on. Students should walk through or be guided through their positions for each set or section of the show. The director may have them walk through while looking at their music so that they know the exact beat or measure number where each maneuver will take place. Once again, it is important that these associations are made early on so that as the students move they will know precisely where they will be at any given time in the music.

7:00 p.m.–8:00 p.m.

Students will reconvene in the band room for a final show review. It is best that this final hour is conducted completely by the drum major(s) so that students can adjust to field-conducting motions and the conducting nuances of the student leaders. The group should play while standing so that breathing and tone production will be the same as on the field (even though they are not moving). The group will also march in place so that they can make necessary embouchure adjustments as the mouthpiece shifts while moving. The group will be dismissed at the conclusion of this session.

RESIDENTIAL CAMPS

Residential marching band camps generally last for one week. For these camps the school rents a camp or retreat for seven days. These camps or retreats have cabins and dining halls and swimming areas (pools or lakes). One of the benefits of residential camps is that you can mix recreational activities with rehearsal activities (swimming, volleyball, horseshoes, badminton, etc.). Team building is the major benefit of residential camps. The entire group and sections of the band can rehearse together but you can also mix in fun team-building activities. Some directors have each section prepare a skit to be presented at the end of the camp (the last night).

Because students are staying at the camp overnight the daily schedule can start and end when you want it to and can be adjusted as the week progresses. During the rehearsal day, breakfast, lunch, and dinner will be one hour each and rehearsals and leisure activities can be scheduled around those times. Adjusting the eight-hour day or split day schedules to include swimming, hiking, and other activities will make the camp as productive as possible. A sample time schedule would be as follows:

7:00 a.m.–8:00 a.m.	Breakfast (morning shower time)
8:00 a.m.–10:00 a.m.	Full Band Rehearsal
11:00 a.m.–12:00 noon	Sectionals
12:00 noon–1:00 p.m.	Lunch
2:00 p.m.–3:00 p.m.	Inside Activity
	(show description/discussion/critique)
3:00 p.m.–5:00 p.m.	Leisure Activities
5:00 p.m.–6:00 p.m.	Dinner
6:00 p.m.–8:00 p.m.	Full Rehearsal
8:00 p.m.–9:00 p.m.	Sectionals
9:00 p.m.–11:00 p.m.	Free Time or Team-Building Activity
11:00 p.m.	Lights Out

Flags and Poms can be scheduled for practice/drills when sectionals are scheduled. How you decide to schedule full band rehearsals and sectionals should be determined based on the weather. The size of indoor spaces will determine if full band rehearsals can be held inside or whether they will be held outside. When selecting a camp or retreat you should find out the capacity of each building and determine whether or not the site will accommodate your group.

Another consideration before planning a residential camp is adult supervision. Generally, you will need to have one adult per sleeping area and you should arrange to have adjunct faculty members to supervise and run sectionals. The size of your band will determine the number of staff members and adults you will need. The daily schedule and itinerary should be preprinted and distributed to your students and their parents. You should also furnish your students with the music to be worked on before leaving for the camp (if practical). As in the case of concert band, if you distribute the music beforehand, make sure that you keep a library copy for each part in case parts are lost or left behind.

Whether you have a nonresidential camp or a residential camp the efficient use of time is important. Having students standing around or nonchalantly reporting to positions during rehearsals will negatively impact on the rehearsals and future performances. If students are expected to react to commands immediately, that training must start during the first marching band rehearsals. Some of the objectives of marching band camp and rehearsals should be to train the band to respond to verbal or whistle commands, march in step together, carry instruments uniformly, and play together.

Each rehearsal should focus on each of these objectives separately or at the same time. You may work on marching without playing or playing without marching while responding to commands for attention, parade rest, or at ease. It is best to have the group assemble at a specified place and time and march to the rehearsal space (field or parking lot) and at the end of the rehearsal march back to the assembly point to fall out. The more marching bands march, the more aware they will become for the need of uniformity at all times. If students react in a lax manner during rehearsals that tendency is transferred to actual performances.

You should use voice commands or whistle commands during all drills and to get students to assemble. The more they have to react to commands the more natural it will become. This will also give your drum majors an opportunity to hone their leadership and command skills.

All terminology used in rehearsals should be terms that students will need to know and respond to during performances. Whether the group is a competitive group or a noncompetitive group, the terminology used will be the same.

MARCHING BAND TERMINOLOGY

The following terms are used when teaching or describing marching band. There are many terms used by different bands and regions but the terms listed here are some of the more basic terms.

About Face – a 180-degree turn to face or march in the opposite direction.

At Ease – instruments may be lowered to a relaxed position; body will not be as erect as parade rest (see "parade rest").

Attention – the process of preparing to receive a command from the director or drum major; standing with feet at a forty-five-degree angle and ready for step off.

Auxiliary – marching units such as color guard, flags/silks, pom-poms, twirlers.

Battery – percussion section and/or drum line.

Cadence – the "beat" played by a drum line or percussion for marching on the field or in a parade.

Carriage – the posture of standing upright while marching, body alignment.

Column – vertical lines formed by marchers directly behind the front rank/horizontal line.

Company – a large group of marchers—(generally the entire marching unit made up of smaller groups (see "platoons").

Cut-off – the stopping of marching or the stopping of sound.

Dress – checking your alignment to form a straight line (see "guide right" and "guide left").

Drill – the on-field show or sets for a marching band performance.

Drill Book – the book used to design or hold designs for a show or sets.

Drum Major – the student who conducts the band and leads drills; on-field director and leader; calls commands and sets the tempo of performance pieces.

Eight to Five – eight steps for every five yards marched on a football field.

Fall In – command given to have the group assemble into parade rest positions preparing for the attention command.

Fall Out – band is released to move about from the attention position (fall out always comes from attention; called to attention from at ease or parade rest then given the command to fall out).

Flags – flags/silks used by marching color guard/auxiliary.

Float – corps style marching step adjusted by size and speed to get from one set to another.

Fronts or Front Ensemble – primarily used by corps style units; the PIT percussion set-up that does not move during marching maneuvers (timpani, large bass drum, xylophones, marimba, etc.); can also refer to the first rank in parade formation (see "rank").

Forward March – command to step off moving forward.

Gait – the distance between steps while marching.

Guide Right – looking to the left shoulder of the person to your right to maintain a straight line while marching.

Guide Left – looking to the right shoulder of the person to your left to maintain a straight line while marching.

Guard – an auxiliary unit of the band that uses flags/silks, rifles, pom-poms, and other props to enhance the marching band show.

Harness – equipment piece used to hold marching percussion in place while marching.

Halt – a complete stop from marching or marking time (always ends on the right foot going down).

High Step – a marching step that comes off the ground at about twenty-two and a half inches, forming a ninety-degree angle bended knee.

Horns High/Horns to the Box – instruments are held high and pointed toward the press box on a football field.

Interval – the distance between marchers (based on steps or arm lengths).

Left Face – a turn to the left on command.

Mark Time – marching in place before or after step off; stepping in place with a cadence or basic pulse being tapped.

Oblique – a forty-five-degree precision move on the field to get from one spot/position to another (generally a show band maneuver).

Parade Rest – an on-field or parade stationary position with legs spaced apart, left hand behind the back, awaiting the command for attention.

Pinwheel – a pivot motion a full 360 degrees.

Pivot – a turn of 45, 90, 180, or 360 degrees.

PIT – the stationary percussion used for marching band shows (generally corps style).

PIT Crew – parents and volunteers who move the stationary percussion instruments on and off the field; in some cases when the instruments are used in a set, they move the field props and percussion instruments into place.

Platoons – two or three large groups that form a company (based on a half of the band or a third of the band).

Plumes – feathers used on hats and often held by hand for a visual effect for a show.

Present Horns – a two-count movement, horns gripped on count one and raised on count two.

Quads – four-piece drum set used by marching drum line (connected).

Rank – the horizontal line formed shoulder to shoulder (generally an arm length or less apart).

Right Face – turn to the right on command.

To the Rear March – a 180-degree turn to march in the opposite direction (turn either to the left or right).

Section Leader – a designated leader of like instruments responsible for implementing commands from the director or drum major.

Sets – the pictures formed by the band on the field (sometimes props are used).

Squads – four- or eight-member groups generally based on like instruments.

Step Off – the initial steps that begin a marching maneuver.

Step Two – A movement based on counting two beats between individuals or groups stepping off.

Step Two Turn – A turn used rather than a swinging gate turn that uses two steps and then a turn to the right or the left. Each rank marches in place until the last member of the rank steps forward to form a straight line. Once the line is formed, the rank steps off.

Swinging Gate Turn – a turn made with a group using a right guide or left guide to maintain a straight line during a turn.

SELECTED COMPOSERS FOR MARCHING BAND

Andy Clark
Ed Huckeby
George Thorogood
Henry Mancini
Isaac Gregg
James Swearingen
John Fogerty
John Philip Sousa
John Williams
Ken Dye
Ken Harris
Larry Kerchner
Louis Prima
Muff Winwood
Robert Browne Hall
Roland Seitz
Spencer Davis
Steve Winwood
The Surfaris
Theodore Mesang
Todd Rundgren

SELECTED MARCHING BAND PUBLISHERS AND COMPOSERS

Alfred Music Publishing
Arpeges Diffusion (IMD)
Arrangers' Publishing Company
Band Music Press
Beriato Music
Boosey & Hawkes

Bourne Music
C. L. Barnhouse
Cherry Lane Music
Echelon Music
Edition Andel
Editions Robert Martin

17

Developing a Jazz Ensemble as Part of Your Overall Band Program

In previous sections of the book, lesson plans and what kinds of things should be taught in band class have been discussed. There are some basics that are taught in all band classes irrespective of the type of music being played. Good tone, intonation, rhythmic accuracy, attacks and releases, precision, and articulation will be focused on daily but the way these elements of music are applied will differ from groups that play popular music and groups that play classical music. Jazz Ensemble is one of the classes that will offer students an opportunity to express themselves musically in a way that is far different from other band classes.

It is difficult to believe that there was a time that jazz ensembles were not considered a part of most schools' band programs. In fact, they had to be justified as having value as part of the total band program. Jazz instruction in schools as a class is still not as prevalent as other classical-based classes. This means that as a music teacher/band director, you will need to incorporate jazz instruction into your overall program objective and possibly offer the class as a before school or afterschool activity. Some school districts allow before school and afterschool rehearsals to be "for credit" classes (rather than an extracurricular activity).

Stating that your program's goal is to develop each student to his optimum level of performance opens the door to your having different kinds of groups to meet each student's need to express himself musically. Jazz, by nature, is a constantly challenging musical endeavor. Improvisation, which is a key to jazz performance, is "spontaneous composition." This means that as performers hear chord progressions, they create musical lines above the progressions. This is what composers do except that jazz players must do it instantly and usually in front of an audience (even if that audience is classmates during class). Not all students will be interested in "exposing themselves" and their weaknesses by improvising, but there is great value in providing them with the tools to try.

Some band directors are reluctant to teach jazz because they feel inadequate or underprepared. This should not keep you from providing this class for your students. In fact, it will help you as a teacher. As you try to perform jazz, you will discover firsthand what your students are experiencing. Because of this, you will be empathetic with your students and have a greater understanding of what they are going through.

Jazz is a class that requires your students to be analytical, use discovery learning (trial and error), and push themselves to their emotional and creative limits. Unlike most classical forms, jazz requires students to incorporate their acquired skills through experimentation rather than simply following the music printed on the score before them. When improvising, students are choosing musical vocabulary that allows them to express themselves. The comparison can be made to a storyteller; some stories are short and to the point (with few words used) while others are more involved (very descriptive). Some jazz improvisers will tell short stories slowly (with a few notes or phrases) while others may choose to use a lot of notes fast. It is up to the teacher to help each student discover how to best tell her musical story. Teaching improvisation will be discussed in more detail later in this chapter.

SELECTING STUDENTS FOR JAZZ ENSEMBLE

Since Jazz Ensemble is an elective, there will be some students who opt to take Jazz Band but chances are there won't be enough for you to get balanced instrumentation. Some of the players you will need in Jazz Ensemble may not be found in your band program (guitars, acoustic bass or electric bass, piano, and singers/vocalists). First, you should poll your current students and find out if any of them play needed instruments (you'd be surprised by the number of guitarists and pianists there are in most schools). If so, discuss with them your plans to form a jazz ensemble and what you think their contributions and benefits would be. If not, post on your website, bulletin boards in the school, or student news media that you are interested in starting a jazz ensemble and need students who play guitar, bass (acoustic or electric), piano, and drum set (all of your percussionists may not play drum set).

Because jazz ensembles by size will fall below class size requirements, you may need to convince your administration to waive minimum class-size requirements. One way to do this is to have them average your classes (band classes are usually above maximum class sizes and should balance your class numbers). Example: If class size minimum is thirty students per class and you have twenty students in jazz band but forty students in concert band, have the administration average the number to thirty students per class. This can also be done by taking the total number of students you have each day and dividing that number by the number of classes you teach to get the average of thirty per class. Do not allow the administration to force you to enroll more students for the jazz ensemble class. Many problems occur because of jazz class overcrowding. Some students will not be able to play during class and discipline problems will occur. It will be very difficult to reach optimum sound balance with unbalanced instrumentation.

Even though most jazz scores call for one player per part, it is possible for you to have two players on rhythm section instruments (guitar, bass, piano, and drums) if you explain to the students that everybody won't be playing on every song every day. Should you double, it will be wise to make sure each player learns each song. Wind players may need to audition for placement in the class and that should be addressed in the class description, syllabus and the band handbook. Jazz ensemble instrumentation usually consists of five saxophones (two altos, two tenors, and one baritone), four trombones (sometimes five), five trumpets, one guitar, one bass, one pianist, and one drum set player. Saxophone players are often expected to double on clarinet and/or flute and soprano saxophone.

There should be audition pieces for each instrument furnished to the students beforehand and students should be told what is expected of them. If possible, furnish the students with a short played example of the audition material so that they can hear the style required. Doing this will help you to determine how well the students will use their "ear" when learning jazz styles and prepare them for using their aural skills while performing jazz.

The mistake a lot of directors make that dooms their jazz groups is to feel as though jazz classes don't require lesson plans or classroom management like concert band classes. In some ways, jazz classes need more structure than classical classes. Jazz can seem less organized based on its free-spirited style, but the seemingly chaotic nature of jazz performance requires as much if not more structure. Jazz allows students to be innovative within a clear structure, and the teacher must set the parameters in which the "chaos" can exist. Improvisers have to be aware of form and structure in the music being performed that classical players are not required to actively detect. Classical music by nature is clearly written out and all players know their responsibilities. In jazz, each player must see his part well defined within the group.

One of the difficult challenges of jazz band is to get students to be willing to take chances. This means that as the director, you must give students the tools they need to develop their jazz skills. Books that are used for classical band warm-ups generally shouldn't be used for jazz band because articulation and expression are different. If you must use the same books (because of a limited budget) you will need to select exercises that you can adapt to jazz performance. If the books use block chords, rewrite some parts to include major-minor seven chords, known as Dominant Seventh chords (ex: C–E–G–B-flat) or Major Seventh chords (ex. C–E–G–B) or minor-minor chords (C–E-flat–G–B-flat). These chords will help your students develop their aural abilities to hear jazz tonalities. If the book uses major scales, instead of starting on the tonic (first note of the scale), start them on the seventh note and ascend to the seventh note an octave higher and without repeating the seventh, descend the scale and end on the seventh an octave lower. When using eighth notes, because the "stress" will be placed on the second half of the beat, students will begin to "hear" how swing eighth notes should be played (stress or emphasis on the second eighth note). This will be discussed in more detail later in this chapter when discussing jazz class lesson plans.

One of the most difficult tasks you will face is getting classical students to hear and comprehend the differences between classical and jazz melodies, harmonies, and rhythmic structures. Because some of the elements of jazz are found in other popular music you can use your students' love of popular music to teach jazz concepts. Having guided listening sessions will help. As you listen to various recordings, point out how the different elements of music are approached by jazz players. Twelve bar blues songs (blues played in twelve measures) are a good starting point. The blues form in twelve measures/bars will have a short motif statement (four bars), slight variation (four measures and repetition of the original statement). You should select model big bands such as Duke Ellington's Orchestra, the Count Basie Band, Stan Kenton's band, and some of the United States military big bands. These recordings will serve two purposes: one, they will give your students a chance to hear what big bands should sound like and two, they will provide an opportunity for students to hear jazz styles and concepts.

ORGANIZING THE FIRST JAZZ BAND REHEARSAL

When organizing the first jazz ensemble rehearsal, one of your first considerations should be to explain the function of each instrument and section in the ensemble. Below is a brief description of selected instruments and their functions. There are books written for jazz ensemble instruction that devote complete chapters to this.

Bass (acoustic or electric) – The function of the bass in the jazz ensemble is to establish and keep the beat. Contrary to common belief, the bass not the drum set is the instrument primarily responsible for keeping time and outlining the chord progressions. One of the most important responsibilities of the bass is to keep a steady, driving beat. The bass is often referred to as the pulse of the jazz ensemble. It will create melodic lines under the chord progressions that will form the basis for harmonization. Sometimes bass lines are written out but the more advanced charts allow the bass player to create her own bass lines. This means that the bass player must have a good concept of chord progressions and how chords are spelled out horizontally rather than vertically. Sometimes all the bass player has written on his part is chord symbols. This is usually done for swing charts (Latin, rock, and fusion generally have parts that are written out). When playing swing charts the bass player becomes the lead player in the rhythm section.

Drum Set – The function of the drum set is to complement the bass and place accents on beats two and four and emphasize important parts of the music. Each part of the drum set serves a different purpose. In general, the hi-hat cymbal establishes beats two and four commonly known as the back beat. The large cymbal known as the ride cymbal is used to add stylistic elements to the music. Each part of the ride cymbal gives a different sound. The closer to the bell of the cymbal the drummer plays (near the top), the less ring the cymbal will have. The farther from the bell the player plays, the more ring the cymbal will have. Drummers need to experiment with stick placement on the cymbal to determine which sound should be used for various styles of music. The pattern known as the "swing pattern" is played in varied eighth note patterns on or near the edge of the cymbal. Another large cymbal is known as the "crash" cymbal. This cymbal is used to add extra emphasis or punctuations to parts of music that are intended to stand out or add a degree of completeness to a musical phrase (sometimes used in conjunction with the ride to create swing patterns). Drummers learn how to use the bell of the crash cymbal played in tandem with the ride cymbal to create different colors. This is especially true when playing rock, Latin, or fusion styles of music.

The bass drum is not used for keeping time (except in rock styles); it is used for extra emphasis referred to as "kicks." These kicks are based on "punches" that are written in for brass sections to establish where beat one is so the winds can accurately come in on the second half of the beat (think boom-pow for two eighth notes).

Piano – The piano is the main chord-playing instrument for the band. The piano is used to complement what the bass and drums are doing and generally doesn't play on the beat. The chords the piano plays will furnish the basis for improvisers to be able to follow the song's chord progressions. Jazz pianists play a pattern based on a dotted quarter note followed by an eighth note known as a "comping" pattern, short for complementary pattern. This means that the way the chords are played should add emphasis in selected places in the music. The piano part is not designed to keep time—that responsibility rests with the bass and drums (depending on the style of music being played).

Piano players, even more than bass players, have to have a thorough understanding of music theory. Most jazz charts only provide a chord sketch, not piano voicings. It's the responsibility of the player to know how to spell out each chord based on the written progressions. It will be helpful to young players for you to take out time to write out chord choices for them (Jamey Aebersold, Dan Haerle, and Jerry Coker have books that can help you). With a little guidance they can design the rhythms they will use for their comping patterns. Remind them (especially in the early stages) that less is more. This means that since chords are written out for wind parts, it's not necessary for them to play a lot of chords. They should be taught to simply "fill in the blanks"—provide chords where none are being played by other instruments.

You can start younger players off playing one note with the left hand and two notes with the right. The lowest note can be the chord's root note and the third and fifth or the third and seventh can be played. The third should be included because it will determine the quality of the chord (major or minor). Once the player becomes comfortable you can have him play two notes in each hand. The pianist must be careful not to play solos or lines while others are soloing, he must rhythmically vary the chords and comping patterns.

Guitar – The function of the guitar is basically the same as the piano, but when the two are playing at the same time, they should voice chords differently. Simply, if one is playing chords in root position, the other should play inversions (starting on any note other than the root). The most used style of guitar playing is named for the long-time guitarist with the Count Basie Band, Freddie Green. Unlike the piano, the guitar in Freddie Green–style will play on each beat of the measure and sometimes play "comping" patterns.

The Freddie Green–style is a lot more difficult than it sounds and you should encourage your guitarist to listen to the Count Basie Orchestra and focus on Freddie Green. There are a lot of players in big bands who play the Freddie Green–style so if you have recordings of other big bands that were recorded after 1970, you will have other examples of the style. Most notably, military bands provide free recordings and as you build your recording library, request recordings from them.

Lead Trumpet – This distinction is given the first trumpet part of a jazz score. The lead trumpet is the color instrument of the big band and generally plays high notes and punctuates specific parts of the music. In jazz band scores, there is a section known as the "shout" section and the lead trumpet has the responsibility to "lead" the band through the "shout." In some advanced scores, lead trumpet parts can go up to D above the staff.

This means that lead trumpet players must be able to not only hit high notes but articulate them in the upper register comfortably.

Lead Trombone – Lead trombone is the distinction given the first trombone part. The function of the lead trombone is to play the highest voice parts of the trombone section and to function as the "big trumpet" complementing the lead trumpet (sometimes playing the same musical lines an octave lower).

Lead Alto – This is the name given the first alto saxophone. The lead alto saxophone's function is similar to the lead trumpet's function but because it does not project in the same way as a trumpet its purpose is to "soften" the effects of the brass section (soften in this case does not refer to volume, it refers to texture). Because of the design of the instrument, the lead alto plays fast lines of music and leads the saxophone section through soli lines (harmonized solos played by the entire saxophone section at the same time).

Jazz Tenor – The jazz tenor designates the main saxophone improviser in the big band. If there is any instrument that can be expected to have solos written in most songs, it is the first tenor saxophone (jazz tenor).

After explaining the function of each of the individual instruments, the next important discussion will be how each section should work together and how they function within the group. The best description of a jazz ensemble (eighteen-piece big band) is that it is a rhythm section and three wind instruments—trumpet, saxophone, and trombone. The most-used band setup has the lead trumpet, lead trombone, and lead alto all lined up from the lead alto on the front row, lead trombone on the second row to the lead trumpet on the third row (in the center of the band). Some bands have the trumpets standing throughout performances; some have trumpets and trombones standing; and some have each section seated with the trombones and trumpets on risers (in graduated heights). There are several different kinds of setups for jazz ensemble, but for the purposes of this book we will use the three-row system with the rhythm section stage left of the conductor.

Function of Each Section

Each section has a specific function and that function is based on the timbre of the instruments in that section. You should explain the function and concepts of each section clearly to your students (explain the functions during a listening session so that students have concrete examples to refer to). The only section that is not made up of "like" instruments is the rhythm section. Though the rhythm section is made up of instruments that are totally different, it is the unity of this section that makes the band "swing." The following is a brief discussion of the function of each section.

The Rhythm Section—Piano, Bass, Guitars, and Drums

There is a description of jazz ensembles that addresses how the band swings. Swing in this case does not refer the period of music known as the Swing Era. If there is any section that is responsible for swing, it is the rhythm section. Swing in this case refers to the feeling of the emphasis on beats two (2) and four (4) rather than on the strong beats of one (1) and three (3) in common time (4/4). This feeling of syncopation is one of the reasons jazz was often referred to as "syncopated music" in the early days of its development.

In the description of each of the rhythm section instruments how they emphasize and play off beats two (2) and four (4) was discussed. Each instrument has a specific way that it creates the swing feel. What takes work from you as the director is getting the instruments of the rhythm section to function as one.

In order to get the rhythm section to play together as one you should start with twelve-bar blues with the bass line written out or a song in thirty-two-bar form that has the bass line written out. As they play four beats per measure, the bass should play on each beat placing a slight emphasis on beats two (2) and four (4). The drummer should play the hi-hat cymbal on two (2) and four (4) while maintaining an eighth note pattern on the ride cymbal and placing slight accents on two (2) and four (4) or on syncopated patterns that complement the melody on the snare. The drummer should use the floor tom and bass drum to emphasize "off beats." Off beats can be described as any weak beat or weak portion of a beat. The piano player should follow the written part and so should the guitar (see above for each instrument separately).

After they become familiar with the written part, the guitarist and pianist should be encouraged to experiment with chord voicings and chord placement. If possible, before rehearsing the entire band you should work with the rhythm section. Jazz players refer to jazz rhythm sections as "making the bed" or "laying the foundation." If you want the band to swing or have drive, it starts with the rhythm section. In order for the rhythm section to function as one, everyone must listen to and communicate with one another (one unchecked ego can ruin the unity).

If the tempo of your band is a problem (speeding up or slowing down), the section you should immediately look to solve the problem is the rhythm section. Most directors walk over and stand in front of the rhythm section and clap or snap their fingers. This alerts the rhythm section of their primary function—keeping steady time. Audiences generally aren't aware of what's going on unless the conductor starts to conduct or loudly count off. Simply standing in front of the rhythm section brings their attention to the problem and helps them to unify around the beat.

The Jamey Aebersold series has recordings available that allow each rhythm section instrument to play along with CDs that will help them learn their function (Jamey Aebersold Music). One of the supplemental books for the series gives piano voicings that are commonly used in jazz (*Piano Voicings from The Volume 1 Play-A-Long*).[1] The Aebersold jazz voicings can be used for basic blues as well as with jazz standards. Dan Haerle also has a book that teaches piano voicings for jazz, rock, and pop piano playing, *Jazz-Rock Voicings for the Contemporary Keyboard Player.*[2] Another book recommended by piano players and jazz educators is *Standardized Chord Symbol Notation* by Clinton Roemer and Carl Brandt.[3] This book has common chord spellings and chord forms used in most music scores. These books are very good for students who have little or no training in playing jazz chord progressions.

The Saxophone Section

If there is a comparison with the function of strings in classical music, the saxophone section in a jazz ensemble would be that comparison. If there is any wind section that colors the band or is used to introduce melodic ideas, it is the saxophone section. When the saxophones are not carrying the melody, they are playing sweeping, moving lines that are counter melodies or are playing complementary lines to the melody.

Because of the nature of saxophone instruments' sound, the saxophone section blends with brass instruments to create a more mellow overall sound. If brass instruments are known for providing the punch for a band, saxophones are known for "rounding out" the sound of the band.

The Trumpet Section

The range and design of the trumpet makes it the instrument that brings "punctuations" and added emphasis to the jazz ensemble. If saxophones add mellowness, trumpets add brashness to the band. It is the careful blending of these two kinds of instruments that gives the jazz band its unique sound. Most big band charts (scores) have sections written in that are punctuated and/or led by the trumpet section with the lead trumpet playing the highest notes of any instrument. During soli sections (harmonized solos or ensemble solos), the trumpet section leads the band. The trumpet section is also the driving force for tutti sections (full ensemble sections).

The Trombone Section

Sometimes overlooked in jazz ensembles, the trombone section has many important functions. Thought of as being "big trumpets," these instruments serve a much more important function. Most arrangers and composers use the trombone section to play block chords or moving chords to reinforce the chord progressions being played by the piano and/or the guitar. Because they are brass instruments, their timbre allows them to "cut through" and bring emphasis to the chord progressions with or without the trumpets. The flexibility of the instrument also allows it to add subtle nuances that other members of the ensemble can't. Since it has a slide rather than keys, it can literally slide from chord to chord, giving the music a special effect.

CHOOSING JAZZ ENSEMBLE LITERATURE

One of the most challenging parts of establishing a jazz ensemble in your school is choosing the right literature for your group. Band directors who have little or no experience with jazz ensembles can be overwhelmed by this task. Before selecting pieces to teach your jazz ensemble, you should listen to as many demo recordings provided by jazz music publishers as possible. You will have an opportunity to follow the score as you listen to determine if the note range is accessible to your brass players; if rhythmic patterns are within your teaching ability and your students' learning capacity and if the music will hold your students' interest. You'll want to choose literature that will serve many purposes. Some songs will be used for festivals; some will be used for children's concerts for elementary school performances; some will be used for in-school concerts; some will be used for out-of-school concerts (such as senior centers); some will be used in class for educational purposes.

Unlike concert band, you probably won't be teaching basic music techniques since most students coming into jazz band will have a grasp of major and minor scales and basic rhythmic counting skills, but you will be teaching articulation and stylistic expression. In order to do this effectively you should establish a group listening session at least twice a week for ten minutes of class. As the group starts to understand basic jazz articulations and expression you can cut the listening sessions back to once a week or once every two weeks (listening should remain a vital part of your teaching). With the availability of videos on youtube.com, you can use videos of some of the top jazz big bands such as Duke Ellington, Count Basie, Woody Herman and others for your listening/viewing sessions.

There are some composers and arrangers such as Sammy Nestico, Les Hopper, Mark Taylor, Mike Kamuf, and Mike Carubia who have dedicated their writing and arranging to making big band charts accessible to student groups. You should start with music by these writers and arrangers first because the techniques you want to focus on are the techniques their pieces are based on. Of course, these are not the only composers and arrangers that put out quality charts but their work has been proven over time to assist greatly in the development and building of good jazz ensembles. Directors who participate in national festivals identify these composers and arrangers as those most consistent in quality and accessibility.

When choosing music for younger groups or inexperienced players, it is wise to avoid trumpet parts that go beyond G above the staff or trombone parts that go beyond C above the staff. Your players should have a range two notes above the highest written note to be assured of being able to play the written notes with power and control. They should not have to strain to achieve high notes because they will tend to "blast" or pinch the notes out of tune. It is difficult enough for bands to play in tune within their comfortable range but when students have to struggle with new concepts and ranges it is almost impossible to get the finished product you wish to have.

Composers and arrangers of high school and middle school jazz ensemble music are aware of the range limitations of some young players and the fact that all jazz ensembles will not have complete instrumentation. There are scores that can be reduced to one or two players per instrument section (trumpet, saxophone, or trombone). These scores are written in such a way that the integrity of the piece remains even with fewer instruments.

Most statewide or national festivals have prescribed literature to be performed for adjudication and you should use that as a guide for programming your performances. All good jazz ensembles are expected to perform three pieces in contrasting styles for adjudication. One song should be a blues based swing selection or a piece in thirty-two-bar form, a Latin piece, a ballad, and/or a pop-rock style piece. More experienced groups should play a ballad. Because ballads make intonation demands on players that require advanced ear training, it is generally wise to avoid them until your group is mature enough to make necessary adjustments (work on them in class until they gain the necessary skills for performance). In order to authentically perform these pieces your group should view or listen to model groups perform in each of those styles. MENC has two publications that are quite helpful for choosing literature for jazz ensembles.

- *Teaching Improv in Your Jazz Ensemble*: A Complete Guide for Music Educators (http://www.menc.org/resources/view/teaching-improv-in-your-jazz-ensemble). Over 180 arrangements of jazz standards are indexed to correlate with the sequence of improvisation study. Complete lead sheets are provided for each chart so you can determine the exact improvisational requirements of the charts before purchasing them.
- *The Jazz Ensemble Companion*: A Guide to Outstanding Big Band Arrangements Selected by Some of the Foremost Jazz Educators (http://www.menc.org/resources/view/the-jazz-ensemble-companion). Recommends and analyzes sixty-seven quality jazz arrangements. Listed alphabetically,

each analysis includes information on instrumentation, ranges, playabil-
ity, and requirements for rendering the score. Includes eight indexes of
musical features to help instructors select repertoire and teaching topics,
and five indexes for quick navigation and reference.

Groups like the Jazz at the Lincoln Center Orchestra, the Bob Mintzer Big
Band, and Gordon Goodwin's Big Phat Band perform music in the big band
style but because the players are contemporary players your students can
hear some modern influences on classic jazz literature (Bob Mintzer uses
an electric bass). This avoids the students labeling the music as "old" and
not relevant to the present time. Younger players can't help but integrate
modern jazz styles (Be Bop, Hard Bop, Cool Jazz), rhythm and blues, pop
and rock styles into their improvising. It is this integration that helps keep
jazz alive and preserves the history for future generations. Jazz ensemble is
another way that your program can teach multicultural styles and encourage creativity.

Teaching style in jazz ensemble requires listening to model groups perform. Notes in jazz are notated exactly the same as classical music but the
way notes are played and articulated are vastly different. Two eighth notes
in jazz are called swing eighth notes and the way they are played resembles
an eighth note triplet pattern with a quarter note followed by an eighth
note (long-short). Jazz articulations are best taught by using syllables to
represent each note in a rhythmic pattern. The most commonly used for a
two eighth note swing pattern is doo-bay for the long-short relationship.
Teaching jazz without teaching a student how to articulate correctly is the
same as teaching a student a foreign language without using the correct
accent or voice inflections. The rubato quality of jazz rhythms is what separates jazz from classical styles. Explanations without listening exercises will
not be effective. There are many books that will provide you with syllables
used to teach jazz rhythmic counting. Space does not allow the complete
discussion on jazz syllables here. One of the first books to address jazz
rhythms and jazz styles was written by Marc Gridely, *Jazz Styles*.[4] There have
been many other books written since but this book was written when jazz
ensemble was first being taught in American schools.

If the score calls for "Latin," it is important that you as director know
whether the style is Afro-Cuban Latin or Brazilian Latin. Looking through
the score to identify common bossa nova patterns, clave or salsa patterns
will help you identify the styles and explain them to your students. Wynton
Marsalis and the Lincoln Center Orchestra have a young peoples' series that
very effectively explains these differences. You should view these videos and
listen to the various styles in order to explain them to your students. You
should not listen to or view any of these recording along with your students
for the first time. Not knowing how to explain or perform these patterns

will damage your credibility as the instructor. Prescreen videos and recordings and if necessary, consult a jazz professional for clarification of difficult concepts.

DEVELOPING IMPROVISATIONAL SKILLS

One of the greatest challenges jazz students encounter is being able to convert things that they have learned in method books to things that can be used in improvised solos. Teachers must try to explain to them that in order to use method books to learn improvisation effectively, they must understand what method books are designed to do.

Most method books are not designed to teach students how to improvise. They are designed to help them develop the skills they will need to draw from in order to become a good improviser. Your students shouldn't expect to learn improvisation directly from a method book any more than they should expect to learn how to read from a dictionary. Method books will help them to understand jazz articulations and phrasing similar to how a dictionary helps them to learn to define words and pronounce words. Dictionaries equip you with a working knowledge of words to use in sentences but they don't teach you how to create sentences or how to read them.

If you can understand this concept, you can teach students to effectively use method books. First, the teacher must decide what skills their students are working on. Method books in general are designed to help the user to gain facility on their instrument. Repetitive digital exercises are designed to help players play fluidly. Once students have gained mastery on their instrument technically they are then ready to start working on creative skills. After working on digital skills they should also start working on aural skills at the same time. This will help "release" players to develop ideas as they play. Most players have difficulty playing ideas they "hear" in their heads because they lack the technical proficiency to play their ideas in cohesive units. Don't have students work on either playing by "ear" exclusively or working on technical studies exclusively without pairing the two. Neither component will work alone for effective soloing. Improvised solos are a way for the soloists to tell their story through sound. The best soloists do this effortlessly because their technique allows them to be fluid in their expression.

There are too many "technical" soloists who sound mechanical when playing because they have concentrated too heavily on technique. At some point an audience should be able to connect with the soloist's playing on an emotional level. If they leave talking about how many notes a soloist played rather than marveling at how the soloist "told their story," it means the soloist hasn't been an effective soloist. This can be compared to listening to someone tell you a story using multisyllabic words that you don't understand. You'll leave impressed by their vocabulary but chances are you'll have no idea what the story was about.

Many great improvisers have a lot of technique but when you listen to their solos you don't just think of the fact that they played a lot of notes, you think about how they used those notes to keep their solos moving along the way they wanted to express themselves. Some students will memorize great players' solos note for note but have absolutely no concept of the logic behind their note selections. Should they happen to take an extra chorus or if the rhythm section alters the progressions they are totally lost. Developing a logical concept is the key to developing as a soloist.

The idea of becoming creative and independent from reading written solos should be the goal of using method books. Most scores written for jazz ensembles include written solos for student musicians. When getting your students to start learning improvisation they can use a combination of ideas from method books and the written solos (the hope is that they will eventually develop their own ideas).

If you are working with your students as they work with method books, you may want to have the students listen to improvised solos in the style of music you're working on. As you listen to the solos, you can identify scales and arpeggios the soloists are using that the student can find in the method book(s) they are using. Remember, the idea of using method books is to develop technique to be used in solos. By listening to how good players use those techniques to effortlessly play solos, your students can start the process of becoming a soloist.

One of the biggest problems in teaching jazz improvisation is getting the novice improviser to relax and let the music flow naturally. The problem starts with the improviser's fear of failure, whether self-imposed or unwittingly imposed by the teacher/director. One of the most frequently asked questions directors have is how to get a student to relax while playing over chord changes. The simple answer is that everybody starts off relaxed until they find out they've done something wrong. Then the fear of failure clouds the issue. When a baby is learning to talk we don't try to teach them grammar and sentence structure immediately. We let them express themselves the way that comes to them most naturally and then we start to shape their language development. How many years of school are dedicated to learning grammar and subject/verb agreement? Most kids have been expressing themselves verbally for five or six years before ever hearing about subject/verb agreement or the proper use of pronouns.

With that in mind, why would we expect someone learning the language of jazz improvisation to be able to immediately understand it and play? Most young improvisers, like kids learning to speak have some experience in communicating with their listeners.

Young players should already have some experience with playing scales before trying to improvise (from using method books or from learning in band class). Kids learning speech have sounds to imitate from hearing their parents and/or siblings talk. The same has to be true about young improvisers, if you want them to learn the language, they must hear the language. Help them develop a discography with players they need to model.

Once you give them the opportunity to listen to jazz players improvise, let them play along with the recording or try to play what they think they've heard the improvisers play. Don't try to edit what they play; let them experiment. It's from this imitation and experimentation that the fluidity needed for improvisation develops. If you try to force the student to adhere to the "proper way" to improvise, inhibition sets in. An inhibited player will not develop the fluidity or the confidence needed for success in improvisation.

If the student is allowed to play in a relaxed setting with you guiding her toward the proper way to speak this new language, success will follow. One of the ways teachers can do this is to bring in an experienced improviser to work with their students. If you don't have access to good, experienced improvisers check with music retailers and instrument manufacturers to get some of the artists who endorse instruments to come to your school. Having an opportunity to interact with a "real" player is much better than playing with a recording. However, being able to hear jazz inflections demonstrated live or on recording is helpful. Several companies have a roster of clinicians/performers who are available by request to visit your school—take advantage of those opportunities.

The most important aspect of this is to have the students play. Eventually with some direction, students will begin to hear what needs to be edited out or added in as they are playing. Just as English teachers don't grade papers until the student has completed putting her ideas down on paper, you'll need to wait until the student has finished playing his solo before you critique him. As was stated earlier, it is very important that students play uninhibited early on.

Use simple melodies working with students to help them develop as soloists. This accomplishes two things. First, they get a "theme" to keep in mind as they develop "variations" that later become crafted solos, and most importantly, they learn the importance of form (there are many songs based on the simple melody "I[ve] Got Rhythm"). Once they are comfortable with melodic form, you can then address harmony and harmonic chord structures. The problem some teachers and students have is trying to do too much too soon. Most students find it difficult to concentrate on learning the melody, form, chord progressions, and patterns at the same time. That would be like trying to jump from simple math to calculus without a thorough progression from one step to the next. With a little structure and design you will be able to help your students learn improvisation.

In summary, it is important when working with young improvisers that you as the teacher create an encouraging, nurturing environment. Soloists should be encouraged to play through chord progressions on the piano. It doesn't matter that they are not pianists, it's only important that they hear the chords spelled out to choose notes for their solos. Improvisation should be taught every day in class.

REHEARSAL PITFALLS TO AVOID

Some problems jazz ensembles experience are caused by the director. Over-teaching and causing students to tighten up as they play is counterproductive and will cause more work than required. Just as with preparing soloists, you don't want to create inhibited players. Don't try to teach too much at one time or drill points by overexplaining. It's better to allow students to hear what's expected of them by listening to sound examples than to try to write exercises on the blackboard and explain what you expect to hear. Thanks to youtube.com, dailymotion.com, and other internet video sites, you and your students can view jazz videos together.

When you're playing CD examples or video examples, insist on your students actively listening—this is not free time between the "real" rehearsal time and the warm-up. Make sure that they understand that listening is an organized part of the rehearsal. It helps drive that point home if you're organized. Before you put a CD on, make sure you know the exact track you want to play and that you have an idea of what you specifically want your students to focus their attention on. Just putting the video or CD on and saying "Listen to how this is played" is not directed listening. Saying that you want them to "listen to how the saxophones are articulating the quarter notes," or "listen to how the group is phrasing the melodic line" serves a better purpose. For this to be a true learning experience for your students, you must point out what you want them to learn. Students won't automatically know what to listen for or how to execute what they've heard without your guidance.

If you choose to talk during the rehearsal or stop the band during the rehearsal make your comments short and to the point. One of the worst mistakes made by directors is to stop the band during a piece and not have a specific reason. This may sound ridiculous but there are some directors who are so intent on repetition and drills that they stop the band just to go back over a part (even though students have performed well). Of course, this stops any continuity or momentum the group has. Sometimes the best teaching occurs when you simply allow your students to put in practice previous lessons. Most jazz ensemble students have been taught how to cross-listen, fix intonation problems, and gain facility with scales from other band classes so there are problems they can correct themselves without you having to stop the band to point anything out to them. By you not stopping it teaches them that you expect them to self-correct. This does not mean that you should allow major mistakes to go unchecked. If minor infractions occur, discuss them at the end of the piece and ask the students to identify corrective measures. If they don't know how to make the corrections you should guide them through the process.

Do not take time out of your rehearsal deciding what pieces you are going to work on. Have your students put their music in order at the beginning of the class period by announcing the rehearsal order or writing the names on the board. As stated earlier in the chapter, it's as important to have lesson plans for jazz ensemble class as it is for symphonic or concert band class. Organization at the beginning of the class will yield an efficient rehearsal. The more efficiently you use your time in what are seemingly small details, the more productive your rehearsal will be. Disorganization generally leads to a nonchalance that carries over to the other aspects of the rehearsal—sloppy entrances, late releases, improper articulation, and so on. Having a rehearsal agenda written on the board will help considerably.

One of the most efficient rehearsal requirements is to have students bring pencils to class and mark their parts based on your instructions. This keeps you from having to repeat the same instructions every rehearsal. You can give concise instructions: "Check out the markings you have for letter B." Insist on students marking their parts and give them specific markings that are clear and unambiguous. Once again, don't ramble; keep your comments as brief and as accurate as possible. Some directors will spend time during every rehearsal discussing the same points. This unintentionally sends the message to your students that they don't have to listen closely the first time because you will say the same things over and over. Why mark their parts if you're going to tell them the same thing? Even if you have insisted on your students listening to you and marking their parts, repeating yourself is counterproductive.

Before moving from one piece to the next during the rehearsal, if there are things your students have done well, praise them. Some directors fear that praise will give their students the idea that there is no need for improvement or home practice but if stated correctly you can achieve a positive mood and reinforce the need for continued work. "Even though there are still things we need to fix, there were some good things we just did. Now, we need to polish this up a little more to have it performance ready." Statements like those above say that you have heard their progress but the group is not quite where you want them to be.

Any director who doesn't think their students can hear or discern that the group sounds better is ignoring how well their students are learning and performing. The statement attributed to Miles Davis, "That's close enough for jazz," is incorrect and taken out of context. Miles Davis was described as a perfectionist so being close enough was not his goal. Standards for jazz performances must be the same as for any classical performance. Jazz standards cannot be perceived by your students as being lower than classical standards. "Close enough for jazz" generally means that the literal interpretation of the music is a bit less exact than classical. Playing swing eighth notes will not be played evenly; they will have a long-short relationship between the first and second note. Because of the rubato, or robbed tempo aspect of jazz, playing eighth notes unevenly is "close enough for jazz."

Try to maintain balance during rehearsals. If you scold students because they have not performed to your expectation, you must praise them with the same emotional level. Yelling or screaming at your students creates what jazz musicians call "a negative vibe." To be effective, you must praise your students enthusiastically. Students need positive feedback to improve, especially if they're insecure doing a new thing such as improvisation or learning jazz phrasing for the first time. The way you react to their performances will either lift their confidence level or discourage them. The best choice seems obvious but sometimes directors get caught up in the moment. Record your rehearsals and listen to yourself and your instruction technique as well as how your students are performing. You may discover a correlation between your reactions and your students' performance level. If your reactions are mostly negative you may discover that your students' energy level gets increasing lower. It is possible to uphold high performance standards without destroying your students' confidence level.

Taking a few minutes before rehearsing each piece to explain the feel of the piece, performance style, and expected rehearsal techniques will help you to have an effective, productive rehearsal.

As stated many times throughout the book, planning and organization are vital to the success of your group. When discussing the rehearsal piece, be as specific as possible as you run down the piece. Be sure to explain any terms that are unique to jazz performance. If there are special techniques that differ from concert band performance you may wish to go over them before starting the piece. You can isolate sections of the band and have them play through a part of the piece so that when they get to a challenging section they have had an opportunity to address it to overcome any fear they may have. You should try to sight read one or two of your performance pieces so that your students have to apply techniques learned in previous classes. This will also help to sharpen your students' analytical approach to the music. Confident players become more willing risk takers and are more likely to improvise when called upon. A lot of jazz ensemble festivals have a sight-reading component. If your students sight read in class regularly they will be able to apply sight-reading techniques learned in class to the festival sight reading exercise.

Don't approach conducting jazz ensemble the same way you conduct symphonic or concert band. The swing feel for jazz depends on the emphasis being placed on beats two and four. Classical conducting techniques emphasize beats one and three. It is difficult for bands to play pieces other than ballads when given a four-beat pattern. Jazz educators refer to this as playing with a vertical feel. Unwittingly groups will react to beat one as the strongest pulse note rather than beat two. Philly Joe Jones, a great jazz drummer, started a feel known as "drop four" drumming. Drop four drumming creates what is considered a linear approach to jazz time. Simply stated, the beat shifts in such a way that beat two begins to feel like the strongest beat in the measure and beat four becomes the second strongest (related to the feel of beats one and three in classical music). To get this concept across to your band, put a metronome on sixty and assign beat two to every click. As the students count, beats one and three will be silent on the metronome and the heard clicks will be two and four (i.e., one-click-three-click). Doing this will help your band develop a "feel" for swing and help them keep better "time." When your soloists start to follow the chord changes it will feel more natural to them because of the shift in emphasis. Increase the tempo on the metronome as you determine that your students are ready for the increase.

So the question is: "How do I conduct my band?" The answer is, count off each piece at the tempo you want it played. Cue important parts of the music: accents; special entrances; dynamics; soloist entrances; tempo changes; fermatas; and cutoffs. Besides counting off the piece, the conductor's responsibility is to end the piece. A good, clean cutoff depends on how clear the conductor's cutoff motion is. Most jazz directors step to the side while soloists are playing or the band is playing a section that does not require special cueing. It's the responsibility of the rhythm section to maintain the tempo and unless the rhythm section speeds up or slows down it isn't necessary for the conductor to stand in front of the group. Should the rhythm section change tempo, most jazz directors will start to clap on two and four rather than "beat the air" with conducting patterns. Jazz festival adjudicators will generally make comments to directors who use a baton or conduct each beat by hand. When bands receive on-stage clinics at festivals, the first thing most adjudicators do is address jazz band conducting if a director has conducted pieces. It is difficult for rhythm sections to communicate with one another through eye contact when their attention is being directed toward the front of the group.

When preparing your group to play a piece during rehearsal or for a sight-reading exercise, you need to "walk" the band through the piece. Tell them about anything special found in the piece such as repeats, D.S. or D.C. marks, modulations, tempo changes, time changes, and any other changes that will affect the performance of the piece. You should establish whether or not the piece should have swing eighth notes or if it is a rock piece or a Latin piece that will be played with "straight" eighth notes. Ballads will also have straight eighth notes and will be the only exception to the nonconducting rule (though you still don't want to conduct from beginning to end).

Unlike Concert Band, which is thought of as a teaching class, Jazz Ensemble is thought of as a performance-based class. It's true that basic music skills and knowledge are required for entry into Jazz Ensemble classes, but it is a mistake not to think of the class as a teaching class. There are many techniques for good jazz performance that must be taught or modeled. If jazz is not one of your strengths, bring in a professional jazz musician to do a master class or clinic. In chapter 1, using guest artists was discussed. Contacting your local music dealer to get a list of available local artists or securing a guest artist from a national company can help. Many companies have a roster of artists spread all over the United States who will visit schools. Because technology is such that you can take video lessons from professional musicians without them leaving their home, you can secure highly competent players for little or no cost to you (see chapter 1 for more details on this). Military jazz ensembles travel all across the United States and if you request that they visit your school they will try to schedule the large jazz ensemble or a smaller ensemble to perform and do a clinic for your students.

USING COMBOS TO HELP DEVELOP
SOLOISTS AND THE RHYTHM SECTION

One of the best ways to develop a good rhythm section and good improvisers is to form a smaller lab group. There are techniques that can be taught during combo rehearsals and performances that are too time-consuming to be taught in a large ensemble setting. There are combo workbooks and methods that are available that you can use for combo playing.

Some teachers use "fake books," which are jazz books that contain songs and chord progressions. The songs included in fake books are generally songs that professional jazz musicians play and they include a discography so that students can locate and listen to the actual recordings of the pieces (commonly referred to as tunes). If you'd like to use these charts as "head charts" for use at the beginning of class, make copies for each student to have (there are fake books in C, B-flat, E-flat, and Bass clef).

Start with the rhythm section learning the changes. *The Real Book*,[5] the most commonly used fake book, has CDs that accompany the books (purchased separately). You can play the song through for the rhythm section and then have them play it (*Real Book* CDs do not have melodies played, just the rhythm section). Once the rhythm section is comfortable playing the changes you can add one or more instruments or have the full band play the melody (head). After the nonrhythm instruments become comfortable playing the melody, form quartets, quintets, or sextets. Encourage each combo member (including the rhythm players) to attempt to play an improvised solo. Some directors will write out a solo sketch for their students to use as a "jump off" point. Encourage your students to think of their initial solos as variations on the melody until they feel comfortable enough to expand their ideas into completely independent melodic lines (see the section above dedicated to improvisation).

Using a smaller number of students will also keep your students from being self-conscious of what they're playing. Since everyone will be attempting a solo, no one will be likely to make fun of someone else's efforts. Combos generally have to meet at lunch time or after school so the students who attend the sessions will be showing their interest just through their attendance.

WRITING LESSON PLANS FOR JAZZ CLASS

Just as with other instrumental groups, lesson plans for jazz ensemble should be stated in behavioral terms with objectives stated very clearly with specified goals and outcomes. Some of the basic teaching objectives for jazz ensemble include working on intonation, articulation, tone quality, expression, rhythmic patterns, and so on. Your lesson plans should state how you will focus on each of these elements and what techniques you will use to teach them. Every jazz class or rehearsal should start off with a warm-up that works on or reinforces jazz styles. Each day you should work on a new technique or style that relates to the music you will be working on. Plans need to be well spelled out with specific goals and projected outcomes.

INTONATION IN JAZZ ENSEMBLE

Intonation is a concern for all instrumental groups and must be addressed every day in every rehearsal. Jazz students who have been part of your other groups should have learned how to tune their instruments and how to make intonation adjustments as they play. In this section we'll discuss the intonation problems that are unique to jazz ensembles. The addition of piano, guitar, bass (acoustic or electric), and possibly vibes means that wind players will have to match pitches with fixed pitched instruments and nontempered instruments.

Trumpets, trombones, and saxophones must be able to hear the pitches produced by the rhythm instruments and make adjustments. Tuning within their sections and with the other wind instruments is challenging enough but having to discriminate electronic instruments' pitches creates even more of a challenge.

A lot of band directors fear having a large number of saxophones in their groups because saxophone players are known for poor intonation. Jazz ensembles have at least five saxophones that are expected to play in tune and blend. Since a lot of saxophone parts are written in unison, any intonation problems are magnified.

Saxophone Intonation

Some of the reasons for saxophone intonation problems are mechanical and can easily be fixed. Starting with the mouthpiece set-up, one of the problems could be the mouthpiece itself. A worn out mouthpiece (yes, mouthpieces wear out), will generally play flat but sometimes will play sharp. Check mouthpieces for calcium build-up along the side walls or for small chips at the base or the tip. Miniscule changes in airflow can negatively affect pitch. Have your students get in the habit of cleaning out their mouthpiece with a mouthpiece brush after playing.

If the cork on the saxophone neck is too thick for the mouthpiece to be pushed in, the instrument will be played flat (pushing the mouthpiece in raises the pitch). One of the little known facts about saxophone tuning is that once a saxophone is tuned with a tuner, you can mark the cork. When tuning in the future, this mark will serve as the point where the horn is in tune (as long as the embouchure is set correctly).

Aside from the mouthpiece and neck, poor reeds or poorly aligned reeds can affect pitch. Check to make sure that the player is not using a reed that is too soft by having the student play a long tone into a tuner. Next, have the player play four quarter notes into the tuner. If the note stays relatively the same (slight or no variation of the pitch), the reed is a good strength for the player. If the quarter notes go flat, the reed is probably too soft. Conversely, if the notes go sharp, the reed strength is probably too strong.

The placement of the ligature (the ring that holds the reed to the mouthpiece) can affect the perceived reed strength so you must be sure it is in the correct place. There is a line on most good mouthpieces that shows where the mouthpiece should be aligned. If the ligature is too high, it won't let the reed vibrate completely and the note will be sharp giving the impression that the reed is too strong (the ligature will restrict the reed's vibration). If the ligature is placed too low, the reed will vibrate too much but at a level that will cause it to play flat. Before making a decision on reed strength, be sure to experiment with ligature placement.

The instrument itself can be a problem for the player's ability to adjust tuning. If there are dents in the neck or the body, they will alter the airflow and cause the player to play flat. It should also be checked for leaks. Leaks cause a problem with the airflow with players overblowing to force the note to come out. This also generally will cause the instrument to play flat unless the player pinches the sound (pressure on the reed tip and mouthpiece). Pinching always results in playing sharp. Needless to say, in order for the player to be able to make necessary intonation adjustments, she must be playing on the best possible instrument with the best possible equipment (reeds, ligature, and mouthpiece). The design of most saxophones is such that the upper register will play sharp and the lower register will play flat. This is pure physics: high notes vibrate in a way that is perceived by the ear as being sharp (frequency of vibration) and the lower notes tend to be perceived as being flat. There are saxophones now that are designed to play well in tune throughout the complete range of the instrument eliminating some of the mechanical tuning issues.

Since every saxophone player in your saxophone section will not be playing on the same brand of instrument, there are individual (human) adjustments that will need to be made. Your first step should be to have each player play into a strobe tuner or digital tuner (one that has a needle) so that they can recognize the tendency of each note on their instrument. They should not use vibrato and the airflow should remain constant throughout the range of the horn.

As the students play, you should check to make sure that they are not making drastic changes to their embouchure while playing. Most saxophone teachers would prefer that the embouchure not change while the student is playing but because jazz requires subtle embouchure changes to alter the sound, students need to know how those changes alter their pitch. In ideal vibrato playing, the vibrato note viewed on a tuner should deviate slightly going below the pitch and back up to the pitch. Incorrect vibrato or uncontrolled vibrato will drop below the pitch and then vary above the pitch never centering.

If the pitch does not center, it will be impossible for another player to match the first player's pitch (this is also the reason you want "straight" tones for tuning). Multiply this problem by five and you have the issue faced by a lot of jazz bands. As in the case of the band's tuning, the best tuning starts from the bottom up. Have the baritone saxophone player tune first but then have the lead alto tune to the baritone. Once the lead alto has tuned to the baritone, have the rest of the section tune to the lead. This conditions them to listen for the lead alto's sound as their sound source for solis and section lines. When the section is playing in unison they should listen to the lead alto but the lead alto should listen for the baritone to make sure that the tuning pitch is centered (both are E-flat instruments so they are playing some notes an octave apart).

Brass Intonation

Brass intonation does not have as many mechanical problems as saxophones (fewer working parts) but there are problems that can be fixed through instrument repair or maintenance. The first thing that should be checked is whether or not the instrument is clean. For trumpets, take all valves, water keys ("spit" keys), and slides out and rinse the inside of the horn out and dry it completely. If you rinse slides out, make sure to keep the spit key open so that none of the pads get wet (you can cover the pads with cellophane paper to protect them).

When you put the valves back in, make sure that you twist them until you hear a click (if you get them mixed up, there are numbers engraved on the bottom of each valve). Once you have cleaned the instrument and checked for dents, next you must address human issues. Place the trumpet tuning slide one half or three-quarters in so that you have room to push in or pull out to adjust the pitch. Have the student play a long tone into a strobe tuner. Check to make sure their posture is such that they can maintain a good airflow. You should have at some point addressed the importance of breathing from the diaphragm but if you haven't, this is the time to address it.

Next, as with saxophones, trumpet players must have the proper embouchure. Sometimes the pure buzz made by taut lips is confused with the pseudo buzz created by an incorrect embouchure. Have the student play a Concert B-flat scale two octaves into a strobe tuner. If the pitches grow increasingly flat, chances are there is a problem with the player's embouchure. Repeat this process using Concert F major. If you are not a brass player, bring in a brass player to assist with corrective embouchure adjustments.

As the players with correct embouchures play the scale into the tuner, have them identify pitches that are not in tune. In most cases, notes played with first and third valves (the note Concert C) will be out of tune and in some cases Concert E-flat. For Concert C, have the player make slight pitch adjustments by sliding the third valve slide out. Once they find the location of the valve that is in tune, it will always be in tune at that position unless there is a mechanical problem that develops. For Concert E-flat, the same is true making an adjustment with the first valve slide. If there is no first valve slide on a lower-quality instrument, an embouchure adjustment must be made.

Intonation problems for most brass instruments originate with a poor airflow. Breath support is of the utmost importance for brass instruments (as with all wind instruments). Most intonation problems for brass instruments are caused by lack of breath support.

Trombone Intonation

The design of the trombone is such that even if the tuning slide is in place after tuning to a strobe tuner, notes can be played out of tune. No two trombones will have matching positions where the notes are played in tune. Because of this, trombone players more than other wind players must depend on their ear to maintain pitch accuracy. It is important that you teach your trombone players to listen to the piano or vibes to hear a tonal source that they can tune by. Not only are trombone players challenged to find the correct pitch, they must fine tune it to play the pitch in tune. Knowing this as the director, you'll need to have your trombone players play each note into a tuner and then make a mental note where the exact position for the pitch is. Obviously, as they play they will have to make subtle adjustments to play each note in tune. The more they play into a tuner the more their ears will be trained to hear correctly tuned pitches.

Acoustic and Electric Bass and Guitar

The tendency of some band directors is to have their bass players and guitarists depend on electric tuners for tuning. This is a very bad mistake. First, if the batteries die or there is no electrical source, your players will be lost attempting to tune up. One way directors help these players develop their ears is to give them the tuning note for the E string and let them tune the other strings based on note positions for the next string to be tuned. After they have pretuned, then have them use the tuner to get the exact pitches. The more they do this, the more accurate their pretuning will be. They should also be taught how to use overtones for tuning each string.

Acoustic bass players face the same challenges that trombone players face. They must be able to immediately locate each pitch quickly and accurately. The same process used to help trombone players develop the ears should be used with bass players. Have them play scales on all four strings slowly checking each pitch against a tuner for pitch accuracy. Inaccurate pitch positions will be sharp or flat based on whether the finger placement is above or below the note's location.

EQUIPMENT NEEDED FOR JAZZ ENSEMBLE

When starting a jazz ensemble, there are instruments and equipment needed that may not be used by other groups (some schools' pep bands and marching bands now use drum sets and electronic equipment for performances). In order to provide the quality of instruments and equipment that you will need, it is best to purchase equipment with school funds or booster provided funds. As you choose instruments and equipment, durability and longevity should be considered. There will possibly be a lot of people using the equipment; it will be transported from time to time and young people will be using it! For this reason, price should not be a determining factor. Less expensive equipment may not survive the rigors of frequent use and may have to be replaced. Whatever savings you may have had will be negated by the need to purchase replacement equipment.

You will need to purchase a bass guitar, a guitar, electric piano, vibraphone, and a drum set with cymbals and stands. You will also need amplifiers for all of the electronic instruments, and for out-of-school performances you will need a complete portable sound system. The sound system will need microphones, microphone stands, cables, speakers and a mixing board. Buying the correct microphones for vocals and instruments is another important consideration. There is no such thing as a universal microphone in the lower price range. Since you will need six to eight microphones minimum, you will need to have microphones for micing instrumental soloists, vocal soloists, acoustic piano, the saxophone section (to balance with brasses), and for you to announce selections. Having a mixing board is very important for you to be able to get a good balance and possibly record performances away from school.

Since your school's auditorium will hopefully have a complete sound system, you will be able to get good sound recordings for concerts. When ordering equipment for the auditorium for a new school or new building, the school administration will need your input. They may not be aware of your needs, and you should not take for granted that they will order equipment with your program in mind. The in-school needs will be the same as your portable needs, but you should be able to get a higher quality since the entire music department and drama department will be using it. The music department and the drama department should meet with a sound professional to consult with in order to get the equipment that best suits your collective needs.

There are high-quality video systems that will make digital audio-video recordings. If the school's budget will support the purchase of one of these systems, have your school's purchasing agent secure one. Having high-quality videos of your jazz ensemble (and other bands) will help with your recruiting and archiving your group's achievements. As you have your band evaluate their progress, it helps to have the highest-quality recordings of the band for the band to critique.

PARENT BOOSTERS' ASSISTANCE WITH THE JAZZ ENSEMBLE

As is the case of marching band and pep band, jazz ensemble needs assistance transporting equipment and with concert set-up. If you have established a public relations committee with your parent boosters group, their services will be greatly needed to promote concerts, report on the outcome of competitions, promote the group to the community, and help with recruiting students. If there is an equipment vehicle or trailer used for marching band and pep band, use it for jazz ensemble. The sound system and amplifiers will need to be transported and set up and you will need an advance team to locate electrical outlets and go through other set-up procedures. Because you and your students will need to spend time warming up, tuning up, and getting the music for the program ready, the more help you can get from parents the better prepared you will be for the performance. Some directors fail to tap into a vital resource and spend their time and energy performing mundane tasks that prevent them from preparing their group adequately for the performance. Even if the performance is at your school you should still enlist the help of parents.

Jazz groups will also have special outfits for performances. Some directors poll their parent group for seamstresses and tailors to have them make vests, dresses, or other parts of the outfit so that the group will match (there are vendors who provide outfits designed especially for jazz groups). If you don't want to make the outfits, the parent group can help raise funds to purchase uniforms or outfits.

Jazz ensembles also use special music stands called "fronts." These fronts are specially made and will usually have the band's name and insignia on the front. Besides helping with the purchase of these fronts, the set-up, transporting, and break down of the fronts can be done by parents or students from other band groups. Of course, your jazz students can participate in the set-up but not at the expense of your warm-up or tuning.

DEVELOPING A JAZZ ENSEMBLE BUDGET

Depending on the size of your band program, jazz ensemble expenses can be included in your overall budget. Second only to marching band, your jazz ensemble will require a moderate to large budget (depending on the number and location of performances). There are jazz ensembles that require a separate budget. This section will give you some information on developing a budget exclusively for jazz ensemble.

As with your concert band, you will need to determine what equipment you will have to purchase and if there is any money available from the school district or the school's budget. In the early years of the development of your band program you should meet with your principal and explain clearly your vision of what the complete band program can become. Bands bring a lot of positive attention to schools and you should make your principal aware of how she will benefit from a successful band program. Principals have discretionary funds that they can tap into to develop new programs and start new school projects. It's your job to sell your program as a good PR source. The more money you get from the school, the less money you'll need to raise. Some schools have a business manager or financial secretary who does the purchasing for the school. Consult this person to find out about what can be requisitioned or purchased with a school purchase order. The financial officer also has the bid list that approves purchases and provides discounted prices for instruments and equipment. They are also the people who meet with the principal to allocate the school's general funds (soda machine profits, concession stand funds, school boosters' funds, etc.). The more you can tap into these funds, the less money comes from your budget.

After meeting with the principal and/or financial officer, you should take a needs inventory. If you're not sure what needs you will have, search out a director of an established jazz ensemble, and ask about starter needs and five-year needs. It is better to spend a lot of money starting the program off than it is to save money that you may lose in the next fiscal year (school budgets are decided based on your past purchase record). If you're in a school that has had a jazz ensemble before, you should check the inventory to see what equipment needs to be replaced. The financial officer should have a record of all large purchases and the band's recent purchase history.

Jazz ensembles have special needs that concert bands don't have. Unfortunately, the music and method books you buy for concert band cannot be used for jazz ensemble. Some scale methods can be used by both groups but it's better to have jazz band methods for jazz ensembles. Music purchases should be your number one priority. As is the case with concert band, jazz band music and method books are your class texts. Your budget should include the estimated costs for one or two method books and forty-five minutes worth of music (enough music for a performance).

You will also need to have a digital recording system and at least two microphones to start the program off (this is a onetime cost until a replacement is needed). As stated before, in the first year there are instrument purchases that have to be budgeted for. Flugel horns, soprano saxophones, congas, electric piano, travel cases for drums, mutes, and amplifiers are immediate needs. You will probably want to add Latin percussion instruments and other color instruments as your music performance level grows and there are more demands in the music.

There will be a need to purchase bass and guitar strings, drum heads, cords, and recordable CDs every year. You will also need to include funds for emergency repairs and replacement equipment. It is better to over budget rather than to under budget. Your parent boosters' group can plan fund raising activities around your needs. Don't be afraid to solicit help from financial specialists (especially parents who responded that they are financially gifted).

SUGGESTED PUBLISHERS FOR JAZZ ENSEMBLE

Advance Music
Alfred Music Publishing
C. L. Barnhouse
Edition Andel
Editions Marc Reift
Hal Leonard
Heritage Music Press
Jalen Publishing
Jazz Lines Publications
JPM Music Publications
Kendor Music Inc
Lush Life
Molenaar Edition
Neil A. Kjos Music Company
Queenwood Publications
Sierra Music
Southern Music Company
The FJH Music Company Inc
Twin Towers Music Publications
Walrus Music Publishing

SUGGESTED COMPOSERS FOR JAZZ ENSEMBLE

Andy Clark
Bill Holman
Dean Sorenson
Doug Beach
Duke Ellington
George Gershwin
Gordon Goodwin
Harry Warren
Howard Rowe
John Edmondson
Larry Neeck
Lennie Niehaus
Les Hooper
Mike Carubia
Mike Lewis
Neal Hefti
Paul Clark

Robert Lowden
Shelly Berg
Victor Lopez

SUGGESTED ARRANGERS FOR JAZZ ENSEMBLE

Andy Clark
Bill Holman
Bob Curnow
Bob Florence
Dave Wolpe
Frank Mantooth
Gordon Goodwin
Jerry Nowak
John Berry (119)
Mark Taylor
Matt Catingub
Michael Sweeney
Mike Carubia
Mike Kamuf
Mike Lewis
Mike Tomaro
Paul Murtha
Peter Blair
Roy Phillippe
Sammy Nestico
Tom Kubis
Victor Lopez

NOTES

1. Jamey Aebersold, *Piano Voicings from The Volume 1 Play-A-Long* (New Albany, IN: Jamey Aebersold Jazz).
2. Dan Haerle, *Jazz-Rock Voicings for the Contemporary Keyboard Player* (Los Angeles: Alfred Publishing, 1984).
3. Clinton Roemer and Carl Brandt, *Standardized Chord Symbol Notation: A Uniform System for the Music Profession* (Sherman Oaks, CA: Roerick Music Co., 1976).
4. Marc Gridely, *Jazz Styles* (Upper Saddle River, NJ: Prentice Hall, 1978).
5. Hal Leonard Corporation, *The Real Book*, 6th ed. (Milwaukee, WI: Hal Leonard Publishing, 2004).

18

Using Technology and Multimedia in Band Class

Using technology available to you today can revolutionize the way you teach and present information to your band. Instead of filmstrips, overhead projectors, slide projectors, tape recorders, and mimeograph machines being used, computers, DVD players, and digital recording and playback devices are now being used. Computer-driven PowerPoint presentations make it a simple task to present instructional materials to your class using digital audio synchronized with a visual score or other visuals. You can start and stop the audio/visual materials wherever you choose and discuss specific parts of the music and point out any issue that may need to be highlighted and corrected.

When introducing a piece of music to your band you may play the piece while your students follow the score on an overhead screen. Seeing the music on the screen as they follow along helps your students to see and hear that their part is a small part of a whole. Once you have started playing the piece you can substitute the model group's performance with your group's performance. As the group watches and listens you can identify sections of the score where the group needs to improve.

This technology has not always been available and many college and university music education student preparation programs and some schools are not aware of the need to teach the use of PowerPoint in the classroom for band instruction.

HOW DO YOU PREPARE FOR A POWERPOINT
INSTRUCTIONAL PRESENTATION?

Preparing for a PowerPoint presentation is not as difficult as you may think. All you need is a laptop or desktop computer, a scanner to scan music scores, a digital recording of your group or the group you want to synchronize with the visual, an overhead screen, and a sound system. Of course, a basic knowledge of how to prepare a PowerPoint presentation is needed. The tutorial for PowerPoint will be of assistance to you. Since most schools offer computer courses that teach PowerPoint you can always ask for outside assistance (some systems offer in-service training at no cost).

In your preparation there are a few things you must consider. It should be clear to your students what skills you are focusing on. By using specific parts of the score you can circle or highlight exact places on the score where the item you're focusing on can be found. PowerPoint allows you to do this in a way that will get your students' attention. The same kinds of graphics and special effects that they see in video games can be used as teaching aids for you.

Once the presentation has been prepared you should coordinate it with your lesson plans. Students react to multimedia presentations and if you use this technology wisely they will remember the points of the lesson you emphasized. If you're focusing on rhythmic patterns, you can extract the rhythm you want to teach and have the class tap, clap, or sing the rhythm on a fixed pitch. Start by showing the rhythm in the context it appears on the score and then isolate the rhythm and display it on the overhead. You can use a bouncing ball or a pointer to show how each note would be counted using beats and partials of beats (e.g., one and two and three and four and). For counting sixteenth notes, using "one-e-and-uh" gives each partial a syllable and keeps the beat and the "and" of the beat in the same place for consistency (some directors use "one-a-n-d" but the syllables aren't consistent for students to recognize). Everything you present should be transferable and functional for future lessons and sight reading.

Once the students have counted the desired rhythmic pattern to your satisfaction, have them play it from the overhead or from their parts on the music. If all of the students don't have the selected rhythm on their part, have them play it from the overhead so that everyone learns the pattern. This will help the students to learn the rhythm for use in future pieces of music where they may encounter it. It also helps them to develop analytical skills they can apply when sight reading.

When using PowerPoint to teach rhythms you are free to adjust the tempo. By doing this, you can make the pattern accessible to your students and give them an opportunity to see and hear how the pattern should be performed and sound. If you want to conduct along with the presentation you should be sure to position yourself and the screen in such a way students can see both you and the screen while playing.

One of the advantages of a PowerPoint presentation is that you can customize it to suit your needs and make adjustments based on the progress your students are making. By being able to include a "click track" (a metronomic beat track), students will all be able to hear the tempo you want followed. You can also repeat the same presentation without the click track and conduct at the tempo you want the students to play to.

RECORDING YOUR REHEARSALS AND USING PLAYBACK TO EVALUATE PERFORMANCE GROWTH

One of the most effective ways of combining high tech with low tech is to digitally video tape or audio tape your band's performances and rehearsals. There are hand-held digital video and audio recorders that can be purchased for a minimal amount. These recorders are small enough to fit into your pocket and record with studio quality sound. During your rehearsals you can set the recorder up on a tripod in front of your band, centered so that you can get a good balanced recording. After recording the group you can add the recording to a PowerPoint presentation and you and your students can evaluate and discuss your performance. If you don't wish to add the music to a PowerPoint presentation, you can play the recording through your sound system and have a quality recording to evaluate. As the students listen to the recording, they can evaluate how well they are balancing as a group, playing in tune, articulating, playing phrases, and performing all of the items bands are evaluated on at festivals and competitions. Recording your band regularly helps your students hear their growth. Sometimes as groups rehearse, their progress is incremental and not easily noticed daily, but when they can compare rehearsals once a week the improvement they have made is noticeable. Guided listening from you will help your students determine what they need to work on during their individual practice sessions.

There are also computer-based recording programs. Computer-based recording is easily integrated into your PowerPoint presentation without any need to transfer the digital recording from one source to another. Compact discs can also be "burned" from the computer. You can use an external microphone or the computer's internal microphone to record. Should you wish to record a live performance or concert the computer can be connected to the control board of your sound system to get a professional quality recording (so can some of the better hand held devices). Depending on your program's budget, there are many options for recording your band, including using a professional recording system with a mixer and playback capabilities (with a professional engineer). There are websites devoted to using technology in the classroom that can give you much more information on purchasing and using technology in the classroom.

A PowerPoint presentation will also allow you to use the music of a college group or professional group for your students to compare themselves with. You must make it clear that you don't expect the band to sound like the higher-level groups but that you do expect them to execute the music at their highest ability level. This means that the same techniques you used to teach rhythms, intonation, articulation, and other musical effects can be employed to demonstrate how the higher-level group is executing. Even in higher-level groups there may be problems your students can recognize as they follow the score during the presentation. While listening to identify problems, your students will use higher-level listening discrimination and hear the positives you are hoping to bring to their attention. It is important that they understand that they are listening for positive qualities as well as points they need to correct.

As was mentioned in an earlier part of the book, when using recordings to assess progress you must make sure that as students do peer and self-assessments they focus on the positive as well as any negatives they might hear (you should also avoid using negative terms and find a substitute phrase describing items that require work). Instead of saying, "The trombones messed up in measure 33," have the students say, "The trombones will need to spend more time working out the problems in measure 33." When discussing retention earlier, it was stated that every effort should be made not to discourage students by criticizing their work in a way that causes embarrassment or sensitivity. This is especially important when critiquing recorded performances because as the saying goes, "tape is forever." As the students listen to previous recordings they should be able to hear personal growth as well as group improvement.

There is also software and hardware available that you can purchase to produce professional quality CDs of your band's performances. As in the case of most technology, it is best to visit a vendor for a demonstration, attend an in-service demonstration, or search the web for information on mixing and mastering equipment, hardware, or software. Comparative shopping will help you get the equipment that best suits your needs for a price that fits your band's budget.

If you're just going to be recording your rehearsals and performances for postperformance evaluation you probably won't need top of the line equipment. If you plan to mix and master CDs or mp3s you may need professional level equipment. Unless your knowledge base includes recording technology knowledge, you probably don't want to purchase advanced equipment. In some cases, it is best to simply hire a recording engineer to come to your school and record your performances. Before you record and distribute recordings of your band you must secure the rights to record all of the music you wish to record. If you sell recordings with copyrighted music for which you have not secured permission to resell, you are in violation of U.S. copyright laws. Unless you have arranged music that is in public domain or your original music, you must be sure that you can receive clearances. There are music clearance companies that will help you secure clearances and give you information on fees that need to be paid. The Harry Fox agency (HFA Songfile), BMI, and ASCAP have data bases that allow you to search for publishing rights and allow you to secure clearances. It can all be done on their websites.

USING NOTATION SOFTWARE

Using recording software and digital recording devices serves the purpose of allowing your students an opportunity to hear the group perform. Notation software will serve two purposes, allowing you to print parts needed for a performance, and allowing your students to discover the composition side of music. Whether it's scoring for your pep band, marching band, jazz band or concert band, notation software is very useful and helpful. Besides being a time-efficient way to write out parts, notation software enables you to print out, copy, and save parts.

Music publishers have teamed with notation software companies to enable you to download and print parts of a piece of music you've purchased and pay a nominal fee per part downloaded. This means that if your students lose a folder or their parts you have access to extra parts instantly. This is a major change from you having to copy a part from the score by hand. Some publishers even allow you to print the amount of copies of each part you need directly from their website into your notation software (though they have a "save protect" that allows you to save and print parts only once). This means that you can get a full package of music without going to a music store. That can be quite helpful should your school be in a rural area or small music market. Visit music publishers websites for details on downloading scores and parts. If your local music store doesn't have the music you need, downloading or ordering online can be quite useful to assure that your students have an opportunity to play the pieces you want to play rather than settling for what's available from your local vendor.

Technology has revolutionized the way music is taught, published, and presented. All you need to do is go online and use a search engine to find what you need. Most music publishers have mp3 recordings available to listen to as you study scores of pieces you wish to buy for your band. Having an opportunity to see the score, listen to the music, and review the cost from your home or office makes the process much easier than it was ten or twenty years ago. Do not be afraid to explore new technology available.

Most state, regional, and national in-service conferences have an area set aside for vendors to demonstrate their products. Before you decide to purchase notation software, try to attend an in-service meeting or convention where these products are showcased. Ask questions about compatibility with different computer platforms, how "user friendly" (easy to use) these programs are, and if you can interface with or download from music publishers. Stand-alone notation software will cost less initially but software that allows you to download and print parts is much better and saves money over time. Either way, clear, easy-to-read parts can be written and printed for your students. Most notation software will give you the option to choose the quality of print to be used. The higher quality of the printing makes it less difficult for students to see and read their parts.

The second valuable use of music notation software is allowing your students to learn composition skills. Students perform better once they understand what went into the composition of a piece. Listening skills can be developed through composition skills when students become aware of the importance of all parts working together. Having students write a simple piece of music and have a small group play their composition, the composer learns to listen carefully to see if all parts are being represented. This then transfers to their playing as they train themselves to listen across the band to hear all parts being represented. Students don't have to be able to write or notate their ideas by hand since most notation software will transcribe music that is entered by MIDI keyboard instruments. Some of the more expensive notation programs can transcribe music sung into a microphone or played into a microphone with a wind or percussion instrument. The better programs will allow you to play your compositions as well as printing the parts or a score.

The use of notation software can also help keep some of your more advanced students engaged while you're working with other students who need remedial assistance or extra work. Once again, retention is an ongoing effort and the use of technology can be quite useful in that endeavor. When choosing notation software, the following questions should be answered:

- Can inexperienced users use the program with a minimal amount of difficulty?
- Will advanced users get bored because the software is limited in scope and its ability to perform advanced tasks?
- Can you add text or lyrics to the score?
- Does the program allow you to extract and print individual parts as well as an entire score?
- Will the program automatically line up measures on the score or must that be done manually?

- Will I be able to input specific markings from a score that I'm printing parts for?
- How many parts or voices can be used or saved?
- Will I be able to output sounds?
- As parts are being entered, can other parts be heard? Can multiple parts be heard on playback?
- Can I print engraved-looking or professional-looking copies of parts?
- Will the program auto-transpose or will I have to do that manually?
- Will the parts on the score be in transposed keys or will they be in concert key?

The answers to these questions will help you to determine the amount you will need to budget to purchase the software and if the software you're considering will be useful for you. Remember, as stated in an earlier chapter, you want to avoid anything that will add work for you or consume more of your time.

USING PLAY-ALONG SOFTWARE AND HARDWARE

Besides being able to transcribe music by playing through a microphone, real-time notation software can help you teach students their individual parts. Play-along software can serve many purposes. Students who are trying to learn their parts can play along with music that has been written or notated; students can work on jazz improvisation playing along with music that has been sampled (input by transferring recordings into the notation program); students can practice for Solo and Ensemble by playing with recorded tracks or notated tracks.

If you want your students to play along with the music you're currently working on, you can scan your score into the computer and have it automatically notated and recorded into the software. The student can then play along with the music at a tempo that you select (most programs allow you to select any tempo you wish without altering the pitch). If there is a need to rewrite music because of missing instrumentation, having the student play along with the score will help him hear the importance of the part he's covering.

There are digital devices that play CDs, mp3s, and other digitally recorded music for your students to play along with. Like the play-along software, the tempo can be adjusted for your students without affecting the pitch. You can also "loop" specific parts of a song that you want to repeat in a continuous pattern until the student has mastered the section being focused on.

Most people think of play-along recordings being for individuals or small ensembles, but if used during band class they can serve the same purpose. Because stand-alone devices and recording software can play prerecorded music, sections of your band or the entire group can play along with a recording. Using the "loop" component of the play-along device or software, you can focus on specific problem areas of the score being rehearsed. This is a "fun" way of working on intricate problems without encountering some of the problems you might encounter while working with one section while other sections have "down time." You can even combine the use of notation software with this exercise by printing the difficult section(s) for the entire band to play along with. A transposable software program can transpose parts that can be played by everyone so that no one has down time. This helps you to avoid some of the discipline problems that accompany boredom during class. It also helps you teach everyone rhythmic patterns they may encounter in the future.

Smart Music is an interactive software program that allows your students to play along with concert band music, solo and ensemble music, method book studies, and scale studies. The program contains many classic band pieces that you can include in your concert programming. The student can record their progress for you to assess. It has an e-mail component that allows the student to e-mail their work to you. The program has a loop component that allows students to repeat sections of the music for repetitious practice. This enables the student to repeat a section until they reach a proficient level. There is also a variable speed component that allows the student to slow down or speed up sections of the music or the entire piece.

Teachers can purchase the educational package and assign students access numbers and the students can purchase the microphone needed to use the program on their home computer. This works very well for advance students and students participating in solo and ensemble. Some states are now using Smart Music for their all-state audition preparations (not the actual audition).Superscope is a digital recording system that allows students to play a CD at variable speeds and also loop sections. Unlike Smart Music, this is a stand-alone piece of equipment. It is not possible for students to e-mail their progress to you but it does allow students to practice to proficiency and then play for you in person or record themselves for you to listen to them later.

Band in the Box is software for jazz students. Like Smart Music, it has a library of songs that students can play along with. It also allows students to program in songs or to compose their own songs. This is a very good way to teach jazz forms and improvisation.

VIDEO TAPING YOUR BAND'S PERFORMANCES AND REHEARSALS

Just as PowerPoint presentations are powerful teaching aids because of the visual element, videotaping your band can be a powerful tool. When your students watch and listen to their rehearsals and performances they will notice things that you cannot tell them to notice. Directed listening is a good exercise for bands but because most people are visually oriented, students will see things more readily than they will hear things. Since most digital video recording devices also provide digital sound, using video of performances and rehearsals can help your students focus and realize the importance of what they look like on stage. Judges and audiences are either distracted by or impressed with the visual from the stage. If you have told your students how foot tapping affects the tempo and they see tapping and hear rushing, you have been effective (as discussed in the section on lesson plans).

Another positive about the visual effects from videotaping is the fact that the group will see the importance of posture, stand positioning, and the group being dressed uniformly, and they can also see whether or not the group is looking up at the conductor. The videotape gives you an opportunity to drive home points that you have discussed that students may not be able to see or notice from their particular vantage point. Viewing the tape gives them a chance to remove themselves from the group as they watch the group on the tape. This "out-of-body" experience gives your students an opportunity to be objective viewers and listeners.

Video recording your band can also be used as a recruiting tool. If the adage "a picture is worth a thousand words" is true, a video is worth a million words. No matter how much printed material you send out or how often you meet with potential students and their parents, nothing matches being able to give them some insight into your program more than a video of you and your class at work.

Giving prospective students an opportunity to see how your band rehearsals are managed and run will help them to visualize themselves in the group as well as get to know your teaching style. Needless to say, you want to show one of your best rehearsals with interaction between you and your students as well as hearing the band play. Hopefully, there will be obvious improvement of mistakes that are pointed out by you during the rehearsal.

SMART PHONES, TABLETS, AND NOTEBOOKS

One of the recurring themes found in this book is the importance of organization. Being able to have access to pertinent information almost instantly is one of the ways technology has started to help band directors. All of the information you need from contacts to policies to minutes from parent meetings can be carried with you at all times. Smart phones such as the Android, BlackBerry, Nokia, T-Mobile, and others have enough memory for you to store or access information when you need it without carrying around printed files or hard copies of information. You have access to e-mail and various applications (known as apps) that allow you to consult with someone the moment a problem occurs. You can access the Internet and instantly search for answers to almost any problem you're faced with. Since organizations such as MENC have websites that have forums, you can consult with other band directors from anywhere you happen to be (as long as you have phone or internet service).

One of the most recent developments in the instant information age is Apple's iPad. The iPad can store your inventory, music library, and students' names and information, among other pertinent items (there are apps that allow you to save a program's song list). You can also write or arrange music and print it on the spot. This is quite helpful if someone loses his part or you find it necessary to write out a part because of someone's absence. There's also an app for recording your group live, an app for a metronome, an app for tuning, and many other helpful apps that keep you from carrying a lot of equipment or files with you. Because of the apps at your fingertips, there is no legitimate reason for you not to be organized. Since smart phones and the iPad have many of the same apps, you can share your files and information on two different devices, giving you a backup for everything.

Apple's iPad can also be used by students for writing music even if their music-reading skills are not at an advanced level. There are apps that can assist students in their personal music development through ear training, rhythmic tapping (percussion apps allow students to tap rhythms on the iPad). Many of these apps can be found at iTunes University and YouTube as well as many other locations. Because the iPad was developed in 2010, there are apps being developed daily; many are being developed by music educators for use in or out of school. Your students can use earphones with the iPad and can use it anywhere in the school (with or without Internet access). These tablets will never replace acoustic instruments, but the sampled sounds used can help students hear parts that they have written or parts that have been written for their particular instrument. MENC.org has multiple listings and evaluations by its members of available technology in the classroom resources.

Listed below are a few websites and books most often mentioned by MENC members in forums. It is advisable to use this site or use an Internet search engine to locate the most recent articles and books since this technology is constantly changing. *Teaching Music* magazine, an MENC periodical, has a Technology Section in every issue, and there's a feature-length article in each February issue.

TECHNOLOGY RESOURCES ON THE INTERNET

www.smartmusic.com
www.sweetwateredu.com

www.soundtree.com
www.ti-me.org
www.menc.org
www.kellysmusicandcomputers.com
www.finalemusic.com
www.sibelius.com
www.bandinabox.com
www.avid.com

TECHNOLOGY RESOURCES IN BOOK FORM

Rudolph, T. E. 2004. *Teaching Music with Technology,* 2nd ed., Wyncote, PA: Technology Institute for Music Educators.

Spotlight on Technology in the Music Classroom: Selected Articles from State MEA Journals. 2003. Reston, VA: MENC.

19

Quick Fixes and Emergency Repairs

No matter what condition your school instruments or students' instruments are in, there will always be an emergency repair needed at the worst possible time. Knowing this will help you and your students avoid going into a panic. There are some simple, temporary fixes with common materials that will help you save a performance and put an instrument in playing condition until you can go to a repair shop. No matter how well an instrument is functioning after an emergency repair, you must get the instrument to a repair shop as soon as possible. These fixes are by no means meant to last beyond the emergency. You or your students should take the instrument to a repair shop as soon after the emergency repair as possible.

Woodwind instruments, because of the number of working parts, are generally most likely to need an emergency repair. From pads falling out, springs breaking, reeds breaking, ligatures being loose because of missing screws, and corks coming off, these instruments will need special attention at some point during the year. You're not expected to be a certified repairperson, but as soon as an instrument breaks your students will come to you. Mouthpieces for brass instruments get stuck, strings on rotary key instruments will break, and corks for "spit valves" or spit keys will fall off.

As a new teacher this can be overwhelming. Most college teacher-preparatory programs don't have a repair course as part of the curriculum. Band directors are faced with on the job training or have a certified repair person on speed dial.

EMERGENCY REPAIR MATERIALS AND THEIR USES

Glues (rubber cement, instant glue, epoxy) – pad falls out and needs to be reset or replaced.

Rubber Bands – spring breaks and key needs to bounce back up after being depressed.

Razor Blade (single edge) – trim the tip of a chipped reed, cut cork.

Sandpaper or Emery Board – sand down the thickness of a reed after trimming or sand down neck cork.

Thin Fishing Line – repair the broken string on rotary valve/rotary key instruments.

Butane Lighter – use to heat the glue on the back of a pad that has fallen out to reuse the original glue.

Mouthpiece Puller – pull out stuck mouthpiece.

Key Spring Hook – pull flute and saxophone springs back into place (a paper clip can be converted into a key hook in an emergency.

Fingernail File – can be used as a flat head screwdriver to tighten loose saxophone screws.

Fingernail Polish – can be applied to the top of saxophone screws to make sure that they don't come out again after being tightened.

Eyeglass Screwdriver – can be used to tighten screws on any instrument that has small flat head screws (some eyeglass-repair kits include a small Phillips head screwdriver).

COMMON PROBLEMS NEEDING EMERGENCY REPAIRS

Cork comes off a saxophone neck – Wrap some notebook paper or newspaper around the neck the size and length of a cork. Do not use glue or tape, and once the mouthpiece has been placed on the neck and the instrument has been tuned, do not move the mouthpiece. The cork should be replaced immediately after the performance.

Saxophone/Clarinet key will not respond – The spring has probably disconnected from its seating. Use a paper clip or something that functions as a hook to pull the spring back into place. Be very careful not to break or bend the spring.

Mouthpiece is stuck – You must use a mouthpiece puller otherwise you take the chance of bending or breaking the barrel or tubing. Do not use pliers, wrenches, or vises to pull the mouthpiece out.

Spit valve won't close – Wrap a rubber band or tape around the valve to keep it closed. Replace spring or key immediately after the performance.

Rotary key will not open – Use thin fishing line of string to wrap around rotary mechanism to operate the key.

Reed has chipped tip – Place on flat surface and trim the reed just beneath the chip with a razor. Use fine sandpaper to gently sand down the tip in light strokes, moving forward only. Be careful not to chip or split the reed. This should be done only if an extra reed is not available.

Pads stick – If there is no nonstick fluid available, place a piece of typing paper (no ink on it) between the pad and the seating and pull it out while lightly depressing the key (with your finger on the key). Using a dollar bill will leave an ink deposit that will build up over time, causing sticking or improper pad seating.

Ligature screw breaks or is lost – Use the bottom screw only and turn it tightly enough to hold the reed in place. If both screws are missing, use several small rubber bands or one large rubber band doubled to hold the reed securely (tightly) to the mouthpiece. As a last resort, use duct tape or masking tape (only if rubber bands are not available).

Snare falls off the snare drum – Use cellophane or masking tape to attach the snare to the bottom drum head. Place the tape at the end of the snare on the metal not the snare itself. If you must place tape on the snare, make sure that the snare can still vibrate. Stretch the snare so that it is taut enough to still function as a snare.

Crash cymbal strap comes off – Study the other crash cymbal to see how to relace the strap.

20

Nonmusic Responsibilities of Band Directors

With all of the "hats" a band director wears to effectively do the job as a music teacher/band director, there are also responsibilities the band director has to perform as a faculty member in her school. Elementary and middle school teachers generally have bus assignments requiring them to supervise students coming to school and leaving the school by bus. This sometimes requires the band director to leave the band room open for students to drop off their instruments or have a student, adult volunteer, or colleague supervise the band room for safety and security. If you receive bus supervision responsibilities and explain to your principal the importance of you being able to open the room and supervise students, band room supervision may be your arrival and departure assignment.

Some of these assigned activities will help you get to know students who are not in your program and can help you with recruiting. When you're new to a school these activities also help you to get to know your colleagues and have a degree of visibility. Before you receive your Instructional Related Activities (IRA) responsibilities you should meet with your principal and explain what your mornings, lunchtime, and afterschool band director responsibilities are. Most band directors use the time before school, lunchtime, and after school for individual and group coaching. Try to find an alternative time and/or activity that will fulfill your responsibilities to the school that will not negatively impact your program-building activities. It's important that you perform these tasks like every other faculty member for many reasons. One, you don't want your fellow staff members to resent the fact that you are exempt from some of the mundane tasks they have to perform. Their resentment may cause them to work against you and your program-building efforts. Second, these activities give you an opportunity to participate in the school's total program. Sometimes band directors are viewed as being aloof or not part of the entire school because they put building a program over participating in activities that benefit the school and community. This is a mistake because in order to build a successful band program you will need the help of the entire school community—faculty, students, and community members.

Another mistake a lot of band directors make is to forgo attending faculty meetings. Faculty meetings are a vital part of being a part of the life of your school. Even if you are excused from faculty meetings because of your rehearsal or performance schedule, it is incumbent on you to keep up with the decisions made and information disseminated in the meetings. This information and these decisions impact on the school and your program. If you're not at the meetings there is no one present to address issues that will affect you and your students. Many of the decisions that are made in faculty meetings will directly affect you and your program. Decisions such as block scheduling, course offerings, class scheduling, and class lengths will all impact on your classes. Without having your input, administrators and the school staff may unwittingly make decisions that could destroy all that you've done to build your program and get students into your classes.

Faculty meetings are generally held once a month and even though a lot of items covered may seem mundane, all it takes is one item to affect your program. Since most music students are involved in high-level academic classes including their music classes, it is important that there are no conflicts or problems with class scheduling and extracurricular time schedules. Athletic directors need your input on field scheduling if your marching band needs access to the football field. Coaches need to know about your practice schedule so that if your students are also involved in sports, they know to expect them to be late for athletic practices.

Drama teachers need to know when and if you will need to schedule use of the auditorium. These schedules can be coordinated at the end of a faculty meeting when all involved are present. Even if you don't meet for scheduling purposes at least your colleagues have an opportunity to get to know you and know what your motives are. This way you can form a cooperative relationship with people you know rather than communicate in an impersonal way such as e-mail.

Communicating with parents is another responsibility all teachers have. If you want your band classes to be viewed and valued as academic classes you must maintain academic standards for your classes. This means contacting your students' parents to let them know the progress of their child in your class. You don't want parents or students to get the impression that your class doesn't have standards that must be met. With the new standards being adopted by different states, your lesson plans should demonstrate the value of music as a subject and how music integrates with other subjects. There are schools that pair subjects together in teaching blocks and music is often paired with English/Literature classes, history classes, and world studies classes. With No Child Left Behind standards and requirements, music can play an important part of helping students achieve their goals. Because music students generally have good attendance in music classes and overall, band classes help them to meet the attendance requirements for most standardized requirements.

RECORD KEEPING, STANDARDIZED TESTS, AND NO CHILD LEFT BEHIND

Record keeping is an important part of accountability for grading and meeting the No Child Left Behind requirements. Taking accurate attendance is an important part of all classes and should be done daily. Band classes are larger than most classes but because of instrumentation and seating, taking attendance can be done quickly. Once your students take their seats you can visually take roll rather than calling out names and waiting for responses. Roll keeping/attendance checking is an important part of accounting for schools as part of No Child Left Behind record keeping and has far-reaching ramifications for schools and school systems.

Some statewide standardized tests also require accurate attendance. For test scores to count for a school and individual students, they must be marked "present" for every day the tests are administered. All faculty members are assigned duties during standardized tests. Once again, as a member of your school's instructional team, you should expect to receive some sort of assignment during testing.

ADVANCED PLACEMENT STUDENTS IN BAND CLASS

There will be students who take band classes who wish to receive honors credit for band class. As in the case of other honors or advanced placement classes, honors band classes receive weighted credit. If there are students who wish to take an AP test, there is a prescribed course of study for these classes. Honors-level and AP classes will help you to maintain students who would otherwise opt out of band in search of a class that will give them weighted credit to raise their grade point average. Being able to participate in a class that stimulates them intellectually and creatively and meets rigorous course requirements will help you to retain students who may drop band in their junior or senior years.

Strategies for Teaching Advanced Students in Band Class

If your school does not offer honors or Advanced Placement classes in music, there are ways to challenge advanced students in band class. As was covered in the chapter on technology, there are computer-assisted music programs that will teach and assess your students individually (without you having to grade assignments). These programs range from theory programs to performance programs. Students can learn part writing, take aural tests (intervals and chords), and play songs or segments of songs with instant feedback on correct or incorrect notes played.

During band class you can allow your advanced players to have release time to work with computer-assisted music programs (CAMP). These programs are designed in several different ways. Some allow you to monitor how long students are logged into the programs and view their progress, and others allow students to have a degree of privacy without their progress being monitored. The cost of the program usually determines which one some schools use but it is best to have a way of monitoring students' time and progress to make sure that students who have been released are using their time wisely.

If there is no computer program available for use, there are ways that you can challenge your students during class. You can assign students outside of class work to research the style of music being played in class; information on the composer; what kinds of chords and chord progressions are being used; if the music is by a contemporary composer, what periodic style does the piece resemble (neoclassical, etc.). Having students do research on the pieces and composers you are working on in class will give them a better understanding of what you expect of them. If you have shared your conductor's notes with them, have them prepare notes on the pieces you are working on. Students tend to listen to their peers when those peers present their notes.

Building relationships with school secretaries, custodial staff, and the athletic department is not a requirement but is a very wise move. This support staff will probably interact with you more than many other faculty members. School secretaries will generally be of assistance in filling out and typing up forms, giving you access to the principal, and keeping you informed of items that need to be completed before school, or district-wide deadlines. The custodial staff will help you with before school and afterschool needs and provide access to parts of the building other than your area, set up for concerts and break down after concerts, room cleanup, and so on.

21

General Program Management

DEVELOPING AND MAINTAINING
AN INSTRUMENT INVENTORY

Maintaining an inventory of quality musical instruments for student use to be assured that you will have needed instrumentation is very important to the life and development of your program. Some schools will only provide large instruments such as tubas, sousaphones, bass clarinets, baritone saxophones, mallet instruments, and marching band percussion, but since the director in most cases will want to assign students to "color" instruments, the band's inventory will need to include these. The instruments that are considered "color" instruments include: oboes, French horns, bassoons, alto clarinet, soprano saxophone, piccolo, flugel horn, E-flat clarinet, and English horns.

If you are starting a new school there will be an equipment budget for stocking your new school. Before purchasing any instruments find out what amount of funding you can expect to receive over the next five years. Some districts have a depreciation list that you can get that will help you to decide how to best spend your funds. If you are inheriting your program from another director, try to locate her inventory list. With or without the list, check the inventory and list all equipment and their condition. You will also want to estimate a time each piece of equipment will need to be replaced. The school's procurement officer can help you with this. He will have a record of each purchase made before you came to the school.

Most music stores and instrument manufacturers have a printed instrument lifespan estimate and a depreciation schedule. Request one so that you will be able to develop your school budget and determine what supplemental funding you are eligible for from your school district. Some school districts will provide one or two large instruments to each middle school and high school in the district.

Make sure that piano purchases for your school come out of your school's furniture budget, not your music equipment budget. One piano purchase can deplete your entire budget for a year. Check with your music supervisor for information concerning new instrument purchases and assistance stocking a new school. Since most districts use vendor bids for purchases, centralized music offices have information you may not be aware of. If you are in a small district that does not have a centralized music office, meet with a representative from your music vendor to find out what recommendations she has based on purchase history (your school and other schools).

FOLDERS AND BINDERS

Most music stores will give you cardboard music folders to use for your band. These folders are generally free but will wear out very quickly if your students carry them to and from school (which you want them to do in order to practice). A better way to keep your music from being ripped or frayed is to order leather folders. These folders can be engraved with part names on them and generally have a four- or five-year life span. The drawback for these folders is that they do not fit into student backpacks. Some band directors have started using three-ring binders instead of music folders. These thin binders serve as protection for the music and allow you to have students keep handouts, class assignments, and other important papers. Choose a binder that has pouches so that your students can place their music inside. If you wish, you can three-hole punch the music to make sure the music does not fall out and get lost. If you decide to use binders you should order enough for each student to have the same kind of folder (even if the students have to pay for them). It is also recommended that students be discouraged from using their school binders for band class. One, those binders are too large to be carried onstage and two, you want students to use the folder as a textbook. A regular school binder will also be difficult for students to keep organized for band use (one of the problems students have is binder organization).

STARTING A CONCERT BAND MUSIC LIBRARY

When starting a music library there are several things you need to consider. Among those things is the educational value from studying classic concert literature, appeal to your students, appeal to audiences, variety of music styles, and music challenges to your students. Before choosing literature for your group you should listen to recordings of the music you are considering. There are recordings by professional groups that are available from music publishers with scores for you to peruse. Most colleges and universities also have recordings of classic concert band literature for you to listen to. You may contact them via their web page.

It is very difficult to locate professional recordings of concert bands but the U.S. military bands record classic band literature every year and make those recordings available by request. Video recordings of military bands and university bands can also be accessed on the Internet on sites such as youtube.com and dailymotion.com. There are a few composers of classic band literature whose work should be found in every band library.

Composers whose works are performed most often at middle school band festivals are: Frank Erickson, John Kenyon, John Edmondson, Anne McGinty, James Ployhar, Clare Grundman, John O'Reilly, James Swearingen, Robert Smith, Claude Smith, Ed Huckeby, Elliott Del Borgo, and Alfred Reed. Composers whose works are performed most often at high school band festivals are: Claude Smith, Charles Carter, Gustav Holst, R. Vaughan Williams, Howard Hansen, Gordon Jacob, Jared Spears, Clifton Williams, Frank Tichelli, Elliot Del Borgo, Alfred Reed, James Barnes Chance, and Francis McBeth. These are not the only good composers of concert band music but they are the names that most often are described by band directors as the composers they perform the most at festivals and concerts.

LITERATURE MOST OFTEN
PERFORMED BY HIGH SCHOOL BANDS

Some of the songs that are most often performed by bands at festivals are also songs that can be performed at concerts. Classic band literature reflects the true character of bands more than orchestral transcriptions because they are written specifically for band instruments and band instrument sonorities. Here are some of the songs written for concert bands grade 4 through 6:

Grade 4

Overture for Winds	Charles Carter
Symphonic Overture	Charles Carter
Chorale and Fugato	Frank Erickson
Toccata and Fugue	Frank Erickson
Irish Tune from County Derry	Percy Grainger
American Folk Rhapsody #3	Clare Grundman

Hebrides Suite	Clare Grundman
Havendance	David Holsinger
Battaglia	Francis McBeth
Chant and Jubilo	Francis McBeth
Second Suite for Band	Francis McBeth
And the Heart Replies	Anne McGinty
Atlantica	Anne McGinty
Festivo	Vaclav Nelhybel
Nocturne	Roger Nixon
A Yorkshire Fantasy	John O'Reilly
A Festival Prelude	Alfred Reed
A Festive Overture	Alfred Reed
Amazing Grace	Frank Ticheli
An American Elegy	Frank Ticheli
Shenandoah	Frank Ticheli
Dedicatory Overture	Clifton Williams
English Folksong Suite	Ralph Vaughan Williams
Rhosymedre	Ralph Vaughan Williams
Chorale and Shaker Dance	John Zdechlik

Grade 5

Proclamation	Charles Carter
Chorale and Variant	John Barnes Chance
Variations on a Korean Folk Song	John Barnes Chance
Satiric Dances	Norman Dello Joio
Be Thou My Vision	David Gillingham
Three Sketches for Winds	Clare Grundman
Chorale and Alleluia	Howard Hanson
Prelude and Rhondo	David Holsinger
An Original Suite	Gordon Jacob
Third Suite for Band	Robert Jager
American Overture	Wilcox Jenkins
A Symphonic Jubilee	Wilcox Jenkins
Andante and Toccata	Vaclav Nelhybel
Chorale Prelude	Vincent Persichetti
A Longford Legend	Robert Sheldon
Sanctuary	Frank Ticheli
English Folksong Suite	Ralph Vaughan Williams
Caccia and Chorale	Clifton Williams
Fanfare and Allegro	Clifton Williams
Symphonic Dance #3	Clifton Williams
Symphonic Suite	Clifton Williams

Grade 6

Fantasy Variations on a theme by Paginini	James Barnes
Toccata Fantastica	James Barnes
Suite of Old American Dances	Russell Bennett
Incantation and Dance	John Barnes Chance
Variants on a Mediaeval Tune	Norman Dello Joio
Galactic Empires	David Gillingham
Canzona	Peter Menin

These are not the only choices of music but, based on directors' responses, they are the most performed at festivals.

CHOOSING METHOD BOOKS FOR CLASS USE

When choosing method books for class use, the books chosen should address specific band-building techniques. There are different books used to teach and reinforce concert band styles and jazz/pop music styles. The methods chosen should not be used for both unless they are specifically written to address multiple styles. Since some concert band music incorporates jazz, show tunes, and popular music into the concert piece, there may be a need to teach general principles in class but method books are designed to teach specific techniques.

One of the best method books for teaching scales and chorales in all major and minor keys is the *Treasury of Scales*.[1] This book provides a warm-up with ninety-six harmonized scales from intermediate to advanced. This means that you can tailor your warm-up to any key of any song you're working on in class. Fortunately, because of its success, there are other books designed like it that are available from major music publishers as well as smaller publishing companies. One of the books that is used and recommended by many band directors is *16 Chorales By J. S. Bach*.[2] This book can be used to teach balance and blend to bands of all levels, but it is an intermediate grade.

Method book studies and exercises can help you to develop good breathing skills for band playing, balance, dynamics, attacks and releases, and phrasing. If you use harmonized scale activities, have your students listen for where each note of the scale being played is. As they track the melody from part to part they will make subtle changes in their dynamic levels without you having to tell them to. You can then make small adjustments from the podium but the real adjustments will be student-initiated.

SUPPLEMENTAL STUDIES

There are many other method books that can be used by individual instruments to work on facility and general playing techniques. A lot of states use these books for audition material for all state bands. Rubank, Inc., Music Publishing has a set of methods for all instruments on the elementary, intermediate, and advanced levels. You can choose books to be used based on your students' playing level. Unlike the band methods, these methods are designed to be standalone books that work on specific challenges faced by each instrument.

NOTES

1. Leonard B. Smith, *Treasury of Scales*, 1 (Los Angeles: Alfred Publishing, 1985).
2. *16 Chorales By J. S. Bach* (New York: Schirmer).

22

Sample Forms

The following forms can be copied or modified for use with your band. If you choose not to use these forms you will need to develop your own or check with your music supervisor to see if any forms exist. For a sample image release or audio/visual release form, go to http://www.sagepub.com/upm-data/22997_MENC_Audio_visual_likeness_release_07_08.pdf.

MEDICAL FORM

Student's Name _____

Parents' Names _____

Parent's Phone Number _____

Parent's E-mail _____

Student's Medical Condition _____ (Good, Fair or Poor)

Does the student have any medical condition that requires attention _____

     If yes, please explain _____

Does the student have any food allergies or special dietary concerns? _____

     If yes, please list and explain _____

Does the student have any condition that may restrict physical activities? _____

     If yes, please explain _____

If parent(s) cannot be reached, please give an emergency contact:

     Name _____ Phone Number _____

In case of an emergency, I give medical care givers permission to perform lifesaving care until I can be reached. Signed _____ (Parent)

The information I have furnished is complete to my knowledge.

Signed _____ Date _____

BAND BOOSTERS FORM

Parent's Name _____

Student's Name and Instrument _____

Parent's Cell Phone _____

Parent's E-mail _____

Parent's Home or Business Phone _____

Parent's Occupation _____

Are there committees that you would be interested in participating in (choose as many as you'd like):

Financial/Budget Committee ___

Public Relations ___

Marching Band Pit Crew ___

Transportation ___

Uniform ___

Prop Construction ___

Sign Making ___

Copy Righting ___

Chaperone ___ (Local) ___ (Out of Town)

Equipment Set Up ___

Concert Ticket Sales ___

Concert Set Up ___

Concert/Performance Promotion ___

Fund Raising ___

Recruiting/Retention ___

Are there skills you have to offer that will help the band program in any way that is not listed above? ___ Yes ___No

If yes, please explain _____

Would you be willing to transport students in your private vehicle if permission is granted by the student's parent? _____ (transportation by private vehicle is subject to the school and school district rules of liability)

Signed _____ Date _____

PERMISSION SLIP (LOCAL)

Student's Name _____

Activity _____

Activity Date and Time _____ (class periods missed)

I give _____ permission to ride on school-provided transportation to _____ with the band on _____(date).

I do not give _____ permission to participate in this
activity with the band. I realize that this is a graded activity and my child will be
penalized for non-participation.

I give _____ permission to participate with the band on
_____ (date) but I will transport him/her to and from the activity.

I give _____ permission to participate in the activity listed
above and would like to be a chaperone.

I give _____ permission to ride in private transportation
(parent/adult driven).

This permission slip must be returned to the school by _____

Signed _____ (parent's signature) Date _____

PERMISSION SLIP FOR AN OUT-OF-TOWN TRIP

Student's Name _____

Activity Name and Date _____

Parent's Name _____

Parent's Phone Number _____

Transportation Vendor _____ (bus, airline, etc.)

Estimated Departure Time _____ Date _____

Departure Location _____

Estimated Return Time _____ Date _____

Detach and return to the school by _____

Is there a health/medical form on file? _____

I give _____ permission to travel with the band to

_____ on _____ .

I do not give _____ permission to travel with the

band to _____ on _____ . I am aware that my child will

be penalized for non–participation.

Signed _____ Date _____

TEACHER FIELD TRIP NOTIFICATION FORM

Dear Colleague,

The band will be participating in _____ on _____(date).

Students will be out of class periods _____through_____. Please mark

_____ excused and allow him/her to make up any missed

work. Thanks for your understanding.

Ron Kearns, Band Director

Period 1 _____Signed

Period 2 _____Signed

Period 3 _____Signed

Period 4 _____Signed

Period 5 _____Signed

Period 6 _____Signed

Period 7 _____Signed

INSTRUMENT LOAN FORM, SCHOOL YEAR 20__TO 20__

Student's Name _____ Grade_____

Parent/Guardian's Name _____

Home Phone _____

Parent/Guardian's Cell Phone _____

Parent or Student's E-mail _____

Instrument Type/Name _____

Instrument Serial Number _____

Instrument Condition _____

Are there scratches, dings or dents _____ Where _____

Loan Length _____ (Semester, Year, or Summer)

Loan Date _____

Return Date _____

Return Condition _____

Student Signature _____ Date _____

Parent/Guardian Signature _____

INVENTORY FORM

Instrument _____   Brand _____

Instrument Serial Number _____ Model Number _____

Year of Purchase _____

Condition _____

Finish _____ (with or without lacquer)

MUSIC LIBRARY CARD

Song Title _____

Style _____

Group: Concert Band _____ Symphonic Band _____ Wind Ensemble _____

Jazz Ensemble _____

Last Performed _____

Grade Level _____

File Number _____

PART TWO

QUICK REFERENCE VERSION

1

So You Want to Be a Band Director!

When you decide to train to become a band director you must realize that there are many responsibilities of the job for which you won't be trained. The job entails tasks that are related to business, personnel management, sales, administration, and marketing. Very few teacher-training programs, if any, have band budget-development courses; office- and staff-management courses; public relations training; sales, marketing, and advertising training or basic administration courses on the undergraduate level. This does not mean that you shouldn't prepare yourself in these areas.

Recruiting for your band will be one of the first and most important jobs you will do. If you can't sell your program to kids from feeder schools or inside your school, chances of your program growing are slim. Good marketing means getting people to realize the value of what you're selling. Before your band plays a single note and you have a real product to sell, you're selling the idea of participating in band. You are selling yourself and your vision. How well you present your ideas and sell your mission will mean attracting students or pushing them away.

At some point you will be hiring adjunct faculty members to coach sections of your band. You will have to review candidates' qualifications and hire the right personnel. You should interview candidates for each position and make sure that they are willing to follow your vision of what the program should be. This is where your best personnel manager/human resources skills come in.

Once you've hired the personnel for your band and put your student leaders in place, you'll need to manage your staff. This means laying out clear expectations and holding everyone accountable for his job performance (the same will be true for your band students performing their jobs). A good manager is also a good motivator. The effective manager creates an environment where people want to do their best and look forward to coming in to do their jobs. Good management skills are vital for today's band director.

Good leaders are good administrators. Good administrators articulate their vision to others and get them to follow their lead. As a band director you will discover the need to develop a plan (such as a mission statement) that incorporates your goals and your vision and sell that vision/plan to your school's administration, students, and parents.

PREPARING YOURSELF FOR YOUR NEW PROFESSION

How do you prepare yourself for success in your new position? How do you go about transforming yourself from student to teacher? What kind of a support system will you need to help you establish yourself in the position and create a strong band program? How will you attract students to your new program? Are you prepared? In order to answer these questions and go about preparing yourself for the first day you stand in front of your class, you must make extensive plans that involve self-preparation and devising a plan for building and maintaining a successful band program. This requires systematic planning and finding external resources and creating a help system or a resource network. The thing you must remember is that you are not alone and there are organizations and services available to you. Creating a resource network should be a major priority.

Creating a Resource Network

One of the first things you should do as a new director is to join your state music teaching association. This provides you with a network of skilled professionals who will be willing to answer your questions and help to allay your fears. State music associations are affiliates of MENC, the National Association of Music Education. MENC and its state affiliates have resources that are designed to provide you with the resources needed to be a successful band director. Attending in-service conventions on the state, regional, and national levels will help you to be able to associate with some of the best and brightest music educators around. State association and the MENC websites have electronic forums that allow you to post specific questions that will be answered by mentors who have faced some of the very problems you are facing or will face. The resource system you've created should be used for feedback before you've gone too far in the process of developing your program's objectives. Waiting for an entire semester to solicit assistance may be too late if there is a problem in your plan, goal, or terminal objective (the objective you hope to achieve by the end of a specified period of time).

2

Building a Program in Your
Current School or a New School

PREPARING FOR THE INTERVIEW

The current trend now for hiring band directors is to have an interview team made up of parents, students, administrators, and the choral director or other music faculty members. Each of these stakeholders will have a different expectation and concern you'll need to address. For a successful interview, you should be sure that you express an understanding for each member of the interview team's interests or concerns. Your first priority should be to clearly articulate what your personal philosophy of music education is.

Personal Philosophy Development

1. State your belief in the importance of music education in the education of the "whole" child. This means that aesthetic education (creative courses) helps to round out a person and gives her a means of expressing herself creatively. Explain why it is important for people to realize themselves through creative expression.
2. Explain how music is a lifelong endeavor. Every student may not become a performer but most will become consumers and/or audience members. In order for the arts to survive and for people to enjoy leisure activities involving music, they must be informed consumers and patrons. State how much value music has in the everyday life of people. Include how music relates to an individual's cultural, ethnic, and nationalistic identity. An act such as singing the national anthem requires a fundamental understanding of music.

3. Address how your personal view of music shapes your understanding of the importance of music as part of the American educational system.

4 Define what music education is in your opinion and how it applies to your personal philosophy of music education. Speak in specific terms, not broad generalizations.

5. State why music is as important as other subjects in American schools. Marching band is not just taught in schools to support athletic activities and events. Music is a stand-alone subject with its own weight and importance. The self-discipline learned in music is important to personality development. Music is the first course of study that requires young students to do serious independent study at an early age. Art starts at an early age but the principles of art learned by younger students are not the same principles learned by older and advanced students. Students who learn to read music in elementary school are reading the same music as older students though it may be at a lower level of difficulty.

Preparing to Meet Your Students

As soon as you are named to the new position, you should prepare a letter to be sent to the homes of current students, post a letter on the school or music department's web page, and plan a meeting with students and parents. An informal meeting as a get-together is a good idea. This gives you an opportunity to mingle with individuals or small groups of students. A pizza party for the students works well and organizing a potluck dinner or cookout for parents and students also works well. In either case the objective is to give your students and their parents an opportunity to get to know you as a person and it gives you an opportunity to get to know them. It is important that you are as open with the students and parents as possible. Connecting on an informal level gives you an opportunity to express how much you are looking forward to what you and your students can achieve and how much you have to offer your students. If you can passionately express your love for music and band and your enthusiasm for doing the job, it will be contagious and your students will feed off of your enthusiasm and passion.

Recruiting

One of the most important activities for building a band program at any level is recruiting. There are several ways to recruit but the common denominator is creating interest in you and your program. When starting a program it is as important that potential students know about you as much as it is important that they know your program goals.

Retaining

Whether on the elementary, middle school, or high school level, retaining students currently in your program is of the utmost importance. One of the best ways to achieve this on the high school level is to have your students actively participate in writing a program mission statement or setting terminal objectives. Students drop out of band most often because the music is too hard or not challenging enough. Finding a balance between those two groups is important for the success of your program. You as the director must be able to identify students at risk of dropping out.

Scheduling Band Classes to Aid in Retaining

One of the most overlooked ways of retention is avoiding scheduling conflicts. Music students tend to be some of the most academically advanced students in most schools. That means that there are chances that music classes will conflict with honors classes or classes designed for higher-level students. Knowing this makes it crucial that you communicate this concern with class schedulers and your administration so that these conflicts can be avoided. As a band director you need to take an active part in your school's scheduling. The first step is to make sure that your administration is aware of the fact that your students are involved in advanced classes.

DEVELOPING A FIVE-YEAR PLAN

Before you set program goals, you need to develop your own philosophy of teaching. What do you want to do as a professional? What do you want your students to gain from working with you? What resources do you need to have to achieve your individual goals? Once you've decided where you want to go personally, you can then decide on what you want to achieve with the program you wish to build. Whenever you set goals, you always start with the end product first and then work your way backward. Simply put, where do you see your program five years in the future? If you can't visualize the finished product, you have nothing to strive toward. This shouldn't be vague; you must specifically state your plan: "In five years I'll have the best band program in my district." Once you establish specifically what you hope to achieve with your group you need to work with them to develop a group "mission statement." You can call this statement whatever you want—that's not important. What is important is getting the group to decide on a unified goal to strive toward.

WRITING A MISSION STATEMENT

A sample mission statement could be written and stated in this manner:

It is the Mission of the Atlantis Middle School Band to promote, enhance, and maximize music performance levels of all students of Atlantis Middle School.

Reclaiming

Reclaiming former students should be an activity of all stakeholders—current members, parents, staff, and you, the director. Having students who are currently in the program "reach out" to students you wish to reclaim is very important. Don't underestimate the effectiveness of personal contact.

1. Identify the students you want to reclaim. As was stated before, you may not want to reclaim all of the students who left your program.
2. Present a united front. You don't all have to say the same things the same way but every "recruiter" should have talking points that highlight your goals. Avoid generalizations and be specific as to why you think the student will benefit your program and benefit from your program.
3. List the program's goals and points from the mission statement and how they relate to the student being recruited. Highlight points that specifically apply to the student. If he is a low brass player and you need low brass players, tell him how much his returning to the program will mean to everyone. Tell him how much he can contribute to the group's attaining their goals.
4. Stress how much they are missed. All students like to know that they are needed. Letting these students know that their contributions to the group were significant and that without them participating things are just not the same. They may or may not have been soloists or leaders but that doesn't mean that their contribution wasn't important to the life of the group. Stress that a group is no stronger than the sum of its parts.

Remember, the important part of reclaiming former students is that it will give your band continuity from year to year. If students don't see band as a four-year commitment you will find yourself rebuilding every year.

WRITING A SYLLABUS

The music supervisor for most school districts has a description or syllabus for each type of band class (e.g., Beginning Band, Intermediate Band,

Marching Band, Concert Band, Symphonic Band, and Wind Ensemble). If there is a class description or syllabus available, you can customize it to apply to your particular school and classes. The syllabus should clearly state your class expectations, the class description, your grading policy, discipline policy, performance attire, and how the final or semester grades will be determined. You may customize your class syllabus to address your objectives for the grade level of music a particular band will study. Since this is a class, it's wise to use the term study to refer to rehearsal pieces so that parents and administrators are aware of the educational value of your class. The misconception of how easy it is to successfully participate in a music class is expelled once your syllabus clearly states that you expect your students to be active learners. Stating your lesson plans in behavioral terms will reinforce this concept.

If there are prerequisites for a class, a limited number of parts, or if the class is by audition only, a description of each of these requirements must be listed and explained in the syllabus. Parents and prospective students may not know the difference between a class listed as Concert Band from a Symphonic Band or Wind Ensemble. If the progression you expect is for students to move from Concert Band to Symphonic Band and then audition for Wind Ensemble, you need to clearly state that. Students may be able to participate in Symphonic Band without participating in Concert Band if your instrumentation needs make that necessary, but to avoid looking as though you arbitrarily made the decision, state that in the syllabus. Since Wind Ensemble sometimes only has one player per part, it may mean that some advanced students will not get to audition for the group due to instrumentation restrictions. Once again, to avoid looking arbitrary, state those restrictions and any exceptions in the syllabus.

Before you set program goals, you need to develop your own philosophy of teaching. What do you want to do as a professional? What do you want your students to gain from working with you? What resources do you need to have to achieve your individual goals? Once you've decided where you want to go personally, you can then decide on what you want to achieve with the program you wish to build. Whenever you set goals, you always start with the end product first and then worked your way backwards. Simply put, where do you see your program five years in the future? If you can't visualize the finished product you have nothing to strive toward. This shouldn't be vague; you must specifically state your plan: "In five years I'll have the best band program in my district." Once you establish specifically what you hope to achieve with your group you need to work with them to develop a group "mission statement." You can call this statement whatever you want—that's not important. What is important is getting the group to decide on a unified goal to strive toward.

3

Creating a Handbook for Band

PROGRAM DESCRIPTION

Your program description should be a clear, unambiguous statement of your expectations of what your program will be. You should make it clear to everyone who reads it what your vision of the program is and what you expect it to become under your leadership. Allow for there to be space for you and your students to develop a mission statement so that they will have a stake in the program's success. This will give them an opportunity to take ownership in the program. This ownership will lead to their having accountability in the success or failure of the program based on a mutual vision.

Grading Policy

Your grading policy and the percentage of the grade each activity will be averaged on should be spelled out completely. Class participation, tests or quizzes, festival participation, concert and performance participation, special class projects, outside-of-school concert attendance, and individual performance assessments are a few of the items that should be included. This list can be customized based on your expectations or requirements stated by your school district. A lot of school districts have standardized grading policies and expectations so print those exactly as stated in your handbook.

4

Developing Lesson Plans

A lot of band directors make the mistake of thinking that they don't need lesson plans. For every rehearsal you and your students must be clear on what you expect to achieve during that rehearsal. The lesson plan should state what you hope to focus on and achieve but also be flexible enough for you to be able to handle problems that may come up during the rehearsal. Example: If your lesson plan is based on articulation for a specific section of a piece but you discover that students are having technical difficulties, clear up the technical problems and return to your written plans. If you are being observed by administrators, it's important that you explain to them the elasticity of your lesson plan for the day. Since they are not always aware of how band classes are managed and how our goals differ from other classes, it's imperative that you make it clear that letting a problem go unresolved in order to stay "true" to the lesson plan negatively impacts the overall goal for your program. You, your class, and any observers must understand that each lesson is building on a measurable goal of excellence and achievement during performances. Audiences may not be aware of your plan but they will be aware of whether or not your band has achieved its goals.

ARTICULATION QUICK FIXES

Articulation is a key to accurate attacks and releases. It is important that you explain to your students the fundamentals of proper articulation. There are a few quick fixes you can use to explain basic articulations and have your students execute them properly.

Simple Articulation Fixes/Explanations

Staccato: Short and detached.

Tenuto: Note held full value until the start of the next note.

Marcato: An accented short and detached note sometimes referred to as a "bell tone." This can also be thought of as an accented staccato note.

Legato: A slurred note; notes that fall under a slur mark should not be tongued except for the first note under each slur mark.

Accent: A full value note that begins with a heavy attack; the decay is determined by the duration of the note.

SCORE STUDY

How well you are prepared before a lesson/rehearsal will determine how effective you are. Just because you performed a piece in high school or college doesn't mean you know the piece. Score study enables you to determine what sections of the piece will be most challenging to the group as a whole or selected instrument sections. Work through how you will present and rehearse these difficult or challenging parts. The more organized you are before the lesson, the more organized your rehearsal will be. If you must consult method books or professional players to determine the best way to help different sections of your band, do it.

As a band director, you may not know the pedagogy of each instrument and many problems are unique to different instruments so seek out help and assistance. Contact another band director who may have experienced similar problems, contact a former college instructor, or contact a master musician if necessary. The bottom line is that once you have studied the score and determined your personal limitations, you can help your students with theirs. If necessary, rewrite or simplify parts that are beyond the technical reach of your students. Some lower-grade pieces may have difficult parts for some instruments and less challenging parts for others. Double parts with instruments of similar sounds (double horn parts with alto saxophones or baritone horn parts with tenor saxophones, etc.).

Make Notes on the Score

The idea that a score must remain pristine gets in the way of score evaluation and score study. Circle sections of the piece that will require special attention. Don't give judges at a festival a copy of your work score because it will provide a guide for them to recognize your group's problems or weaknesses. On your work score, write in the solutions you have prepared to explain the challenges of the piece to your students. An annotated score provides you with a narrative to be used to explain the challenges to your students. You may forget something important if you depend solely on your memory. Score study will also help you to create program notes for concert audiences. The notes that you prepare for audiences should be based on the same narrative you have used to introduce the piece to your students.

PACING YOUR REHEARSAL

Many directors have difficulty determining the pace at which student learning should take place. Because students in your band class will have varying abilities, the pace at which they learn will vary. Determining when to press on with a lesson and when to pull up is difficult. You must gain a sense for when you should step away from your quest for perfection. Some lessons will be immediately grasped by your students and others may take quite a while to be achieved. One solution for this problem is to break your lessons/rehearsals down to manageable short units. Trying to achieve too much too soon can be discouraging to you and your students.

5

A Successful First Performance

PLANNING FOR A SUCCESSFUL FIRST PERFORMANCE

The success of your students' first performance has long-term ramifications. If elementary school students step away from a good first performance with positive feelings, they will strive to repeat those feelings in subsequent performances. It also determines whether or not they want to remain in band and continue through their school career. At every level these students will strive to recapture the joy of that first experience and measure their enjoyment based on the feeling they had during their first concert.

Much care must be taken to choose literature (at any level) that will be challenging but accessible to your students. If the music is too easy your students won't be motivated to practice or prepare for the performance, and if the music is too challenging they will be discouraged by the lack of individual or group success. In every group there will be students who can play well or who are motivated to practice to master the music you choose. Conversely, there will be students who find it very difficult to master the same piece of music and some who do not like to practice. Finding a "happy median" is a challenge for you. One way to challenge the advanced players is to transcribe parts for missing instruments or underrepresented parts. You can also have the advanced students peer coach students at the lower levels. When having students pair up for peer coaching you must prepare the coaches to be nurturing rather than highly critical of the lower-level players. There can be strong bonds formed between these students and they will be protective and supportive of one another. If not managed correctly, this can have a negative impact on your band. You must closely monitor what's going on in these peer coaching sessions. Once the students return from the peer coaching session you should have them play the parts they worked on for the rest of the band. Praise their accomplishment when they have had an effective session and use nurturing, encouraging words to steer them in the direction that you wish to see them move toward.

Most elementary and middle school groups have very few low brass players and an overabundance of trumpets, alto saxophones, clarinets, and flutes. If you need to rewrite parts to boost the group or represent missing parts, the following substitutions can be used. (You should also encourage some of the better players to switch to one of the needed/missing instruments.) Trumpets and alto saxophones can be used to cover F horn, clarinet, and baritone horn parts. Alto and tenor saxophones can cover F horn, baritone horn and trombone parts. Flutes and clarinets can cover trumpet parts and the melody no matter what part the melody is written for (they can be doubled by trumpets, alto saxophones, and tenor saxophones). If the melody is written for low brass, saxophones can give you the desired color based on the composer's intent (tenor saxophone can cover a tuba melody much better than a flute). Based on the Fair Use section of the United States Copyright Law, "Printed copies which have been purchased may be edited or simplified provided that the fundamental character of the work is not distorted."[1] In order to maintain the integrity of the piece your rewriting should be done in such a way that the substitutions sound musically logical.

The success of that first performance will depend on how musical your transcriptions are and how well parts are presented. Should you be fortunate enough to have the scored instrumentation, your task is still to make sure that the balances of your group maintain the integrity of the piece. During the rehearsal you need to maintain focus so that students develop cross listening skills that will make them conscious of where the melody is and how it travels through the band. Once students identify the melodic line(s) they will be more sensitive to adjusting the dynamics of the "supporting" parts. After you've made every attempt at balance and part representation then you can work on intonation, articulation, rhythmic accuracy, facility, and many other points that will be constants in subsequent performances.

Every performance you have should build on the success of the first performance. Whatever problems and successes you have in that first performance should be discussed the very next time the group rehearses. If you video or audio tape that performance have a guided listening session during the next rehearsal. Have the students listen critically to the performance and share their impressions. Then, have them play the sections they discussed and make the corrections that you feel are needed. If a student made the correct observation, credit him and praise his observation and solution. This simple exercise helps reinforce the "ownership" part of the mission statement. This is why participants are called "stakeholders." Stakeholders have a vested interest in the success of the group. Passive participants generally don't care how well or how poorly things go. Most groups will do what they are told to do from the podium but unless they "buy into" the finished product, the group won't be as successful as it should be.

On the high school level, marching band is involved in the first performance. Whether it is for a pep rally, parade, or football game, the success of your program depends on how your students feel walking away from that performance. You should choose literature that will be of interest to your students and the audience. Marching band/pep band should be the only time that the audience's reaction will be the determining factor for your music choice.

A lot of bands participate in competitions during the fall and choose music for the competitions and ignore playing for school activities. This is a mistake. Judges at competitions will award points or trophies; school students will talk about your band's performance in the halls, cafeteria, and stadium stands. The positive feeling your students get from peer acceptance goes a lot farther than having trophies in trophy cases (though trophies have value also). Students who stay in the program stay because their peers reinforce the fact that band is a cool place to be.

Band is only a competitive activity when directors make it a competitive activity. In competitions, there are winners and losers. In band you should nurture individual and group achievements that help students feel good about how well they have done in comparison to what they did previously (irrespective of what place you come in). This is different from how well they do in comparison to other groups. Competitions can help you set a standard for where you want your group to go and what you want to achieve but the reason for participating in competitions should be made clear.

If you choose music for competitions you should also choose songs that will help with school spirit during pep rallies and games. A video from a home football game or a pep rally can go a long way with your recruiting and retention. If students remember how well received they were during their first pep rally or game, their self/group esteem will rise. Students who enjoy activities are more likely than not to continue in those activities.

NOTE

1. *The United States Copyright Law: A Guide for Music Educators.* New York: Music Publishers' Association. Revised 2003 Copyright Act, 17 U.S.C., §107 Appendix A. www.menc.org/resources/view/united-states-copyright-law-a-guide-for-music-educators-appendix-a-g#a

6

Developing a Support System for your Band Program

STARTING A BAND BOOSTERS CLUB

When forming a boosters group, it is important that you establish rules and bylaws. These bylaws and rules should clearly state the purpose and function of the group and the group's administrative limitations. It is important that it is clear that the group must abide by school policy and cannot make decisions concerning your group without your approval. The bylaws should be consistent with your school's policies and must be approved by your administration.

Here is a sample of how to form your bylaws.

The _____ Band Boosters Club is established to offer support to the _____ band. The function of the group is to provide financial support, a pool of chaperones, organize support activities, provide awards and recognition, and perform tasks specified by the band director as needed. A checking account will be established in the name of the _____ Band Boosters and two signatures will be needed to conduct any business or write/ endorse any checks. One of those signatures must always be the band director's. No business or official meetings may be held without the band director's presence or knowledge. This does not include committee meetings as designated by the director or the Band Boosters Club.

Marching Band Support from the Boosters Club

Marching band season has special needs, especially if you have a competitive band. If you have equipment that needs to be loaded and unloaded, moved to and from the field, set up and dismantled, these are jobs that parents and other supporters can do. Parents can also help you secure a truck to transport equipment to and from away football games and competitions; a golf cart and trailer to transport equipment to and from the band room to the football field; and just offer bodies to physically carry large equipment. Parents with vans, SUVs, station wagons, and other large vehicles should be encouraged to form a transportation committee. This committee can be used to transport instruments and sets used for competitions. They can also be used to transport uniforms to and from the cleaners or transport rain gear to games and/or competitions. Anything you need picked up or delivered can be done by this committee. It is better to use this adult resource than face the liabilities involved in using student drivers. Check your school district for rules and liabilities governing parents transporting students before having them transport any student(s).

Some special needs unique to marching band are:

- Uniform purchases and fundraising to purchase uniforms
- Uniform cleaning costs (unless students are required to clean them)
- Providing cooling aids for hot weather performances
- Providing rain wear
- Outdoor heaters for cold weather performances
- Providing costumes for special performances
- Securing flags or silks
- Getting footwear
- Paying contest entry fees
- Securing cold weather protection
- Purchasing materials used for building scenery or props
- Setting up scenery or props for performances or competitions
- Transporting instruments and equipment to away from school performances

Fundraising Committee

Even though every group requires fundraising, there should be only one fundraising committee with several subcommittees. The financial officer should head all of the fundraising activities. Having a central location for fundraising information you and your supporters have an opportunity to pool resources. You should establish a percentage of funds raised by each group's subcommittee that will go into the program's main treasury. Parents generally don't like funds raised for their child's group to be applied to another group, so establishing this percentage upfront is very important. This also helps you to have an amount of funds that can be applied to any group that may need financial assistance during the year. If you have parents who are tech savvy, they can maintain a spreadsheet for you to have instant access to the amount of ready cash you have on hand. Canvass your parents and take advantage of any accountants or financial experts you may have at your disposal. During the first parent meeting be very clear about the expertise you will need. You may be surprised by the resources that parents bring to the table.

7

Festival Participation and Preparation

BAND FESTIVAL PREPARATION

Planning for Festivals

Festivals are a good way to assess your band's progress toward your goal. You, your students, and three independent music educators will analyze your execution of two judged pieces and your sight-reading ability. Preparing your students for a positive festival experience is important to gaining the most educational value from festival participation.

- Record the band and have them listen critically to evaluate their progress.
- Have students maintain a festival score sheet and grade themselves the way the judges would grade them.
- Fill out a festival grade sheet yourself the day before the festival and grade the band. Seal your sheet in an envelope and share your comments with them, comparing what you said with what the judges said. If the judges said the same things you said, point that out. If the judges said something that you didn't say, use that to prepare your students for the next performance.
- Play the tape of the band's performance without the judges' comments before playing the tapes with their comments. Have your students write their comments on the evaluation form and compare what they heard with what the judges said.

The worst mistake you could make would be to discount or dismiss the judges' comments. This diminishes the festival experience value. Your students don't elevate you when you make disparaging remarks about the judges; they simply dismiss the value of participating in the festival, and preparing for the next festival will be more difficult. The educational value of a festival is based on how well your students have learned to execute the music and how well they presented it. The two cannot be separated and it is important that you openly discuss their success and/or failure. You can't praise the judges for their positive comments or grades at one festival and criticize their comments at another festival.

8

Developing a Budget for Your Band

In order to effectively establish a working budget, it is important that you list expected income and expenditures. There are standing expenditures that will go from year to year. Some of these expenses include uniform cleaning, instrument maintenance and repairs, festival and/or competition registration fees, bus rentals, and music purchasing.

Here is a sample of the kinds of items that your budget should include. Because every school district is unique, you may have to add or subtract items. This is not an absolute budget; it is only designed to provide you with an outline of expected expenditures so that you may calculate the income needed to maintain your program. Some directors use a two-year budget.

Supplies and Materials: photocopy paper, audio tapes and/or recordable compact discs, football field lining materials, simple repair kit materials, music notation pads and/or workbooks, pencils, markers, and music notation software.

Maintenance: piano tuning, instrument repairs, drum heads and marching band equipment needs, office equipment repairs and maintenance, audio-visual equipment maintenance and repairs, stand repairs or replacements.

Festival and Competition: bus rental, festival fees, solo and ensemble fees, festival music purchases, extra scores for judges.

Equipment Replacement/Purchases: inventory replacement needs, uniform purchases, mouthpieces, mallets and sticks, music stand purchases, sound equipment for recording, sound equipment for playback and classroom use, chairs, music cabinets, instrument storage cages, television monitors, DVD or video tape machine, CD player/recorder, video camera or recording equipment, marching band flags, flag poles, and so on.

Travel Expenses: transportation costs, meals, lodging, shipping costs.

Costs unique to marching band:

- Uniform purchases and fundraising to purchase uniforms
- Uniform cleaning costs (unless students are required to clean them)
- Providing cooling aids for hot weather performances
- Providing rain wear
- Outdoor heaters for cold weather performances
- Providing costumes for special performances
- Securing flags or silks
- Getting footwear
- Paying contest entry fees
- Securing cold weather protection
- Purchasing materials used for building scenery or props
- Setting up scenery or props for performances or competitions
- Transporting instruments and equipment to away from school performances

9

Developing Musicianship in Band Class

One of the most important things to remember about band is that it is a class. Students must be challenged and engaged at all times. A lot of directors feel that teaching comprehensive musicianship in class takes away from practice time. It is time-consuming and involves preparing conductor's notes on the music you're rehearsing, but in the long run your rehearsals will be a lot more productive. Once students understand the periodic style of a piece, the composer's intent, the nationalistic background, and so on, the more interested they may become in their individual preparation. Every band student is not just interested in music; some like history and receiving information on different cultures. As you discuss these points you appeal to a group of students you may not keep engaged with just discussing musical terms and performance techniques. Your question may be, "Isn't this a band class and isn't that what I'm supposed to do?" Yes, it is to an extent but you must keep in mind every band student will not pursue music beyond high school. Keeping nonmusic majors engaged will help the overall performance level of your group.

10

Classroom Management

In your efforts to maintain students in your program the classroom environment plays a major role. As was stated earlier, students lose interest in programs where they feel their time is being wasted. Lesson plans give you an outline to follow that will keep you and your students focused on immediate goals. Most disciplinary problems occur in an environment that is disorganized. If students get bored or feel that their time is not valued, they tend to act out. This acting out can manifest in many ways—from harmless talking in small groups to arguments and fights. When discipline gets out of control, you'll be forced to take immediate action. How you react can escalate the situation or diffuse it. Of course, the best situation is to avoid the need to take action altogether.

Your level of organization will directly affect the level of discipline in the classroom. Effective teachers are organized and know how to manage time. Efficient use of time is important in keeping your students engaged and productive. The time you take to present an organized, well-planned rehearsal will reap great benefits.

When choosing literature for your band, you must be mindful of your instrumentation and your students' playing ability. Start the rehearsal by telling your students how much time you expect them to take getting their instruments out, getting their music, and taking their seats prepared to start the warm-up. The more organized you are, the better the rehearsal environment will be. The key to this is writing clear lesson plans. Of course, if you expect them to be in place and ready to rehearse, you must be ready to start the rehearsal once they are. If you start your rehearsals at the time you have established as the class start time, your students will gather their materials and instruments in a time efficient way. From the start of the rehearsal until the end time of the rehearsal before the bell, your students should have a clear focus on the objectives you have established for that day's lesson.

MANAGING DISCIPLINE

Discipline in band rehearsals is a challenge for new teachers and experienced teachers alike. You don't want the classroom environment to be such that it stifles creativity or inhibits students' performance, or so loose that students' unrest distracts other students. Every time the director has to stop the rehearsal to handle a discipline problem, time is taken away from constructive work time. Discipline is based on the director's rapport with the class and the amount of respect students have for the director and their classmates. The simple act of stating clear directions of what you expect to accomplish during a class period can head off some behavior problems.

Self-discipline is the most important factor to avoiding class discipline problems. If students can manage their behavior, there won't be any discipline problems that require the director's attention. Problems generally start from small infractions that go unchecked. If the director permits an undercurrent of talking to go on unchecked, that talking will get increasingly louder and involve more students.

The best way to handle disciplinary problems in band rehearsals is to remove the causes of those problems or avoid them completely. Time-management problems and a disorganized rehearsal lead to most problems. Boredom and lack of focus by students cause other problems. When students know that they will be held accountable, they will very seldom cause problems. One strategy is that while working with one group of students, remind the other students that you will come to their section next or ask them to evaluate how well the section you're working with has followed your instructions. This simple act serves to keep them engaged and focused. If they don't see how the work you're doing with one section applies to them, they'll become disengaged. Assign a specific amount of time you're going to spend on a problem and have a student in another section be your timekeeper to make sure you don't run over the allotted time. This gives the students the message that you respect their time and that they are expected to achieve results in a reasonable amount of time. If students feel that they don't have a limited time to resolve an issue, they may not focus fully on resolving the problem. If you want your students to be organized and efficient in their practice time, you must model that behavior. If you're not focused on what you expect to achieve, they won't be either.

Far too often, discipline problems are not caused by students. There are times that discipline problems are caused by the teacher. Here are some of the teacher-caused discipline problems:

- The teacher fails to be organized by outlining class expectations, management, and class rules.
- The way the teacher reacts to in-class problems shows favoritism or is not enforced uniformly throughout the group.
- The teacher enters the classroom late or leaves the class unattended.
- Class instructions are not stated clearly for students to understand.
- The teacher uses sarcasm that students interpret as the teacher "putting them down."
- The teacher corrects musical errors in a way that students feel is unfair or arbitrary.
- The teacher confronts a student one on one in front of the class and the student feels a need to "save face" in front of their peers.
- There is a lack of lesson plans or statement of class objectives.
- The teacher fails to start class on time or dismiss class on time.
- The teacher talks too long or discusses a problem to the point that students become restless, reeds dry up, or numerous other problems to instruments occur.
- The teacher is obviously not prepared for class and students feel their time is being wasted.

You may notice that some of the same issues that cause discipline problems are also the reason some students decide not to enroll in class for the next term or semester. There is a relationship between class morale and discipline. If the director allows class morale to drop, productivity and efficiency will also drop. The teacher's attitude is contagious. Negative behavior and negative reactions spread through the band. Sometimes the teacher's nonverbal communication affects the band and the director has no idea he has caused the problem. Just as your enthusiasm for the job yields positive reactions and enthusiasm from your students, so does your negative attitude about your students, their actions, and their playing have a negative impact.

Strategies for Avoiding Discipline Problems

The simplest way to avoid discipline problems is to do the opposite of what causes discipline problems. This may sound simple but in reality it takes much work on the teacher's part. The most difficult thing to avoid is allowing your body language to betray you and show negative reactions to classroom problems. Positive reinforcement for positive behavior and good work will help students to feel good about their work and their participation in class. Avoiding the use of sarcasm, embarrassing students in front of the class, and criticizing students' performance will help avoid confrontation. Some band directors choose to use intimidation tactics that they heard were used by some legendary band directors. This practice will very seldom create the kind of environment that is needed for a positive band experience for your students.

If students perceive your rules to be fair and evenly enforced, they will follow them with minimal problems. Directors who know how to manage their class in a positive way usually discover that students respond in a like manner. Realizing that you can't and shouldn't shame students into practicing or preparing for class is discovered by inexperienced teachers very quickly. Negative generally breeds negative and positive usually breeds positive. Your use of positive reinforcement should not be perceived as your condoning bad behavior, and you should make that clear if you choose to handle the problem at the end of class. Make it clear to the offending student and the rest of the class that you will address the problem but that you don't wish to waste more class time due to this discipline problem.

Of course, there will be some students who are discipline problems irrespective of what the director's strategy is. In these cases, the teacher should quickly act to diminish the effect of these discipline problems. The first way to address the problem is to speak with the student one on one. If that doesn't work, the teacher should arrange a parent–teacher conference. As a last resort (depending on the severity of the problem), the teacher should refer the student to the administration for corrective actions. This should be the last resort so that it doesn't appear to your students or the administration that you can't handle discipline in the classroom. Classroom management is a major part of your teaching responsibilities.

During the first week of school you should:

- Establish your expectation for entering the classroom.
- Describe the procedure for getting instruments out and pretuning.
- Describe how to get music folders from the music shelves.
- Establish that when you are on the podium, all talking and playing stops.
- Establish consequences for not following the rules.
- Describe how to return music to the shelves and instruments to storage areas.
- Establish that the bell does not dismiss class—you dismiss class.

11

Improving Your Band's Performance

Preparing for the first performance and establishing standards for future performances lay the groundwork for improving your band's performance level. Once you have provided your students with the tools they will need for individual preparation and performance, it is important that you constantly remind them of these principles and reinforce them.

After every performance, you'll need to set aside time in the next rehearsal to evaluate and discuss the strengths and weaknesses of the performance. It's important that you stress that the evaluation is for recognizing the good qualities of the performance as well as using constructive criticism to help improve future performances. As the moderator, you should strive to focus on the positive rather than the negative. If your students point out a few problems with attacks and releases, have them listen further to determine if there were places where the attacks and releases were better than they had been in rehearsals leading up to the performance. This stresses the point that even though they may have fallen short of the objective, there was still improvement on the group's part. Do not allow the discussion to become personal; refer to sections or parts only, not individual players even if there is only one player per part. Stress that audiences don't hear individuals, they hear a band.

VIDEO AND AUDIO TAPE PERFORMANCES

It is difficult to critique the band based on memories of the performance. Everyone will have a different perspective based on where they sit in the band. An audio tape or a video tape will give everyone an opportunity to listen objectively and focus on the group as a whole, not section by section or part by part. Video tapes give the added visual effects that audiences have during the performance. If there are visual distractions that cause problems in the performance, the video will give you and your students an opportunity to see them. Foot tapping, besides being a visual distraction, will also cause rushing. As you watch the tape, you as the director can make a point about the relationship between rushing in a particular section of the piece and the foot tapping or other visual distractions that caused the band to rush. Peripheral vision causes players to see things that will distract their attention from the podium. If the group misses entrance cues or expression cues because they weren't looking at the podium due to a visual distraction, point out the importance of being focused on the conducting and listening to what's going on around them musically.

Audio tapes provide you and your students with an opportunity to listen to the performance without being distracted by visuals. If you have an audio and video tape of the performance, it is wise to listen to the audio tape first. Have your students follow their music as they listen to the tape. Once the tape has been played, use a guided activity to have them state their observations. An example of this would be to ask the students how well they followed the expression marks in the music for a specific section of the piece. Another example would be to have the students identify where the melodic line was obscured by the balance being improperly executed. All of the principles of a good performance that you have outlined previously should be touched on. This will cause your students to listen more discriminately and hopefully it will cause them to self-correct going into the next performance.

12

Developing an Elementary Band Program

Some school districts with small budgets assign one instrumental music teacher to multiple schools. Many of these teachers have very little experience or knowledge of developing a band program at the elementary level. Unlike middle school or high school, elementary band classes are usually "pull-out" classes, meaning that students are pulled out of their classroom to go to band for thirty or forty-five minutes. Because art, band, orchestra, and some physical education classes are all pull-out classes, careful planning must be done. Another problem arises when teachers are assigned to more than one school. The schedule must be based on when the teacher is in the school.

Some music supervisors plan the days and times each elementary teacher is assigned to a school but in smaller districts the teacher and principals of each school must agree on a schedule. If the teacher is also assigned to a middle school and/or high school, this further complicates the problem.

One of the first priorities for developing an elementary school schedule is to determine the number of students in each school. This will determine class size and groupings (all brass in one class, all woodwinds, all percussion, or mixed instrumentation).

When starting a beginning band at the elementary level, the teacher must be aware of the fact that students will start off on one instrument and later move on to another instrument. Here are some of the instruments students will move to along with the "jump off" instruments:

Starting instruments—Trumpets or cornets, B-flat clarinets, flutes, alto saxophones, trombones, snare drum, baritone horn, or tuba

Instruments to change to—French horn, oboe, bassoon, bass clarinet, alto clarinet, timpani, xylophone, tenor saxophone, baritone saxophone and contra-bass clarinet, tuba (if not used as a starter instrument)

13

Structuring Your Concert Band, Symphonic Band, and Wind Ensemble

LARGE INSTRUMENTAL PERFORMANCE GROUPS

When going into a new school, it is your hope that you will have the instrumentation that you need to form a band that is able to perform music that is scored for concert band. Unfortunately, when building a band program you will probably not have ideal instrumentation. If this is the case, you have two options: one, you can adjust the score to match the instrumentation that you have or two, you can choose to have small, mixed, or homogenous ensembles.

Should you decide the latter, there is literature written for mixed instruments that can be performed at ensemble festivals not band festivals. If your band is under thirty members, you may wish to teach band literature in class but prepare small-ensemble literature for ensemble festivals. This may require more work on your part, but having model groups in your program to present publicly will help with building your program by quality and quantity. Getting enough instrumentation to form a concert band is a major priority for the new director. You need to have at least one band in your school that performs classic band literature.

Bands that perform classic band literature and classical music can be called by different names at different schools but most school districts have course descriptions that describe Concert Band, Symphonic Band, and Wind Ensemble as different courses. The term "concert band" is used to describe all three of these bands, without distinction. Depending on the size of your band program's enrollment, your band may be called Concert

Band or Symphonic Band; Wind Ensemble is generally reserved to describe an elite band group.

When describing Concert Band in school districts, the distinction is made that Concert Band is the lowest-level band class in a school. This is the class that incoming freshman students are automatically enrolled in when they sign up for band. Unfortunately, if there are only a few students enrolled in your band program, securing ideal balance on parts will be difficult. Students coming into high school directly from middle school or middle school directly from elementary school will probably be playing flute, clarinet, trumpet, or alto saxophone (the most popular and manageable instruments for younger players). Having oboes, trombones, bassoons, bass clarinets, alto clarinets, French horns, English horns, and contra-bass clarinets in most middle school bands or elementary school bands is rare. Because of this, you will probably have to convert some of your students to a new instrument in order to achieve good balance and meet the instrument requirements of most scores.

OBJECTIVES FOR BANDS IN CONCERT STYLE

Objectives for Concert Band, Symphonic Band, and Wind Ensemble will be the same. It should be that the expectation for execution of these objectives improves as the group level gets higher.

Some of the things you want your bands to be able to do are as follows:

1. Play in tune with themselves and others
2. Listen across the band to trace melodic lines
3. Follow expression markings accurately
4. Adhere to phrase markings
5. Play with rhythmic accuracy
6. Play in the correct style using articulation that complements that style
7. Control dynamic ranges even though outside projection is important
8. Play with good tone control and note shadings
9. Balance within the section and through the entire band
10. Develop good breathing techniques and breath control

WORKING ON INTONATION FOR BAND CLASSES

Intonation is one of the most important elements of good musicianship and good band performances. Standing in front of your band and having them play a given tuning note and telling each student if he or she is sharp, flat, or in tune serves no real purpose. It tells them that the mechanical device you are holding says that they are or are not in tune but does little to help them understand how to hear it for themselves.

One of the best ways to train your students on how important tuning is will be to set up a tuner in the instrument storage room and let the students pretune before taking their seats. Once they have been seated and have warmed up, tune them starting from the lower instruments upward. It's best to tune to two different pitches, Concert B-flat and Concert F. After playing the first rehearsal piece, have your first chair clarinet play a tuning pitch and fine tune the band once more. This lets your students know that tuning is an ongoing process and is a constant concern for bands.

14

Using Small Ensembles to Improve Your Band's Sound

Using small ensembles to improve the overall performance level of your band is a valuable tool for many reasons. The smaller ensemble enables your students to put to use all of the skills required for good band playing. Being able to hear things in a smaller setting is the most valuable aspect of small-ensemble playing. Students can focus on intonation, attacks and releases, balance, rhythmic accuracy, and many other skills needed for accurate large ensemble playing. Not having the distractions of many instruments and being able to concentrate on a small group of instruments allows your students to apply the skills you've taught in the larger group and implement those skills with a high degree of accuracy. They can then apply these skills acquired in small-ensemble playing to the larger ensemble. The subtle ways they are learning these techniques enable them to internalize them and apply them naturally and almost effortlessly.

In the smaller setting of a trio, quartet, quintet, septet, or octet, students can make eye contact with other players as they prepare for entrances. This eye contact reinforces the need to watch for visual cues (such as those provided by a conductor) in order to enter at the right time. These attacks must be precise and can be easily heard if they are not. This may not be as evident in a larger group as it is in a smaller setting, but by hearing it in a smaller setting your students learn to realize how important accurate attacks and releases are. A sloppy or late attack can negatively impact on the small ensemble immediately. Students will hear how important an accurate attack is and how a late attack spreads through a larger group because others are dependent on someone else's attack. Hearing this for themselves in a small ensemble has a greater impact than you trying to describe it in the abstract. As stated earlier, this kind of learning by discovery is invaluable.

15

Developing Satellite Groups for Your Band

Every successful band program offers musical opportunities for its students that vary from solo performances, small-ensemble performances, marching band, pep band, and jazz ensemble. Each of these satellite groups offers a different way of musical expression for your students. In order for your band program to grow you should make every effort to attract students with a wide range of musical interests. Most students don't just want to participate in only one style of music; they have a desire to explore as many styles as are available to them. Some satellite groups include pep band; marching band; jazz ensemble; and woodwind, brass, and percussion ensembles.

Before you start offering classes or extracurricular groups for your students to participate in, you should make sure that you will be able to provide the best participation experience possible. This means making sure that each group maintains the integrity of the style of music they perform. If you do not perform a particular style of music that's being offered, it is your responsibility to learn as much about that style as possible or bring in someone who can assist you. Poor instruction leads to poor performance levels and poor performances will do your program harm.

PEP BAND

When establishing a pep band, your main concern is to select players to cover the instrumentation required by the score and students who will bring pep to school activities. If you cannot get the instrumentation needed for the score, then you must write an arrangement substituting for the missing parts (this will be discussed in more detail in the section on technology and notation software). If the pep band is performing outside during football games, brass instruments and saxophones should be used to carry the melody. Sound projection is the most important element of what instruments should be used. Since flutes and clarinets don't carry well outside, they should be used to double the melody, not carry it alone. For performances inside, flutes and clarinets can be used to carry any melody that is underrepresented by instrumentation. Since gymnasiums are the sites of pep band performances during basketball season, you should limit the number of brasses used. Even though many band directors use marching band arrangements for pep band, there are many published pep band scores. There are music books that are written specifically for pep band. Rather than having to purchase individual songs for use by pep band, select books that have several songs in them. Some of these books specialize in music of specific styles and periods (e.g., '70s, show tunes, etc.)

The typical pep band instrumentation will be twenty to thirty-six members in size, but there is no maximum size. The minimum size would depend on the minimum instrumentation on the score (one player per part). Smaller groups are generally used for indoor performances (basketball games and volleyball games). Most pep bands use three (3) to six (6) trumpets; two (2) to four (4) alto saxophones, one (1) or two (2) tenor saxophones; one (1) baritone saxophone; six (6) clarinets; four (4) to eight (8) flutes; one (1) piccolo; one (1) baritone horn; two (2) French horns; three (3) trombones; one (1) tuba; one (1) drum set or one (1) snare drum, one (1) bass drum and one (1) cymbal. The positioning for playing should have woodwinds in the front rows; trumpets and horns on the next row; trombones, baritone, and tuba on the last row. If you use a drum set, it will be placed on the floor (best at the corner of the band not in front). If you use a snare, bass, and cymbals, they should stand behind the last row or in the side corner beside the band. Remember, sound inside will be amplified by acoustics so you don't want percussion instruments and brasses in the front. Since one of the things you're going to work with your band on is sound projection, you don't want to create balance problems by your setup. If the band plays outside at football games you want to use a larger number of players.

JAZZ ENSEMBLE

Jazz ensemble is a satellite group of your concert band that will give your students a different way of expressing themselves musically. Like pep band and marching band, jazz ensemble plays music that is not classically based. Improvisation is an important component of jazz ensemble and gives students an opportunity to express themselves creatively by doing "spontaneous composition."

MARCHING BAND

Marching band is the "face" of band in most schools. More people will see your marching band than any other group or groups you'll have. Because of this, marching band requires a great deal of planning.

16

Developing a Marching Band as Part of the Complete Band Program

Developing a marching band as part of your band program can be tricky. In most schools, the marching band is the most visible component of the complete band program and the entire band program is judged by its success or failure. Since this is the case, you'll want to make sure that the principles of a good band program are used in the development of the marching band.

During football season, more people will see your marching band at one game than will see any other component of your program during the entire year. Marching bands are viewed by audiences as entertainment but most music educators view them as educational activities. Because of the balance required to have the band be an educational tool for music students and entertainment for audiences, the band director must choose music, show designs, and marching styles that provide both.

One of the decisions the band director must make is what style marching band she will have. The two basic marching band styles fall into two categories—show style, also known as high step, and corps style, known as heel to toe. Each style is unique and requires knowledge of language that is specific to that style. These terms will be described in detail later in this section. Choosing which style to use for your marching band should be decided upon by the make-up of your band and the appeal to your community and the style of music you plan to perform. You should develop knowledge of both styles so that you will not force your group or community to adjust to a style that they won't enjoy. This may not seem practical but remember, this will be your first recruiting tool and the way the community reacts to your band will determine how much support you will receive.

In order to teach musical skills during marching band, the band director must decide on what skills need to be taught. Those skills will be the same skills that will be needed for good band performance for concert band and other inside instrumental performance groups. Students in all bands need to be able to:

1. play in tune with themselves and others;
2. play with rhythmic accuracy;
3. play in the correct style using articulation that complements that style;
4. control dynamic ranges even though projection outside is important;
5. play with good tone even when projecting sound outside;
6. develop good breathing techniques and breath control;
7. have accurate attacks and releases.

These skills need to be taught and reinforced from the first rehearsal until the end of the year. Even though the reality is that marching band has been preparing in a relatively short amount of time, they will be judged as if they have practiced a complete year before their first performance. This may not seem fair but it is a reality. Explaining this to your band will help you to keep them focused.

MARCHING BAND TERMINOLOGY

The following terms are used when teaching or describing marching band. There are many terms used by different bands and regions but the terms listed here are some of the more basic terms.

About Face – a 180-degree turn to face or march in the opposite direction.
At Ease – Instruments may be lowered to a relaxed position; body will not be as erect as parade rest (see "parade rest").
Attention – the process of preparing to receive a command from the director or drum major; standing with feet at a forty-five-degree angle and ready for step off.
Auxiliary - marching units such as color guard, flags/silks, pom-poms.
Battery – percussion section and drum line.
Cadence – the "beat" played by a drum line or percussion for marching on the field or in a parade.
Carriage – the posture of standing upright while marching.
Column – vertical lines formed by marchers directly behind the front rank/horizontal line.
Company – a large group of marchers (generally the entire marching unit made up of smaller groups (see "platoons").

Cut-off – the stopping of marching or the stopping of sound.

Dress – checking your alignment to form a straight line (see "guide right" and "guide left").

Drill – the on-field show or sets for a marching band performance.

Drill Book – the book used to design or hold designs for a show or sets.

Drum Major – the student who conducts the band and leads drills; on-field director and leader; calls commands and sets the tempo of performance pieces.

Eight to Five – eight steps for every five yards marched on a football field.

Fall In – command given to have the group assemble into parade rest positions preparing for the attention command.

Fall Out – band is released to move about from the attention position (fall out always comes from attention; called to attention from at ease or parade rest then given the command to fall out).

Flags – flags/silks used by marching color guard/auxiliary.

Float – corps style marching step adjusted by size and speed to get from one set to another.

Fronts or Front Ensemble – primarily used by corps style units; the PIT percussion setup that does not move during marching maneuvers (timpani, large bass drum, xylophones, marimba, etc.).

Forward March – command to step off moving forward.

Gait – the distance between steps while marching.

Guide Right – looking to the left shoulder of the person to your right to maintain a straight line while marching.

Guide Left – looking to the right shoulder of the person to your left to maintain a straight line while marching.

Guard – an auxiliary unit of the band that uses flags/silks, rifles, pom-poms, and other props to enhance the marching band show.

Harness – equipment piece used to hold marching percussion in place while marching.

Halt – a complete stop from marching or marking time.

Heel to Toe – a marching step that places the heel down first and rolls to the toe as the individual steps forward.

Oblique – a forty-five-degree precision move on the field to get from one spot/position to another (generally a show band maneuver).

Parade Rest – an on-field or parade stationary position with legs spaced apart awaiting the command for attention.

Pinwheel – a pivot motion a full 360 degrees.

Pivot – a turn of 45, 90, 180 or 360 degrees.

PIT – the stationary percussion used for marching band shows (generally corps style).

PIT Crew – parents and volunteers who move the stationary percussion instruments on and off the field; in some cases when the instruments are used in a set, they move the field props and percussion instruments into place.

Platoons – two or three large groups that form a company (based on a half of the band or a third of the band).

Plumes – feathers used on hats and often held by hand for a visual effect for a show.

Present Horns – a two-count movement, horns gripped on count one and raised on count two.

Quads – four-piece drum set used by marching drum line (connected).

Rank – the horizontal line formed shoulder to shoulder (generally an arm length or less apart).

Right Face – turn to the right on command.

To the Rear March – a 180-degree turn to march in the opposite direction (either to the left or right).

Section Leader – a designated leader of like instruments responsible for implementing commands from the director or drum major.

Sets – the pictures formed by the band on the field (sometimes props are used).

Squads – four- or eight-member groups generally based on like instruments.

Step Off – the initial steps that begin a marching maneuver.

Step Two – a movement based on counting two beats between individuals or groups stepping off.

Swinging Gate Turn – a turn made with a group using a right guide or left guide to maintain a straight line during a turn.

17

Developing a Jazz Ensemble

It is difficult to believe that there was a time that jazz ensembles were not considered a part of most schools' band programs. In fact, they had to be justified as having value as part of the total band program. Jazz instruction in schools as a class is still not as prevalent as other classical-based classes. This means that as a music teacher/band director, you will need to incorporate jazz instruction into your overall program objective.

Stating that your program's goal is to develop each student to his optimum level of performance opens the door to your having different kinds of groups to meet each student's need to express himself musically. Jazz, by nature, is a constantly challenging musical endeavor. Improvisation, which is a key to jazz performance, is "spontaneous composition." This means that as performers hear chord progressions, they create musical lines above the progressions. This is what composers do except that jazz players must do it instantly and usually in front of an audience (even if that audience is classmates during class). Not all students will be interested in "exposing themselves" and their weaknesses by improvising, but there is great value in providing them with the tools to try.

Some band directors are reluctant to teach jazz because they feel inadequate or underprepared. This should not keep you from providing this class for your students. In fact, it will help you as a teacher. As you try to perform jazz, you will discover firsthand what your students are experiencing. Because of this, you will be empathetic with your students and have a greater understanding of what they are going through. Jazz is a class that requires your students to be analytical, use discovery learning (trial and error), and push themselves to their emotional and creative limits. Unlike most classical forms, jazz requires students to incorporate their acquired skills through experimentation rather than simply following the music printed on the score before them. The comparison can be made of a storyteller; some stories are short and to the point while others are more involved. Some jazz improvisers will tell short stories slowly while others may choose to use a lot of notes fast. It is up to the teacher to help each student discover how to best tell her musical story.

18

Using Technology and Multimedia in Band Class

Using technology available to you today can revolutionize the way you teach and present information to your band. Instead of filmstrips, overhead projectors, slide projectors, tape recorders, and mimeograph machines are being used, computers, DVD players, and digital recording and playback devices are now being used. Computer-driven PowerPoint presentations make it a simple task to present instructional materials to your class using digital audio synchronized with a visual score or other visuals. You can start and stop the audio/visual materials wherever you want and discuss specific parts of the music and point out any issue that may need to be highlighted and corrected.

When introducing a piece of music to your band, you may play the piece while your students follow the score on an overhead screen. Seeing the music on the screen as they follow along helps your students to see and hear that their part is a small part of a whole. Once you have started playing the piece, you can substitute the model group's performance with your group's performance. As the group watches and listens, you can identify sections of the score where the group needs to improve.

This technology has not always been available and many college and university music education student preparation programs and some schools are not aware of the need to teach the use of PowerPoint in the classroom for band instruction.

SMART PHONES, TABLETS, AND NOTEBOOKS

One of the recurring themes found in this book is the importance of organization. Being able to have access to pertinent information almost instantly is one of the ways technology has started to help band directors. All of the information you need from contacts to policies to minutes from parent meetings can be carried with you at all times. Smart phones such as the Android, BlackBerry, Nokia, T-Mobile, and others have enough memory for you to store or access information when you need it without carrying around printed files or hard copies of information. You have access to e-mail and various applications (known as apps) that allow you to consult with someone the moment a problem occurs. You can access the Internet and instantly search for answers to almost any problem with which you're faced. Since organizations such as MENC have websites that have forums, you can consult with other band directors from anywhere you happen to be (as long as you have phone service).

One of the most recent developments in the instant information age is Apple's iPad. The iPad can store your inventory, music library, and students' names and information, among other pertinent items. You can also write or arrange music and print it on the spot. This is quite helpful if someone loses his part or you find it necessary to write out a part because of some-one's absence. There's also an app for recording your group live, an app for a metronome, an app for tuning, and many other helpful apps that keep you from carrying a lot of equipment or files with you. Because of the apps at your fingertips, there is no legitimate reason for you not to be organized. Since smart phones and the iPad have many of the same apps, you can share your files and information on two different devices, giving you a backup for everything.

Apple's iPad can also be used by students for writing music even if their music-reading skills are not at an advanced level. There are apps that can as-sist students in their personal music development through ear training and rhythmic tapping (percussion apps allow students to tap rhythms on the iPad). Many of these apps can be found at iTunes University and YouTube as well as many other locations. Because iPads were developed in 2010, there are apps being developed daily; many are being developed by music educators for use in or out of school. Your students can use earphones with the iPad and can use it anywhere in the school (with or without internet ac-cess). These tablets will never replace acoustic instruments, but the sampled sounds used can help students hear parts that they have written or parts that have been written for their particular instrument.

19

Quick Fixes and Emergency Repairs

No matter what condition your school instruments or students' instruments are in, there will always be an emergency repair needed at the worst possible time. Knowing this will help you and your students avoid going into a panic. There are some simple, temporary fixes with common materials that will help you save a performance and put an instrument in playing condition until you can go to a repair shop. No matter how well an instrument is functioning after an emergency repair, you must get the instrument to a repair shop as soon as possible. These fixes are by no means meant to last beyond the emergency. You or your students should take the instrument to a repair shop as soon after the emergency repair as possible.

Woodwind instruments, because of the number of working parts, are generally most likely to need an emergency repair. From pads falling out, springs breaking, reeds breaking, ligatures being loose because of missing screws, and corks coming off, these instruments will need special attention at some point during the year. You're not expected to be a certified repairperson, but as soon as an instrument breaks your students will come to you. Mouthpieces for brass instruments get stuck, strings on rotary key instruments will break, and corks for spit valves or spit keys will fall off.

As a new teacher this can be overwhelming. Most college teacher-preparatory programs don't have a repair course as part of the curriculum. Band directors are faced with on the job training or have a certified repair person on speed dial.

EMERGENCY REPAIR MATERIALS AND THEIR USES

Glues (rubber cement, instant glue, epoxy) – pad falls out and needs to be reset or replaced.

Rubber Bands – spring breaks and key needs to bounce back up after being depressed.

Razor Blade (single edge) – trim the tip of a chipped reed.

Sandpaper or Emery Board – sand down the thickness of a reed after trimming.

Thin Fishing Line – repair the broken string on rotary valve/rotary key instruments.

Butane Lighter – use to heat the glue on the back of a pad that has fallen out to reuse the original glue.

Mouthpiece Puller – pull out stuck mouthpiece.

Key Spring Hook – pull flute and saxophone springs back into place (a paper clip can be converted into a key hook in an emergency).

Fingernail File – can be used as a flat head screwdriver to tighten loose saxophone screws.

Fingernail Polish – can be applied to the top of saxophone screws to make sure that they don't come out again after being tightened.

Eyeglass Screwdriver – can be used to tighten screws on any instrument that has small flat head screws (some eyeglass-repair kits include a small Phillips head screwdriver).

COMMON PROBLEMS NEEDING EMERGENCY REPAIRS

Cork comes off a saxophone neck – Wrap some notebook paper or newspaper around the neck the size and length of a cork. Do not use glue or tape, and once the mouthpiece has been placed on the neck and the instrument has been tuned, do not move the mouthpiece. The cork should be replaced immediately after the performance.

Saxophone/Clarinet key will not respond – The spring has probably disconnected from its seating. Use a paper clip or something that functions as a hook to pull the spring back into place. Be very careful not to break or bend the spring.

Mouthpiece is stuck – You must use a mouthpiece puller otherwise you take the chance of bending or breaking the barrel or tubing. Do not use pliers, wrenches, or vises to pull the mouthpiece out.

Spit valve won't close – Wrap a rubber band or tape around the valve to keep it closed. Replace spring or key immediately after the performance.

Rotary key will not open – Use thin fishing line of string to wrap around rotary mechanism to operate the key.

Reed has chipped tip – Place on flat surface and trim the reed just beneath the chip. Use fine sanding paper to gently sand down the tip in light strokes, moving forward only toward the tip. Be careful not to chip or split the reed. This should be done only if an extra reed is not available.

Pads stick – If there is no non-stick fluid available, place a piece of typing paper (no ink on it) between the pad and the seating and pull it out while lightly depressing the key (with your finger on the key). Using a dollar bill will leave an ink deposit that will build up over time, causing sticking or improper pad seating.

Ligature screw breaks or is lost – Use the bottom screw only and turn it tightly enough to hold the reed in place. If both screws are missing, use several small rubber bands or one large rubber band doubled to hold the reed securely (tightly) to the mouthpiece. As a last resort, use duct tape or masking tape (only if rubber bands are not available).

Snare falls off the snare drum – Use cellophane or masking tape to attach the snare to the bottom drum head. Place the tape at the end of the snare on the metal not the snare itself. If you must place tape on the snare, make sure that the snare can still vibrate. Stretch the snare so that it is taut enough to still function as a snare.

Crash cymbal strap comes off – Study the other crash cymbal to see how to relace the strap.

20

Nonmusic Responsibilities of Band Directors

With all of the "hats" a band director wears to effectively do the job as a music teacher/band director, there are also responsibilities the band director has to perform as a faculty member in her school. Elementary and middle school teachers generally have bus assignments requiring them to supervise students coming to school and leaving the school by bus. This sometimes requires the band director to leave the band room open for students to drop off their instruments or have a student, adult volunteer, or colleague supervise the band room for safety and security. If you receive bus supervision responsibilities and explain to your principal the importance of you being able to open the room and supervise students, band room supervision may be your arrival and departure assignment.

On the high school level, teachers are also assigned to bus duty, but band directors can usually be exempted from this because of the additional number of faculty and staff members assigned to parking lots and bus stops. Most high schools have safety-and-security staff members whose responsibilities are parking lots and bus stops. Safety-and-security staff cover some of the responsibilities band directors and other teachers would have. Smaller districts and smaller schools have to require teachers to perform safety-and-security staff members' jobs. Teachers are assigned cafeteria duty, study hall duty, open gym duty (watching students in the gym before school starts or during lunch), and Instructional Related Activities (known as IRA responsibilities). IRA responsibilities involve supervising study halls, student activities (chess club, math club, etc.), in-school detention halls, and mentoring sessions.

Some of these assigned activities will help you get to know students who are not in your program and can help you with recruiting. When you're new to a school these activities also help you to get to know your colleagues and have a degree of visibility. Before you receive your IRA responsibilities you should meet with your principal and explain what your mornings, lunchtime, and afterschool band director responsibilities are. Most band directors use before school, lunchtime, and afterschool times for individual and group coaching. Try to find an alternative time and/or activity that will fulfill your responsibilities to the school that will not negatively impact your program-building activities.

It's important that you perform these tasks like every other faculty member for many reasons. One, you don't want your fellow staff members to resent the fact that you are exempt from some of the mundane tasks they have to perform. Their resentment may cause them to work against you and your program-building efforts. Secondly, these activities give you an opportunity to participate in the school's total program. Sometimes band directors are viewed as being aloof or not part of the entire school because they put building a program over participating in activities that benefit the school and community. This is a mistake, because in order to build a successful band program you will need the help of the entire school community—faculty, students, and community members.

Another mistake a lot of band directors make is to forgo attending faculty meetings. Faculty meetings are a vital part of being a part of the life of your school. Even if you are excused from faculty meetings because of your rehearsal or performance schedule, it is incumbent on you to keep up with the decisions made and information disseminated in the meetings. This information and these decisions impact on the school and your program. If you're not at the meetings, there is no one present to address issues that will affect you and your students. Many of the decisions that are made in faculty meetings will directly affect you and your program. Decisions such as block scheduling, course offerings, class scheduling, and class lengths will all impact on your classes. Without having your input, administrators and the school staff may unwittingly make decisions that could destroy all that you've done to build your program and get students into your classes.

Faculty meetings are generally held once a month and even though a lot of items covered may seem mundane, all it takes is one item to affect your program. Since most music students are involved in high-level academic classes including their music classes, it is important that there are no conflicts or problems with class scheduling and extracurricular time schedules. Athletic directors need your input on field scheduling if your marching band needs access to the football field. Coaches need to know about your practice schedule so that if your students are also involved in sports, they know to expect them to be late for athletic practices. Drama teachers need to know when and if you will need to schedule use of the auditorium. These schedules can be coordinated at the end of a faculty meeting when all involved are present. Even if you don't meet for scheduling purposes at least your colleagues have an opportunity to get to know you and know what your motives are. This way you can form a cooperative relationship with people you know rather than communicate in an impersonal way such as e-mail.

Communicating with parents is another responsibility all teachers have. If you want your band classes to be viewed and valued as academic classes you must maintain academic standards for your classes. This means contacting your students' parents to let them know the progress of their child in your class. You don't want parents or students to get the impression that your class doesn't have standards that must be met. With the new standards being adopted by different states, your lesson plans should demonstrate the value of music as a subject and how music integrates with other subjects. There are schools that pair subjects together in teaching blocks and music is often paired with English/Literature classes, history classes, and world studies classes. With No Child Left Behind standards and requirements, music can play an important part in helping students achieve their goals. Because music students generally have good attendance in music classes and overall, band classes help them to meet the attendance requirements for most standardized requirements.

RECORD KEEPING, STANDARDIZED TESTS, AND NO CHILD LEFT BEHIND

Record keeping is an important part of accountability for grading and meeting the No Child Left Behind requirements. Taking accurate attendance is an important part of all classes and should be done daily. Band classes are larger than most classes but because of instrumentation and seating taking attendance can be done quickly. Once your students take their seats you can visually take roll rather than calling out names and waiting for responses. Roll keeping/attendance checking is an important part of accounting for schools as part of No Child Left Behind record keeping and has far-reaching ramifications for schools and school systems.

Some statewide standardized tests also require accurate attendance. For test scores to count for a school and individual students, they must be marked "present" for every day the tests are administered. All faculty members are assigned duties during standardized tests. Once again, as a member of your school's instructional team, you should expect to receive some sort of assignment during testing.

ADVANCED PLACEMENT STUDENTS IN BAND CLASS

There will be students who take band classes who wish to receive honors credit for band class. As in the case of other honors or advanced placement classes, honors band classes receive weighted credit. If there are students who wish to take an AP test, there is a prescribed course of study for these classes. Honors-level and AP classes will help you to maintain students who would otherwise opt out of band in search of a class that will give them weighted credit to raise their grade point average. Being able to participate in a class that stimulates them intellectually and creatively and meets rigorous course requirements will help you to retain students who may drop band in their junior or senior years.

Strategies for Teaching Advanced Students in Band Class

If your school does not offer honors or AP classes, there are ways to challenge advanced students in band class. As was covered in the chapter on technology, there are computer-assisted music programs that will teach and assess your students individually (without you having to grade assignments). These programs range from theory programs to performance programs. Students can learn part writing, take aural tests (intervals and chords), and play songs or segments of songs with instant feedback on correct or incorrect notes played.

During band class you can allow your advanced players to have release time to work with computer-assisted music programs (CAMP). These programs are designed in several different ways. Some allow you to monitor how long students are logged into the programs and view their progress, and others allow students to have a degree of privacy without their progress being monitored. The cost of the program usually determines which one some schools use but it is best to have a way of monitoring students' time and progress to make sure that students who have been released are using their time wisely.

If there is no computer program available for use, there are ways that you can challenge your students during class. You can assign students outside-of-class work to research the style of music being played in class; information on the composer; what kinds of chords and chord progressions are being used; if the music is by a contemporary composer, what periodic style does the piece resemble (neoclassical, etc.). Having students do research on the pieces and composers you are working on in class will give them a better understanding of what you expect of them. If you have shared your conductor's notes with them, have them prepare notes on the pieces you are working on. Students tend to listen to their peers when those peers present their notes.

Building relationships with school secretaries, custodial staff, and the athletic department is not a requirement but is a very wise move. This support staff will probably interact with you more than many other faculty members. School secretaries will generally be of assistance in filling out and typing up forms, giving you access to the principal, and keeping you informed of items that need to be completed before school or district wide deadlines. The custodial staff will help you with before school and afterschool needs, and provide access to parts of the building other than your area, set up for concerts and break down after concerts, room cleanup, and so on.

21

General Program Management

DEVELOPING AND MAINTAINING AN INSTRUMENT INVENTORY

Maintaining an inventory of quality musical instruments for student use to be assured that you will have needed instrumentation is very important to the life and development of your program. Some schools will only provide large instruments such as tubas, sousaphones, bass clarinets, baritone saxophones, mallet instruments, and marching band percussion but since the director in most cases will want to assign students to "color" instruments, the band's inventory will need to include these. The instruments that are considered "color" instruments include: oboes, French horns, bassoons, alto clarinet, soprano saxophone, piccolo, flugel horn, E-flat clarinet, and English horns.

If you are starting a new school, there will be an equipment budget for stocking your new school. Before purchasing any instruments find out what amount of funding you can expect to receive over the next five years. Some districts have a depreciation list that you can get that will help you to decide how to best spend your funds. If you are inheriting your program from another director, try to locate her inventory list. With or without the list, check the inventory and list all equipment and their condition. You will also want to estimate a time each piece of equipment will need to be replaced. The school's procurement officer can help you with this. He will have a record of each purchase made before you came to the school.

Most music stores and instrument manufacturers have a printed instrument lifespan estimate and a depreciation schedule. Request one so that you will be able to develop your school budget and determine what supplemental funding you are eligible for from your school district. Some school districts will provide one or two large instruments to each middle school and high school in the district.

Make sure that piano purchases for your school come out of your school's furniture budget, not your music equipment budget. One piano purchase can deplete your entire budget for a year. Check with your music supervisor for information concerning new instrument purchases and assistance stocking a new school. Since most districts use vendor bids for purchases, centralized music offices have information of which you may not be aware. If you are in a small district that does not have a centralized music office, meet with a representative from your music vendor to find out what recommendations she has based on purchase history (your school and other schools).

FOLDERS AND BINDERS

Most music stores will give you cardboard music folders to use for your band. These folders are generally free but will wear out very quickly if your students carry them to and from school (which you want them to do in order to practice). A better way to keep your music from being ripped or frayed is to order leather folders. These folders can be engraved with part names on them and generally have a four- or five-year life span. The drawback for these folders is that they do not fit into student backpacks. Some band directors have started using three-ring binders instead of music folders. These thin binders serve as protection for the music and allow you to have students keep handouts, class assignments, and other important papers. Choose a binder that has pouches so that your students can place their music inside. If you wish, you can three-hole punch the music to make sure the music does not fall out and get lost. If you decide to use binders you should order enough for each student to have the same kind of folder (even if the students have to pay for them). It is also recommended that students be discouraged from using their school binders for band class. One, those binders are too large to be carried onstage and two, you want students to use the folder as a textbook. A regular school binder will also be difficult for students to keep organized for band use (one of the problems students have is binder organization).

STARTING A CONCERT BAND MUSIC LIBRARY

When starting a music library, there are several things you need to consider. Among those things is the educational value from studying classic concert literature, appeal to your students, appeal to audiences, variety of music styles, and music challenges to your students. Before choosing literature for your group you should listen to recordings of the music you are considering. There are recordings by professional groups that are available from music publishers with scores for you to peruse. Most colleges and universities also have recordings of classic concert band literature for you to listen to. You may contact them via their web page.

It is very difficult to locate professional recordings of concert bands but the U.S. military bands record classic band literature every year and make those recordings available by request. Video recordings of military bands and university bands can also be accessed on the Internet on sites such as youtube.com and dailymotion.com. There are a few composers of classic band literature whose work should be found in every band library.

Composers whose works are performed most often at middle school band festivals are: Frank Erickson, John Kenyon, John Edmondson, Anne McGinty, James Ployhar, Clare Grundman, John O'Reilly, James Swearingen, Robert Smith, Claude Smith, Ed Huckeby, Elliott Del Borgo, and Alfred Reed. Composers whose works are performed most often at high school band festivals are: Claude Smith, Charles Carter, Gustav Holst, R. Vaughan Williams, Howard Hansen, Gordon Jacob, Jared Spears, Clifton Williams, Frank Ticheli, Elliot Del Borgo, Alfred Reed, James Barnes Chance, and Francis McBeth. These are not the only good composers of concert band music but they are the names that most often are described by band directors as the composers they perform the most at festivals and at concerts.

LITERATURE MOST OFTEN
PERFORMED BY HIGH SCHOOL BANDS

Some of the songs that are most often performed by bands at festivals are also songs that can be performed at concerts. Classic band literature reflects the true character of bands more than orchestral transcriptions because they are written specifically for band instruments and band instrument sonorities. Here are some of the songs written for concert bands grade 4 through 6:

Grade 4

Overture for Winds	Charles Carter
Symphonic Overture	Charles Carter
Chorale and Fugato	Frank Erickson
Toccata and Fugue	Frank Erickson
Irish Tune from County Derry	Percy Grainger
American Folk Rhapsody #3	Clare Grundman
Hebrides Suite	Clare Grundman

Havendance	David Holsinger
Battaglia	Francis McBeth
Chant and Jubilo	Francis McBeth
Second Suite for Band	Francis McBeth
And the Heart Replies	Anne McGinty
Atlantica	Anne McGinty
Festivo	Vaclav Nelhybel
Nocturne	Roger Nixon
A Yorkshire Fantasy	John O'Reilly
A Festival Prelude	Alfred Reed
A Festive Overture	Alfred Reed
Amazing Grace	Frank Ticheli
An American Elegy	Frank Ticheli
Shenandoah	Frank Ticheli
Dedicatory Overture	Clifton Williams
English Folksong Suite	Ralph Vaughan Williams
Rhosymedre	Ralph Vaughan Williams
Chorale and Shaker Dance	John Zdechlik

Grade 5

Proclamation	Charles Carter
Chorale and Variant	John Barnes Chance
Variations on a Korean Folk Song	John Barnes Chance
Satiric Dances	Norman Dello Joio
Be Thou My Vision	David Gillingham
Three Sketches for Winds	Clare Grundman
Chorale and Alleluia	Howard Hanson
Prelude and Rhondo	David Holsinger
An Original Suite	Gordon Jacob
Third Suite for Band	Robert Jager
American Overture	Wilcox Jenkins
A Symphonic Jubilee	Wilcox Jenkins
Andante and Toccata	Vaclav Nelhybel
Chorale Prelude	Vincent Persichetti
A Longford Legend	Robert Sheldon
Sanctuary	Frank Ticheli
English Folksong Suite	Ralph Vaughan Williams
Caccia and Chorale	Clifton Williams
Fanfare and Allegro	Clifton Williams
Symphonic Dance #3	Clifton Williams
Symphonic Suite	Clifton Williams

Grade 6

Fantasy Variations on a Theme by Paginini	James Barnes
Toccata Fantastica	James Barnes
Suite of Old American Dances	Russell Bennett
Incantation and Dance	John Barnes Chance
Variants on a Mediaeval Tune	Norman Dello Joio
Galactic Empires	David Gillingham
Canzona	Peter Menin

These are not the only choices of music but they are the most performed at festivals.

CHOOSING METHOD BOOKS FOR CLASS USE

When choosing method books for class use, the books chosen should address specific band-building techniques. There are different books used to teach and reinforce concert band styles and jazz/pop music styles. The methods chosen should not be used for both unless they are specifically written to address multiple styles. Since some concert band music incorporates jazz, show tunes, and popular music into the concert piece, there may be a need to teach general principles in class but method books are designed to teach specific techniques.

One of the best method books for teaching scales and chorales in all major and minor keys is the *Treasury of Scales*[1]. This book provides a warm-up with ninety-six harmonized scales from intermediate to advanced. This means that you can tailor your warm-up to any key of any song you're working on in class. Fortunately, because of its success, there are other books designed like it that are available from major music publishers as well as smaller publishing companies. One of the books that is used and recommended by many band directors is *16 Chorales by J. S. Bach*.[2] This book can be used to teach balance and blend to bands of all levels but it is an intermediate grade.

Method book studies and exercises can help you to develop good breathing skills for band playing, balance, dynamics, attacks and releases, and phrasing. If you use harmonized scale activities, have your students listen for where each note of the scale being played is. As they track the melody from part to part, they will make subtle changes in their dynamic levels without you having to tell them to. You can then make small adjustments from the podium but the real adjustments will be student-initiated.

SUPPLEMENTAL STUDIES

There are many other method books that can be used by individual instruments to work on facility and general playing techniques. A lot of states use these books for audition material for all state bands. Rubank, Inc., Music Publishing has a set of methods for all instruments on the elementary, intermediate, and advanced levels. You can choose books to be used based on your students' playing level. Unlike the band methods, these methods are designed to be standalone books that work on specific challenges faced by each instrument.

NOTES

1. Leonard B. Smith, *Treasury of Scales*, 1 (Los Angeles: Alfred Publishing, 1985).
2. *16 Chorales By J. S. Bach* (New York: Schirmer).

22

Sample Forms

The following forms can be copied or modified for use with your band. If you choose not to use these forms, you will need to develop your own or check with your music supervisor to see if any forms exist.

MEDICAL FORM

Student's Name _____

Parents' Names _____

Parent's Phone Number _____

Parent's E-mail _____

Student's Medical Condition _____ (Good, Fair or Poor)

Does the student have any medical condition that requires attention _____

    If yes, please explain _____

Does the student have any food allergies or special dietary concerns? _____

    If yes, please list and explain _____

Does the student have any condition that may restrict physical activities? _____

    If yes, please explain _____

If parent(s) cannot be reached, please give an emergency contact:

    Name _____ Phone Number _____

In case of an emergency, I give medical caregivers permission to perform lifesaving care until I can be reached. Signed _____ (Parent)

The information I have furnished is complete to my knowledge.

Signed _____ Date _____

BAND BOOSTERS FORM

Parent's Name _____

Student's Name and Instrument _____

Parent's Cell Phone _____

Parent's E-mail _____

Parent's Home or Business Phone _____

Parent's Occupation _____

Are there committees that you would be interested in participating in (choose as many as you'd like):

       Financial/Budget Committee ____

       Public Relations _____

       Marching Band Pit Crew ____

       Transportation _____

       Uniform ____

       Prop Construction _____

       Sign Making ___

       Copy Righting _____

       Chaperone _____ (Local) _____ (Out of Town)

       Equipment Set Up _____

       Concert Ticket Sales _____

       Concert Set Up ___

       Concert/Performance Promotion _____

       Fund Raising ____

       Recruiting/Retention _____

Are there skills you have to offer that will help the band program in any way that is not listed above? _____ Yes _____No

       If yes, please explain _____

Would you be willing to transport students in your private vehicle if permission is granted by the student's parent? _____ (transportation by private vehicle is subject to the school and school district rules of liability)

Signed _____ Date _____

PERMISSION SLIP (LOCAL)

Student's Name _____

Activity _____

Activity Date and Time _____ (class periods missed)

I give _____ permission to ride on school provided transportation to _____ with the band on _____(date).

I do not give _____ permission to participate in this activity with the band. I realize that this is a graded activity and my child will be penalized for non-participation.

I give _____ permission to participate with the band on _____ (date) but I will transport him/her to and from the activity.

I give _____ permission to participate in the activity listed above and would like to be a chaperone.

I give _____ permission to ride in private transportation (parent/adult driven).

This permission slip must be returned to the school by _____

Signed _____ (parent's signature) Date _____

PERMISSION SLIP FOR AN OUT-OF-TOWN TRIP

Student's Name _____

Activity Name and Date _____

Parent's Name _____

Parent's Phone Number _____

Transportation Vendor _____ (bus, airline, etc.)

Estimated Departure Time _____ Date _____

Departure Location _____

Estimated Return Time _____ Date _____

Detach and return to the school by _____

Is there a health/medical form on file? _____

I give _____ permission to travel with the band to

_____ on _____.

I do not give _____ permission to travel with the

band to _____ on _____. I am aware that my child will

be penalized for non-participation.

Signed _____ Date _____

TEACHER FIELD TRIP NOTIFICATION FORM

Dear Colleague,

The band will be participating in _____ on _____(date).
Students will be out of class periods _____through_____. Please mark
_____ excused and allow him/her to make up any missed
work. Thanks for your understanding.

Ron Kearns, Band Director

Period 1 _____Signed
Period 2 _____Signed
Period 3 _____Signed
Period 4 _____Signed
Period 5 _____Signed
Period 6 _____Signed
Period 7 _____Signed

INSTRUMENT LOAN FORM, SCHOOL YEAR 20__ TO 20__

Student's Name _____ Grade _____

Parent/Guardian's Name _____

Home Phone _____

Parent/Guardian's Cell Phone _____

Parent or Student's E-mail _____

Instrument Type/Name _____

Instrument Serial Number _____

Instrument Condition _____

Are there scratches, dings or dents _____ Where _____

Loan Length _____ (Semester, Year or Summer)

Loan Date _____

Return Date _____

Return Condition _____

Student Signature _____ Date _____

Parent/Guardian Signature _____

INVENTORY FORM

Instrument _____   Brand _____

Instrument Serial Number _____ Model Number _____

Year of Purchase _____

Condition _____

Finish _____ (with or without lacquer)

MUSIC LIBRARY CARD

Song Title _____

Style _____

Group: Concert Band _____ Symphonic Band _____ Wind Ensemble _____

Jazz Ensemble _____

Last Performed _____

Grade Level _____

File Number _____

RESOURCES

Concert Band Resources in Book Form

Colwell, R. 1969. *The Teaching of Instrumental Music.* New York: Appleton-Century Crofts.
Garofalo, R. 1996. *Improving Intonation in Band and Orchestra Performance.* Ft. Lauderdale, FL: Meredith Music Publications.
Labuta, J. 1972. *Teaching Musicianship in the High School Band.* West Nyack, NY: Parker Publishing Company, Inc.
Labuta, J. 1997. *Teaching Musicianship in the High School Band.* Galsville, MD: Meredith Music Publications.
Levitan, D. 2006. *This is Your Brain on Music: The Science of a Human Obsession.* New York: Dutton, Penguin Group.

Marching Band Resources in Book Form

Buyer, P. 2009. *Marching Bands and Drumlines: Secrets of Success from the Best of the Best.* Galsville, MD: Meredith Music Publications.
Hopper, D. 1977. *Corps Style Marching.* Oskaloosa, IA: C. L. Barnhouse Company, Music Publishers.
Snoek, K. M. 1981. *Contemporary Drill Design.* Oskaloosa, IA: C. L. Barnhouse Company, Music Publishers.

Jazz Resources in Book Form

Kuzmich, J., and L. Bash. 1984. *Complete Guide to Instrumental Jazz Instruction.* West Nyack, NY: Parker Publishing Company, Inc.
Lawn, R. 1981. *The Jazz Ensemble Director's Manual.* Oskaloosa, IA: C. L. Barnhouse Company, Music Publishers.

Technology Resources in Book Form

Boody, C. G. 1990. *Tips: Technology for Music Educators.* Reston, VA: MENC.
Rudolph, T. E. 2004. *Teaching Music with Technology,* 2nd ed. Wyncote, PA: Technology Institute for Music Educators.

Internet Resources

www.menc.org
www.harryfox.com/public/MechanicalLicenseslic.jsp
www.jwpepper.com
www.kennedy-center.org/education/
www.alfred.com
www.halleonard.com

www.manhattanbeachmusic.com
www.americanbandmasters.org
www.asbda.com
www.banddirector.com
www.jazzednet.org
www.pas.org
www.sbomagazine.com
www.bands.army.mil/music

Technology Resources on the Internet

www.smartmusic.com
www.sweetwateredu.com
www.soundtree.com
www.ti-me.org
www.menc.org
www.kellysmusicandcomputers.com
www.finalemusic.com
www.sibelius.com
www.bandinabox.com
www.avid.com

Index

About the Author

During his thirty-year teaching career, Ronald E. Kearns (Ron Kearns) has taught students of many socio-economic levels. He began his career teaching inner city students in Baltimore (MD) City Public Schools and retired from teaching in the Montgomery County (MD) Public Schools. After teaching elementary school for five months, Ron Kearns began teaching high school band. Over the next twenty-nine and a half years, Ron taught band, orchestra, and jazz in high schools in Maryland.

Ron Kearns's bands won several national awards including being selected as a Grammy Signature School (twice) and a Grammy Partner School. The Grammy Signature School award recognizes the top fifty music programs in the United States. His bands and orchestras were chosen as some of the Washington, DC, metropolitan area's top ten groups for three consecutive years (one year he had three of the top ten groups receiving $1,000.00 per group).

Ron was also selected as one of 50 Directors Who Make a Difference by *School Band and Orchestra* magazine, and he was selected as a recipient of *Down Beat* magazine's Excellence in Jazz Education award. He was nominated by four students in four years to be selected for Who's Who in Teaching (selected all four times). For twenty-eight of his thirty years teaching, Ron's groups never scored less than superior ratings for sight-reading at local, state, or national festivals.

Ron adjudicates national and international festivals and performs clinics throughout the United States and Canada. He is a Vandoren of Paris Performing Artist and has produced over forty jazz recordings including five under his own name. Ron has written several articles for the Maryland

Music Educators Association, New Jersey Music Educators, Maine Music Educators, whyvandoren.com, and MENC.

Ron Kearns received his B.S. degree in music education from Knoxville College (Knoxville, TN) and his master's in Music Education from The Catholic University of America (Washington, DC). He also received a certificate in music and dance from the University of East Africa (currently the University of Nairobi, Nairobi, Kenya). He is a member of MENC and NARAS (National Association of Recording Arts and Sciences).

Made in the USA
Lexington, KY
21 December 2014